THE HEAVY LIFTING

A Boy's Guide to Writing Poetry

THE HEAVY LIFTING

A Boy's Guide to Writing Poetry

Jeffrey Burghauser

Published by New English Review Press
a subsidiary of World Encounter Institute
PO Box 158397
Nashville, Tennessee 37215
&
27 Old Gloucester Street
London, England, WC1N 3AX

Cover Art and Design by Kendra Mallock

ISBN: 978-1-943003-78-5

Library of Congress Control Number: 2023930734

First Edition

NEW ENGLISH REVIEW PRESS
newenglishreview.org

"We must first determine what buildings are to be considered Augustan in their authority. Their modes of construction and laws of proportion are to be studied with the most penetrating care. Then, the different forms and uses of their decorations are to be classed and catalogued, as a German grammarian classes the powers of prepositions. And under this absolute, irrefragable authority, we are to begin to work, admitting not so much as an alteration in the depth of a cavetto,[1] or the breadth of a fillet. Then, when our sight is once accustomed to the grammatical forms and arrangements, and our thoughts familiar with the expression of them all; when we can speak this dead language naturally, and apply it to whatever ideas we have to render, that is to say, to every practical purpose of life; then, and not till then, a license might be permitted, and individual authority allowed to change or to add to the received forms, always within certain limits. The decorations, especially, might be made subjects of variable fancy, and enriched with ideas either original or taken from other schools. And thus in process of time and by a great national movement, it might come to pass that a new style should arise, as language itself changes. We might perhaps come to speak Italian instead of Latin, or to speak Modern instead of Old English. But this would be a matter of entire indifference, and a matter, besides, which no determination or desire could either hasten or prevent."
—**John Ruskin**, *The Seven Lamps of Architecture*

"My purposes / Are chaste, exact, sublime, and beautiful[.]"
—**Anthony Thwaite**, "The Studio"[2]

---

1 cavetto] A type of concave moulding.
2 19-20. *Collected Poems*. Enitharmon Press, 2007, p. 223.

"And if they hit in order by some chance, / They call that Nature, which is Ignorance."
—**John Dryden**, "Prologue to the University of Oxford"

"Nothing [by Abraham Cowley] is far-sought or hard-labored; but all is easy without feebleness, and familiar without grossness."
—**Samuel Johnson**, "The Life of Cowley"

"Let no man build himself a spurious self-esteem on his contempt or indifference for acknowledged excellence."
—**William Hazlitt**, "On Egoism"

"[M]en first found out they had minds by making and tasting poetry."
—**Charles James Fox**

CONTENTS

I

INTRODUCTION

TO THE ANXIOUS READER

I F POETRY IS new to you, this book may seem slightly intimidating, with its strange nouns and alien ideas tornadoing about. My passionate tone may be particularly bewildering. There's nothing more ridiculous than somebody else's passion.

But please don't worry. Take a deep breath, and simply read. If there's a term you've never heard before, you can decide to Google it (which is fine), or you can decide not to Google it (which is also fine). Just read. One word follows the next.

Trust me. You're in good hands.

TWO

QUOTED TEXTS

S INCE WE CAN'T hope to write good poetry without reading a lot of good poetry, this book is stocked with specimens, concerning which:

1. I've modernized spelling, capitalization, and punctuation.

2. I've converted British spellings into American spellings. While updating the spelling of Early Modern English texts (i.e., texts written between the fifteenth and seventeenth centuries), I faced the question of which current spelling to use. I'm American, and chose accordingly. Since it seemed odd to have modernized texts presented in American spelling, and post-Restoration texts (which didn't need modernization) in British spelling, I opted for consistency.

3. This isn't a work of scholarship. To prevent it from becoming a hellscape of academic machinery, I've decided against providing complete citations, except when quoting copyrighted materials.

4. When quoting an excerpt from a longer poem, I number the first line of the quote "1" and use a footnote to indicate what the line numbers are in the original text.

"A SIMULTANEOUS ORDER"

I n "Tradition and the Individual Talent," T.S. Eliot writes:

> [Tradition] cannot be inherited, and if you want it you must obtain it by great labor. It involves, in the first place, the historical sense, which we may call nearly indispensable to anyone who would continue to be a poet beyond his twenty-fifth year; and the historical sense involves a perception, not only of the pastness of the past, but of its presence. The historical sense compels a man to write not merely with his own generation in his bones, but with a feeling that the whole of the literature of Europe from Homer (and, within it, the whole of the literature of his own country) has a simultaneous existence and composes a simultaneous order.

In other words, someone who is serious about poetry should discipline his mind to experience all great poets as being, essentially, colleagues. Shakespeare's Sonnets should seem as fresh as Philip Larkin's "Aubade," and "Aubade" should stimulate the kind of scrutiny we normally apply to the Sonnets.

To help us reorient our minds in this direction, when I'm discussing a particular work, I'll try to exclude its publication year, and any other details which would otherwise shackle it in Time. This isn't always possible; historical context is sometimes necessary. And when citing a copyrighted text, the publication year is essential.

"[A] simultaneous order," however, remains my goal.

FOUR

TO ALL THE BIG AND LITTLE BOYS

W HEN I WAS IN graduate school back in 2002, I attended a seminar where H. Rider Haggard's adventure novel, *King Solomon's Mines*, was discussed. The seminar's tenor was established early, when the professor, her tone viscous with contempt, recited the novel's dedication:

> *This faithful but unpretending record*
> *of a remarkable adventure*
> *is hereby respectfully dedicated*
> *by the narrator,*
> ALLAN QUATERMAIN,
> *to all the big and little boys*
> *who read it.*

Although I couldn't have foreseen the ideological havoc that this type of contempt would eventually diffuse across Christendom, I was certain that it was wicked. Instead of *reading* the novel, she was using it to prop up the leg of a poorly built dogma. It was obvious to me that boys and girls are different—a fact that's no more "good" or "bad" than the fact that each season has its own character. It was obvious to me that boys are more inclined than girls to tales of pith-helmeted derring-do. And it was obvious that the differences didn't end there.

Experience vindicated these instincts—a courtesy that Experience seldom vouchsafes me. I've spent nearly twenty years nudging students to write poetry; the most sullenly steadfast resistance has come from boys. Notwithstanding my dear professor's exertions, boys still tend to want to appear tough and taciturn; poetry can seem effeminate. Boys don't want to discuss their feelings.

And who can blame them? Some of us have experienced the unease of sitting down at a café only to discover (once your curried chickpea melt has already been ordered, and there's no graceful means of escape) that it happens to be "Open Mic Night" and that you will be forced to dine while some emotionally incontinent buffoon hyperventilates into a badly calibrated PA system.

It's no surprise that poetry is unattractive to boys.

But word games? Puzzles? Mechanical contraptions to tinker with? A poem (especially a formal poem, a poem that has ordered rhyme and meter, a *real* poem) is the ultimate contraption. And if you master *this* type of contraption, you can (theoretically, at least) inspire girls to fall in love with you.[1] You can inspire men to sacrifice themselves for an ideal. You can provide your fellow man with intimations of the divine.

My purpose in this book is twofold. Firstly, I'll argue that poetry belongs among the manly arts. In *Sesame and Lilies*, John Ruskin writes about the human male:

> His intellect is for speculation and invention; his energy,
> for adventure, for war, and for conquest—wherever war
> is just, wherever conquest is necessary.

I will attempt to persuade you that writing poetry is consonant with these tendencies. Secondly, I'll provide the practical resources that the novice will find useful in getting underway.

Those of you who are already familiar with poetry will notice the debt this volume owes to Ezra Pound's *ABC of Reading*; like Pound's book, this is an idiosyncratic blend of polemics and pedagogy. What I lack in Pound's erudition I hope I compensate

---

1 The dos and don'ts of love poetry will be addressed in chapters 35 through 39.

for in sobriety, irony, and clarity.

When I was a college freshman at the State University of New York at Buffalo, I had a masterful poetry teacher, George R. Levine, who once gave us a guided tour of Robert Frost's "Stopping by Woods on a Snowy Evening." Professor Levine began by reading it aloud:

> Whose woods these are I think I know.
> His house is in the village, though;
> He will not see me stopping here
> To watch his woods fill up with snow.   4.
>
> My little horse must think it queer
> To stop without a farmhouse near
> Between the woods and frozen lake
> The darkest evening of the year.   8.
>
> He gives his harness bells a shake
> To ask if there is some mistake.
> The only other sound's the sweep
> Of easy wind and downy flake.   12.
>
> The woods are lovely, dark and deep,
> But I have promises to keep,
> And miles to go before I sleep,
> And miles to go before I sleep.   16.

"Comments? Questions?" he said after a well-timed pause.

"Why did Frost repeat that last line?" someone asked.

It turned out that, as a graduate student, Levine had actually availed himself of the unique opportunity to ask the poet this very question.

"It just sounded right," was Frost's purported response.

I relay this story because it tells the truth about creativity, which plays by its own elusive rules. It's highly idiosyncratic. No real poet's process is diagrammable. Robert Creeley was once asked what a particular line of his "meant." His imperishable reply:

"How should I know? I only work here."

I know the feeling. As I confessed earlier, this book is idiosyncratic, for it reflects only what I've observed, and what's worked for me, as a poet. It aspires neither to academic authority nor panoptic omniscience. I'm not attempting to justify the ways of God to Men. I'm more like a master plumber, or someone who makes good Japanese kitchen knives. My guidance may be odd and fragmentary, but it will remain specific.

There's no shortage of books on how to write poetry. And the internet certainly isn't barren of resources; you can even download simple templates that will enable you to work in any poetic form simply by filling in the blanks.[2]

Mastery, however, involves substantially more than filling in the blanks, and this book will teach you those practices and perspectives that will help you to produce things of actual beauty.

Since this book emerges from my years of teaching, I'm indebted to my students for consistently verifying the cliché: the teacher learns more from his students than the other way around. When an author is asked why he's written a book, he will sometimes reply that there was a particular book he wanted to read, and, finding such a book unavailable, undertook to write it himself. When I'm asked why I became a teacher, I'm often tempted to reply analogously that, arriving in the Midwest and finding no interesting people to talk to, I had no choice but to manufacture them myself. It's a cute line—cute, but unjust. My students are remarkable, and I owe them a great deal. I'm fortunate to live within their orbit, where things are always an adventure.

I like adventure, after all; poetry is an adventure—a remarkable adventure. My limits being what they are, the best that this record can hope to be is faithful and unpretending. Therefore:

---

2   A collection of my own (superior, I hope) templates appears in these pages.

This faithful but unpretending record
of a remarkable adventure
is hereby respectfully dedicated
by the author,
JEFFREY BURGHAUSER,
to all the big and little boys
who read it.

FIVE

THE BRICKLAYER

I ARRIVED AT CAMPUS absurdly early on my first day as a professor and found myself beguiling the time in smoking cigarettes, drinking coffee, and chatting with a laborer—the only other person on campus at that ungodly hour. He was there to repair some brickwork, and, after I asked a few questions, he gave me a useful lecture on what can go wrong with brick. Quite a lot, apparently. When a brick's surface is porous, rainwater is absorbed into the first few millimeters. When the temperature drops, the water expands, and the thin layer of brick that's absorbed the water "pops." This explains what one often sees in an exterior brick wall: the odd brick that seems to have shed its surface. My laborer was on campus not only to repair "popped" bricks but to apply a waterproof sealant to thus-far-uncompromised bricks.

The conversation was so fascinating because it made me realize that I'd been around brickwork my entire life without knowing a thing about it. It made me realize that this bricklayer experienced the urban landscape in a much deeper way than I. "A fool sees not the same tree that a wise man sees," says William Blake. It's as true of bricks as it is of trees, and when it came to bricks, I was the perfect fool.

After years of teaching writing, I've discovered that most people experience language just as I experienced brickwork: an obvious component of everyday life—so obvious, in fact, that it's seldom noticed by the average man. But to a maker, that part of the commonplace in which he specializes isn't common at all. What do you make?

SIX

COULD I TROUBLE YOU FOR A LIGHT?

I WAS ALREADY IN my mid-20s when I discovered that sensitivity to language was considered effeminate by anyone. In high school, my only poetically minded classmates were boys, and our English teacher (a real mensch and a proper scholar) was a former U.S. Marine, and resembled a Visigothic warlord.

Once enrolled at the State University of New York at Buffalo, I fell into the orbit of American poet Robert Creeley, who was decidedly manly. He once got into a fistfight with Jackson Pollock and had a robust record of drunken hell-raising. The other students in Creeley's circle were almost exclusively male, and ostentatiously heterosexual.

I was well-prepared for this, having been raised in an Orthodox Jewish milieu in which the written word was a matter of general manly concern. The *beis medresh* (synagogue study hall), an explicitly male zone, was animated late into the night, with everyone from doctors to refrigerator repairmen applying themselves to Hebrew or Aramaic texts with painstaking care. Young men of scholarly distinction married well, sired many children, and enjoyed social esteem equal to that of lawyers.

To employ poets as paid spokesmen for Smith & Wesson revolvers and Camel cigarettes would be more consistent with historical norms than our current imagination of the poet as a preposterous milksop.

SEVEN

MY DECISION TO EXCLUDE HIP-HOP

"We are equally precluded from adopting styles essentially infantine and barbarous, however Herculean their infancy, or majestic their outlawry[.]"
—John Ruskin, *The Seven Lamps of Architecture*

I T'S NATURAL TO expect hip-hop to figure prominently in a book highlighting the connections between verbal facility and swaggering virility. It's necessary, therefore, to explain my decision to exclude it.

I discovered Baltimore's American Visionary Art Museum soon after it opened in 1995. Their collection of "outsider art" includes a remarkable anonymous sculpture called "Recovery." The official AVAM literature describes it thusly:

This lone figure was carved from a single apple tree trunk. It was created as a self-portrait by a British mental patient who had a distinctive concave chest from years of tuberculosis. His doctor remembered that he took no interest in making art until he encountered a fallen apple tree during a walk on the hospital grounds and asked for help in dragging it indoors and getting simple carving tools. At that time, there was hospital prohibition for mental patients handling what could be "lethal" instruments. However, Edward Adamson, a pioneer in using art to treat mental illness, persuaded the authorities to relax this rule, and trust the patient. The result, "Recovery," was a vindication of Edward's remarkable insight. For a month, the patient whittled the wood down to this figure. The artist, in his thirties, committed suicide about two years after leaving the hospital. This applewood figure is his only known work of art.[1]

Recovery, unknown artist[2]

Indeed, most of the works at the AVAM are made by lunatics, criminals, and other eccentrics. There's Adolf Wölfli, a Swiss gravedigger and pederast. There's Calvin Black, a roadside doll-carver from Possum Trot, California. There's Charles Dellschau, a Prussian-born butcher and UFO enthusiast. The

---

1   www.avam.org /
2   Courtesy of the American Visionary Arts Museum, Baltimore.

works are by turns primitive, whimsical, meticulous, grotesque. There's something not quite "right" about many of them, and the few "right" ones feel somehow wrong in their very rightness. Everything smells vaguely of Hell. I love it.

In the opening paragraph of "Self-Reliance," Ralph Waldo Emerson writes:

> To believe your own thought, to believe that what is true for you in your private heart is true for all men,—that is genius. [...] A man should learn to detect and watch that gleam of light which flashes across his mind from within, more than the lustre of the firmament of bards and sages. Yet he dismisses without notice his thought, because it is his. In every work of genius we recognize our own rejected thoughts: they come back to us with a certain alienated majesty.

Indeed, the highest art addresses something universal in the human breast. There's another type of art, however: art that engages us not by its universality but by its individual pathology. This is what "outsider art" is. And hip-hop should be understood as a category of "outsider art."

It's a shame to have distinctions like "High" and "Low" in culture. I've played the five-string banjo for many years, and old-time Appalachian music is essential to me. The tunes of Dock Boggs and Roscoe Holcomb have more heart, integrity, and dynamism than most of today's "highbrow" music. However, it's absurd to mention Dock or Roscoe in the same breath as Beethoven or Bach. To propose that hip-hop can attain the majesty of Keats or Donne is to demonstrate disbelief in the very idea of majesty.

Impatience with high art is perfectly creditable. To everything there is a season: a time for Dr. Johnson's essays, a time for Bernini, a time for the Oxford Lieder Festival…but also a time for frozen pizza and reruns of *Law & Order*. It's also perfectly creditable to disagree with any critical consensus—to argue that *Moby-Dick* is garbage, or that Ohio State football is better than

Russian ballet.

I won't tolerate, however, the claim that standards are themselves pernicious. Our ancestors expect better of us. And that's why there's no hip-hop here.

EIGHT

"THE VAIN SEARCH"

I KNOW HOW obnoxious a poet can be while pronouncing upon those characteristics distinguishing a "real" poet from the undifferentiated heap. The poet-essayist usually ends up with a piece of defensive, passive-aggressive self-portraiture—a riposte to criticism that nobody ever cared enough to level.

What you'll find in these pages isn't any kind of self-portraiture. If I dimly resemble the sketch, it's only because it represents an ideal to which I've long aspired. Life is an ordeal, which, however you choose to live it, will reduce you to a pathetic husk. If this will happen anyway, there's no excuse not to gallop toward your fate while attempting the impossible.

And it's nearly impossible to write "real" poetry. But, in the words of English philosopher Michael Oakeshott (paraphrasing Pascal): "It is good to be tired and wearied in the vain search for the true good, so that in the end we may stretch our arms to the Redeemer."[1]

---

1 Quoted by Paul Franco. *Michael Oakeshott: An Introduction*. Yale University Press, 2004, p. 36.

EDEN

I N W.H. AUDEN'S ESSAY, "Reading," he argues that a critic can only evaluate a work of art according to his own totally subjective Good-Bad axis. Since the Garden of Eden represents the epitome of the Good, the critic should disclose his personal vision of Eden. After all, if a food writer is dispatched to review an Indian restaurant, the whole thing will be compromised if it turns out that he dislikes Indian food—if (in other words) Indian food doesn't figure within his Eden.

Auden prepares a questionnaire that's meant to ascertain a critic's idea of Eden. Before this book gets properly underway, I owe it to you to provide my own answers:

LANDSCAPE: Irrigated Levantine hills, studded with olive trees, and dusted with cyclamen; access to a seashore where fresh-caught shrimp can be purchased.

CLIMATE: Like San Francisco.

ETHNIC ORIGIN OF INHABITANTS: Completely immaterial.

LANGUAGE: Any language in which it feels possible to discuss God and Love without embarrassment—a language in which sentimentality doesn't feel quite so barbarous.

WEIGHTS AND MEASURES: There shall be no exact measurement of any kind.

RELIGION: Amiable Roman polytheism. In the real world (Columbus, Ohio, where it's raining today, and I'm fresh out of green peppers), I'm a monotheist. Were I in Eden, however, I'd be free from the disturbances that make me need God in the first place; indeed, I'd exist in a dimension entirely beyond Need itself. And if metaphysical commitments are purely discretionary, I'll pick Roman polytheism. President Bill Clinton once said (with more charm than truth), "If you want to live like a Republican, you have to vote Democratic." Likewise, if you hanker after pagan ease, you've got to be a Christian.

SIZE OF CAPITAL: Sufficiently small that there's no traffic; sufficiently small that restaurants can space tables generously enough that chatting with your companion doesn't feel like exhibitionism.

FORM OF GOVERNMENT: Reasonable, clever people (elected or unelected; it doesn't matter), completely devoid of charisma, petrified of public speaking, overseeing an omni-competent, invisible technocracy.

SOURCES OF NATURAL POWER: Solar.

ECONOMIC ACTIVITIES: Anything that can be accomplished in a traditional Arab *souq*.

MEANS OF TRANSPORT: Walking.

ARCHITECTURE: Gothic: a great deal of stone performing the trick of appearing weightless.

DOMESTIC FURNITURE AND EQUIPMENT: Hypermodern, unobtrusive, and comfortable.

FORMAL DRESS: Classical togas.

SOURCES OF PUBLIC INFORMATION: Broadsides pasted to public walls.

PUBLIC STATUES: Numerous and diverse.

PUBLIC ENTERTAINMENTS: Plays performed by troupes of itinerant players, such as we meet in *Hamlet* 3.2 or in Ingmar Bergman's *The Seventh Seal*.

TEN

ARTIST STATEMENT

I WAS ONCE CALLED upon to prepare an "Artist Statement," the general idea being that no work of art can reasonably be expected to speak for itself, and that the "consumer" (presuming that he even exists) might benefit from some polemical handholding. Since those already interested in poetry might find it useful to have my aesthetic GPS coordinates, I provide the statement here. Neophytes are encouraged to skip to the next chapter.

There are two categories of poets: Clarifiers and Ramifiers. Clarifiers attempt to make sense of a situation—whether it be personal, social, political, or existential. Clarifiers include W.H. Auden, Joe Brainard, Leonard Cohen, Countee Cullen, John Donne, T.S. Eliot, James Fenton, Thomas Hardy, E.A. Housman, Philip Larkin, Irving Layton, C. Day Lewis, Louis MacNeice, John Milton, Vladimir Nabokov [as poet], John Frederick Nims, Ron Padgett, A.E. Robinson, John Greenleaf Whittier, and Walt Whitman. Whether their scope is modest (Brainard) or vast (Milton), Clarifiers synthesize and condense. In the conventional sense, Clarifiers are "good communicators;" they have something particular to say. Whatever jokes they make tend to be identifiable as such, and are often funny.

Not so with Ramifiers. As the etymology suggests (*rāmus*

[branch] + *faciō* [make]), their investigation of a subject forks, spreads, and subdivides. Examples include John Ashbery, Emily Dickinson, H.D., Robert Duncan, Geoffrey Hill, Charles Olson, Ezra Pound, and Louis Zukofsky. The effect may be both insistent and diffuse. Ramifiers avoid cliché by renouncing the frames of expression in which cliché is even possible. In other words, they seldom attempt to say anything. The adjective "hermetic" (which in current usage describes a poem whose willful, quasi-bookish obscurity is redeemed by its sound, its texture, the suggestiveness of its diction, the experimentalism it shows evidence of, or its general ability to float alongside a subject without ever crossing paths with it) is only applied to the work of Ramifiers.

Where a particular poet exists on the Clarifier-Ramifier axis does not correlate with other tendencies—aesthetic, political or cosmological. T.S. Eliot and Irving Layton share a column.

Some poets are situated outside the Clarifier-Ramifier axis, including some of my favorites: Robert Creeley, Gerard Manley Hopkins, and Dylan Thomas.

Nevertheless, I am a Clarifier. The Clarifier is a craftsman. Craftsmen make things. Ultimately, poetry cannot be a process; it's a product—perhaps even a luxury item, presenting itself for connoisseurial scrutiny. "Artificial" (literally "made with skill") was available as a term of approval until the Industrial Revolution, when human ingenuity came to be associated with squalor and the systematic abuse of the human spirit. Likewise, "product" hasn't done well in the Age of Walmart. "Artifice," however, is long overdue for revival. Let us have gracefully artificial poetry.

Some of the craftsmen I most revere are banjo luthiers. And one of my favorites is Bill Rickard. After misplacing both legs and his left arm in a motorcycle accident, he designed equipment enabling him to build world-class instruments using his right arm alone. What emerges from his workshop is superior by any standard. While his story is fascinating, the "process" would be of zero interest were his banjos shoddy—or even just okay. The New Testament injunction to judge trees by their fruit is as useful in banjo-making as it is in poetry.

ELEVEN

THE ILLUSION OF DIFFICULTY

I N THE ANNALS OF klezmer music, few inspire awe and esteem quite like clarinetist Naftule Brandwein, who was born in 1884 in present-day Ukraine. His genius wasn't lost on the Jewish gangsters of the era, the Murder, Inc. crowd, who often hired him to perform in their social clubs. Tales of his drunken, endearing weirdness abound. He once, for the sake of showmanship, had himself wrapped in Christmas lights for the duration of a set. However, he perspired so heavily when playing that the wires began to smoke and crackle while those otherworldly melodies spiraled from his instrument. My favorite Naftule Brandwein story involves his frequent decision to play with his back to the spectators so that they wouldn't be able to see his fingerings—so that they wouldn't be able to see how the magic is made.

Although I'm scarcely as good a poet as Brandwein was a clarinetist, I understand the temptation to keep mum about the tricks, especially those tricks that may seem absurdly easy, considering how insanely effective they are. We resist letting people peek behind the curtain, especially when the curtain conceals very little. For that reason, I wouldn't even consider giving away my secrets. But I'd certainly sell them, and, presuming that you're neither a thief nor a book critic, you've paid the retail price.

So let's get down to business.

II

THE HEAVY LIFTING

TWELVE

PROSODY

"PROSODY. Noun. \ 'prä-sə-dē \ [a] The study of versi-
fication, especially the study of metrical structure. [b] A
particular system, theory, or style of versification. [c] The
rhythmical and intonational aspect of language."
—*Merriam-Webster Dictionary*

W HEN IT'S A GOOD teacher who introduces us to an
idea or a book, that teacher's legacy walks along-
side the memory of that subject matter, gently recommending
it, asking you to accord it renewed attention. But when a bad
teacher gets ahold of an idea or book, their legacy is no less te-
nacious. A bad teacher doesn't render you merely indifferent to
a subject; he makes you despise it.

The topic of prosody is hardly a saturnalia, to say the least.
Since some form of literary education remains compulsory, and
since most teachers are bad, we have the perfect storm. Assum-
ing you've ever heard of prosody in the first place, it's unlikely a
topic which you are impatient to explore further.

One of the reasons for this is that you regard prosody as
a barrier to self-expression. You once wanted to say something,
when some dowdy English teacher, some hives-inducing har-
ridan, waddled into your line of sight, expatiating upon The
Rules. I get it.

That said, you might have had the experience of overhear-
ing a rookie violinist, age nine or ten, attempting to "express

himself." It's a sound that can raise the dead—and then make the dead regret having been raised. What I'm attempting in this book is not dissimilar to a course of violin lessons; I'm trying to help you develop a few fundamentals so that they become integrated in the mental version of "muscle memory." That's when the fun begins.

And besides, self-expression is overrated. What is this "self" that demands "expression"? If you're anything like me—

But, come to think of it, you're *everything* like me! That's the whole point. With the exception of protagonists from Werner Herzog movies, we all have the exact same "factory settings." We all find ourselves alive and vulnerable, scuttling about in search of respect, companionship, security, and meaning, attempting to evade pain, bearing implacable hungers, all the while beneath the inescapable shadow of our own mortality.

In many ways, there's nothing more tedious than a self. The fine thing about real poetry is that it's an enemy of the self's expression. You're thwarted in your thin drizzle of confession ("Woe is me!"), because the next word needs a stressed syllable in just the right place. Now, you must lay aside your pathetic self, and actually make something.

Poetry is the enemy of the self's expression—enemy, not conquistador. Poetry requires a well-balanced confrontation between Feeling and Technique. Without Technique, you have flaccid kvetching; without Feeling, you have bloodless experimentalism. Poetry requires the contribution of a self. But that self needs strenuous policing. And prosody is among the means by which you accomplish that.

There's a certain music that's inherent to language. It's not added, like caraway seeds to a loaf of rye bread; rather, it belongs to the dough itself. The poet's job is to arrange language so that its inherent music can be mobilized to some effect. The poet is like a master woodworker, studying the grain patterns of each individual piece of wood so that these patterns can contribute to an overall scheme.

There are two types of syllables: stressed and unstressed.

"Until" isn't pronounced "UN-til" (stressed, unstressed), but "un-TIL" (unstressed, stressed). To pronounce it incorrectly violates the word's music.

In one sense, the poet masters language, imposing himself upon it; in another sense, however, he's *engaging* with language, and establishing a consensual relationship with it. Language has certain priorities, tendencies, and quirks that must be yielded to. The poet takes language to a quiet ethnic restaurant, drinks wine with it, and asks it questions in a rich, NPR-ready baritone until it's comfortable exposing its nature to him.

Sometimes language can feel like an adversary. But do remember the sad wisdom that John Milton puts in Satan's mouth in *Paradise Lost*: "Who overcomes / By force hath overcome but half his foe."[1]

A poem is made of stanzas, a stanza is made of lines, and a line is made of...words? Close: a line is made of "feet." A foot is a rhythmic unit, usually of two syllables: one stressed, the other unstressed. I'll mark a stressed syllable "/" and an unstressed syllable "u."

A foot that's stressed-unstressed is called a "trochee:"

    "PHA-llic"   / u
    "MON-ster"   / u
    "WHIM-pers"   / u

A foot that's unstressed-stressed is called an "iamb," which is the most common foot in English verse:

    "a-LAS"   u /
    "e-RECT"   u /
    "a-LONE"   u /

"Iambic pentameter" refers to a pattern of five iambs per line ("penta" = five; "meter" = rhythm). Here's the opening line of Shakespeare's over-quoted Sonnet 18:

Shall I compare thee to a summer's day?

If we mark the prosody, it looks like this:

---

1 1. 647 – 648.

```
 u  /    u  /    u  /   u  /     u  /
Shall I com--pare thee to  a sum--mer's day
 1.       2.      3.      4.      5.
```

Notice that the borders between feet aren't necessarily coincident with those between words; "summer" straddles the fourth and fifth iamb.

Here's another little quirk of prosody: a syllable, stressed under some circumstances, may become unstressed in others. For example, here are the first two lines of Shakespeare's Sonnet 55:

Not marble nor the gilded monuments
Of princes shall outlive this powerful rhyme[.]

Let's focus on the second:

```
 u  /     u  /    u  /     u  /      u  /
Of prin- -ces shall out- -live this pow'r- -ful rhyme
 1.       2.      3.       4.         5.
```

Although "shall" appears as a stressed syllable, it's a function of rhythmical context. In the following example from Sonnet 3, "shall" appears as an unstressed syllable:

So thou through windows of thy age shall see[.][2]

We can notate it thusly:

```
 u  /    u   /    u  /  u  /  u  /
So thou through win-dows of thy age shall see
 1.      2.      3.    4.    5.
```

The eagle-eyed and bat-eared among you will have noticed some apparent anomalies in the sample from Sonnet 55:

---

2 11

Not marble nor the gilded monuments
Of princes shall outlive this powerful rhyme[.]

If the rhymical scheme is to be obeyed scrupulously, then "powerful" doesn't fit at all; Shakespeare pronounces the trisyllabic—

```
  /    u    u
po- -wer- -ful
```

—as a bisyllabic:

```
  /     u
pow'r- -ful
```

And furthermore, Shakespeare wants us to pronounce "monuments"—

```
  /   u   /
mon--u--ments
```

—rather than how it's actually pronounced:

```
  /   u   u
mon--u--ments
```

How to account for this?

Here's Robert Herrick's "Delight in Disorder:"

> A sweet disorder in the dress
> Kindles in clothes a wantonness;
> A lawn[3] about the shoulders thrown
> Into a fine distraction;
> An erring lace, which here and there   5.
> Enthralls the crimson stomacher;[4]
> A cuff neglectful, and thereby
> Ribands to flow confusedly;
> A winning wave, deserving note,

---

3 lawn] Shawl.
4 stomacher] A garment bound over a woman's bodice.

In the tempestuous petticoat;   10.
A careless shoestring, in whose tie
I see a wild civility:
Do more bewitch me, than when Art
Is too precise in every part.

Although we resist chaos, it's possible for something to be too orderly. Spectacles like North Korea's mass gymnastics strike us as so horrifying because we see in their perfect choreography something inhuman. Herrick's ardor for his lady wouldn't be enhanced were she an utter slob; it's those subtle deviations from symmetry that he finds so fetching.

This explains the metrical irregularities in our excerpt from Sonnet 55. The occasional deviations, contortions, and rhythmic protuberances humanize the text. After all, perfect prosody is a defining characteristic of what's called "doggerel:" vernacular, occasional, or novelty verse that was never meant to be taken very seriously.

THIRTEEN

ADDENDUM: ON DACTYLS

WHILE THE IAMB is our dominant foot, there are a few trisyllabic feet, the most interesting of which is the dactyl: stressed-unstressed-unstressed. "Dactyl" means "finger," because a finger has three bones, just as a dactylic foot has three syllables. Some examples:

"EN-trop-y"   / u u
"MAN-i-fests"   / u u
"DIRT-i-ness"   / u u

FOURTEEN

THE PROPER REGARD FOR THE PAST

M Y DENTIST HAS a wry sense of humor, maintaining in his lobby a display case of premodern dentistry tools. The gulf between the type of dentistry represented by those *auto-da-fé* implements and the type of dentistry practiced inside the good man's office is so sweeping that (beyond the fact that both endeavors have human teeth as their subject) they scarcely have anything in common.

As a poet, I've always found it impossible to accept what most of my peers took so easily for granted: "Back Then Poetry" and "Now Poetry" must be similarly estranged. Take Edgar Allan Poe's "The Raven:" why (I wondered) should that entire mode of expression be off-limits? Do people not fall in love now as they did then? Do soulmates not die now as they did then? Do the survivors not grieve now as they did then? Are mystical visitations unheard of today? Was there some point around 1953 when average people became invulnerable to the spell of metrically regulated language?

Certain things do seem to have changed, of course. The age of the 36,000-line narrative poem (like *The Faerie Queene*) seems irrevocably gone. Overt bigotry is discouraged. Since, amid the regnant nihilism, religions seem to have increasingly more in common, we're unlikely to encounter new poems in which one kind of Christian animadverts, on purely doctrinal grounds, against a different kind of Christian. And in the Age of YouTube, I'm afraid that the didactic poem is extinct. I don't know if there's anything out there explaining, by means of sprightly iambic couplets, how to change the sparkplugs on a 2011 Honda Fit, but I'm headed to Google—and then (truth be told) to a professional.

To be clear, I won't miss long-winded narrative, bigotry, *odium theologicum* [theological hatred], and didacticism. But is the entire tradition contaminated?

Postmodernists believe so. They argue that the past is not only a foreign country, but a particularly barbaric foreign country, and that anything originating there must be wicked.

As every well-adjusted adult knows intuitively, this view of the past is insane. But let's assume it isn't; let's assume that the past really is an endless hellscape of bigotry, colonialism, and all the rest of it. I maintain that not even *that* would invalidate traditional modes of expression. The fact that John Donne once wrote, "Spit in my face, you Jews, and pierce my side,"[1] cannot begin to delegitimize poetic convention itself.

To reject poetic form because it's been used to articulate unpleasant things is like having a bad meal, and then deciding that tastiness as such is distasteful, and then having the temerity to call yourself a gourmand. Traditional poetic form will seem contaminated only if you assume a worldview that, if persevered in, will strip from the world everything that's even potentially good, consoling, and delightful.

Although postmodernists have certainly made dispiriting headway in this regard, the odds are ultimately stacked against them. Real poetry is like bacon. It's as if the Left is attempting not just to ban bacon, but to convince you that it was never all that tasty in the first place—that it really tastes like styrofoam. With sufficient time and effort, you could (I suppose) convince yourself that bacon tastes bad, and that the universal consensus to the contrary is wrong, and that the whole idea of a universal consensus regarding *any* food deserves the sternest skepticism.

In so convincing yourself, however, you'd also end up with some corollary convictions: that "taste" itself cannot be possible, that (by extension) common sense is an illusion, and

---

1 Holy Sonnet 11, line 1.

that (finally) nothing is quite knowable. Half of the population would replace bacon with styrofoam cubes. Twenty-five percent would continue eating bacon, but only in private. The remaining twenty-five percent would eat bacon openly, and would start a cash-hemorrhaging magazine in which to hold forth on the subject. Many companies trafficking in bacon would go bankrupt. Most remaining companies would chemically alter their bacon to taste vaguely like styrofoam.

A few real men, however, would remain, unapologetically making good bacon, motivated not by bloody-mindedness, but rather, by an earnest inability to see what the censorious fuss is about.

I'm one of those men, and I'd like to convince you to join me.

FIFTEEN

FORM

I DEFINE "poetic form" loosely, using the term to refer not exclusively to specific poetic structures (sonnets, sestinas, villanelles, etc.) but to the poem's broader character, texture, and mode of address. Poetic form includes structure, just as it includes prosody and rhetoric.

William Drummond of Hawthornden recalls that Ben Jonson "cursed Petrarch for redacting[1] verses to sonnets, which he said were like that tyrant's bed, where some who were too short were wracked, others too long cut short."[2]

Robert Creeley would agree. His influential dictum that "[f]orm is never more than an extension of content"[3] implies a similar argument. The subject of a poem isn't like a quart of milk that can be poured into differently shaped vessels without changing the nature of the milk. Rather, according to Creeley, the "content" of a poem comes first, and the "form" of the poem should be an outgrowth of what's being said. He elaborated in a 2004 interview with Leonard Schwartz:

Well, content is never more than an extension of form[,]

---

1 redacting] In this context, "redact" means to reduce.

2 Quoted in Ian Donaldson. *Ben Jonson: A Life*. Oxford University Press, 2011, p. 48.

3 Quoted in Charles Olson's "Projective Verse," reprinted in *Collected Prose*. University of California Press, 1997, p. 239.

and form is never more than an extension of content. They sort of go together[.] [...] It's really hard to think of one without the other; in fact, I don't think it's possible.[4]

Although Creeley would reject the use to which I'm putting his dictum, it's clear to me that the solution to the problem of form mutilating content isn't the abandonment of form, but its more scrupulous use.

---

4 In *Jacket* 25, 2004.

SIXTEEN

(FORM, CONTINUED)
ADAM HURT'S GOURD BANJO

DAVID HYATT IS a luthier specializing in a primitive version of the five-string banjo, the "pot" of which isn't made of a wooden hoop, but of a dried, hollowed gourd. I first became aware of his work when I saw virtuoso Adam Hurt performing with one of Hyatt's instruments.

Many gourd banjos are uncomfortable to hold. Not only are they awkwardly shaped, but the neck is heavier than the body, which is not only disconcertingly light, but has a slippery texture, so that a certain amount of concentration that should be channeled into your actual musicianship ends up diverted into the struggle to keep the thing well positioned on your lap.

But Hurt's banjo wasn't like that. You see, Hyatt didn't just select a gourd, but actually raised it according to his specifications. The gourd was forced to grow in-between two panes of glass. That way, it had two perfectly flat sides. The growing thing was forced to negotiate around formal limits, thereby producing something that's simultaneously organic and artificial, shapely and misshapen.

That's what a poem is like when it's been properly disciplined by form.

Photo credit: Jesse Andrews

SEVENTEEN

(FORM, CONTINUED)
BODY AND SOUL: FORM AND CONTENT

I N *The Marriage of Heaven and Hell*, William Blake says something wise:

> Man has no Body distinct from his Soul. For that called
> Body is a portion of Soul discerned by the five senses[.]

This proposal about the relationship between the Body and the Soul is something like the relationship between poetic Form and Content.

EIGHTEEN

FORMALITY

I WRITE THIS AT my desk at the school where I teach. It's late May, and I'm wearing shorts and sneakers. Summer vacation is days away, and it seemed preposterous to bother with a necktie, proper trousers, and professional shoes. And it's clear that I'm not the only teacher who feels this way. All of us are spending these final days dressed like slobs—which is to say, the same way our students are dressed all the time.

We like to be comfortable, and we associate comfort with honesty; formality, with deception. If I wear sweatpants at home (we reason), it would be affectation to do otherwise at school. In friendly, informal, first-name-basis America, how can we argue that poetry, which makes the most ambitious claims to Truth, should be formal?

Perhaps the solution can be found in *Hero and Leander*— not in the main body of Christopher Marlowe's mini-epic, but in the bit added by George Chapman after Marlowe received a lethal dagger in the eye.

The story of Hero and Leander comes from Ovid and Musaeus, and involves two lovers. Hero is a priestess of Venus who lives in Sestos; Leander is an ardent young man who lives in Abydos, on the opposite side of the Hellespont, a waterway in present-day Turkey. The story is archetypal: thwarted love, burning passion, the whole nine yards. And, Marlowe being Marlowe, there's a transgressive sensuality running through it.

When Marlowe died, Chapman was brought in. And

Chapman was a bit of a moralizing spoilsport; his contribution to the poem has a radically different character from what preceded it.

Or perhaps he's not quite the spoilsport that he may at first seem, for it isn't on the usual grounds that Chapman objects to the premarital slap-and-tickle. There isn't the precious poeticizing about chastity that we find, say, in John Milton's *Comus*. There isn't the specter of dishonor and social ruin that Laertes and Polonius invoke when lecturing Ophelia on why she ought not canoodle with Hamlet. There isn't any of the inverted puritanism we sometimes get from John Wilmot, the hedonistic 2nd Earl of Rochester, who (unintentionally) can make sex seem so revolting that we feel lucky if we're not getting lucky.

No, Chapman is saying something else entirely. Here's where he outlines his argument:

> But as he[1] shook with passionate desire
> To put in flame his other secret fire,
> A music so divine did pierce his ear
> As never yet his ravished sense did hear:
> When suddenly a light of twenty hues   5.
> Brake through the roof, and like the rainbow views
> Amazed Leander, in whose beams came down
> The goddess Ceremony, with a crown
> Of all the stars, and heaven with her descended.
> Her flaming[2] hair to her bright feet extended,   10.
> By which hung all the bench[3] of deities,
> And in a chain, compact[4] of ears and eyes,
> She led Religion.

Ceremony is personified as a goddess. Notice that she isn't subordinate to Religion; indeed, it's the other way around.

---

1 he] Leander.

2 flaming] The word is being used figuratively.

3 bench] A seat of dignity.

4 compact] Made by connecting.

> All her body was
> Clear and transparent as the purest glass,
> For she was all presented to the sense: 15.

Ceremony hides nothing. She makes things visible. Indeed, among the *OED*'s peripheral definitions is "[a]n external accessory or symbolical 'attribute' of worship, state, or pomp." In other words, it's a public symbol representing a private reality.

> Devotion, Order, State,[5] and Reverence
> Her shadows were. Society, Memory;
> All which her sight made live, her absence die.

We're given a catalogue of those qualities that separate us from animals: "devotion," "order," "state," "reverence," "society," and "memory." Their common denominator is something so easily overlooked (and so easily dismissed) as ceremony.

> A rich disparent[6] pentacle[7] she wears,
> Drawn full of circles and strange characters.[8]   20.
> Her face was changeable to every eye:
> One way looked ill, another graciously;
> Which, while men viewed, they cheerful were and holy,
> But looking off, vicious and melancholy.

Ceremony isn't like some Victorian imagination of God, invoked simply to prevent decent people from having fun. No; Ceremony's goal is our happiness.

---

5 state] Health.

6 disparent] "Unlike, diverse; of various appearance" (*OED*). Interestingly, its first recorded use is in Chapman's 1611 translation of Homer's *Iliad*.

7 pentacle] Apparently a generic name for a magical symbol.

8 characters] "Distinctive mark[s] impressed, engraved, or otherwise made on a surface" (*OED*). It was around this time when "character" began to refer to an individual's moral qualities.

The snaky paths to each observed law   25.
Did policy in her broad bosom draw.

The observance of a law is, after all, a performance—but to call
it "only" a performance would miss the point.

One hand a mathematic[9] crystal sways,
Which gathering in one line a thousand rays
From her bright eyes, Confusion burns to death,
And all estates[10] of men distinguisheth.   30.
By it Morality and Comeliness[11]
Themselves in all their sightly figures dress.

One of the best surprises at my college graduation cere-
mony was the sight of my professors in full academic regalia.
Although they'd dressed like everymen in the lecture hall, here,
each professor resembled a giant walking *boutonnière* of daz-
zling complexity. There were black gowns adorned with import-
ant colored geometries; there were medals, tassels, tufts of white
fur, and berets resembling crushed velvet mushrooms.

These costumes distinguished "all estates of men" (or all
estates of professors, at any rate), rendering visible what had
once been abstract. The *Ordre des Arts et des Lettres* is so ab-
stract as to be almost meaningless; a medallion pinned to a pro-
fessor's gown is real. That medallion is the equivalent of a hand-
ful of chalk powder you can toss into a well-lit room so that an
individual shaft of light will announce its shape.

---

9 mathematic] Mathematical.

10 estates] Conditions.

11 comeliness] "Attractiveness, beauty; grace; courtesy. Occasionally also:
pleasant but not strikingly beautiful appearance" (*OED*).

Her other hand a laurel rod applies,[12]
To beat back Barbarism, and Avarice
That followed, eating earth, and excrement,   35.
And human limbs, and would make proud ascent
To seats of Gods were Ceremony slain.
The Hours and Graces bore her glorious train,
And all the sweets of our society
Were sphered and treasured in her bounteous eye.   40.
Thus she appeared, and sharply did reprove
Leander's bluntness in his violent love[.]

In addition to the routine definitions of "violent," the *OED*
offers some illuminating surprises:

> 1. "Characterized by or involving tyranny or oppression."
> 2. "Characterized by great physical force or strength and
> (typically) speed; not gentle or moderate."
> 3. "Of the use, occupation, or taking possession of anoth-
> er's property: carried out or occurring without the own-
> er's consent, esp. by forcible means; wrongful, illegal."
> 4. "[Of something] [t]hat distorts or corrupts the mean-
> ing of a word, text, etc.; forced, artificial, strained."

Violence is at odds with Ceremony because the latter represents
the power that underwrites law, whereas the former is charac-
terized by lawlessness. Bluntness (which we sometimes regard
as a virtue) is violent, since violence is "not gentle or moderate."
And finally, even though Ceremony may seem tyrannical, we're
led to deduce that Ceremony is in fact incompatible with tyr-
anny, for tyranny is implied in violence. To permit yourself to
be bound by Ceremony is to be liberated in your most essential

---

12 laurel rod] This, from Volume I of John Addington Symonds's *Studies of
the Greek Poets*:

> Hesiod, at the opening of the Theogony, tells us how he had received
> a staff of this kind from the Muse upon Mount Helicon. Either, then,
> the laurel rod had already been recognized in that part of Greece as the
> symbol of the poet's office, or else, from the respect which the followers
> of Hesiod paid to the details of his poem, they adopted it as their badge.

nature.

> Told him how poor was substance without rites,
> Like bills unsigned, desires without delights;

There's a tradition that elevates "desires without delights" into a perverse sort of achievement. The poetry of courtly love is all about desire sans consummation. For John Keats, who came along a few hundred years after chivalry's heyday, the ability to experience "desires without delights" was among the cardinal joys in being alive. In his sonnet, "When I Have Fears That I May Cease to Be," he addresses his beloved:

> And when I feel, fair creature of an hour,
> That I shall never look upon thee more,
> Never have relish in the faery power
> Of unreflecting love [...][13]

To romanticize frustration seems dishonest, for it attempts to make a virtue of necessity. Men often fall in love; since these spasms of longing seldom yield much, it's useful to have some consoling half-truths at the ready. Chapman, however, is less of a masochist; he delights in delights. And he argues (paradoxically, it may seem) that delights only come via the self-discipline involved in Ceremony. He continues:

> Like meats unseasoned; like rank corn[14] that grows   45.
> On cottages, that none or reaps or sows:

Carnivores eat meat; they're happy when they can acquire it, and they don't seem interested in asking too many questions. For human beings, however, food isn't simply a delivery system for nutrition. The simple act of seasoning our meat is a kind of rite—a ceremony that reifies our claim to be superior to ani-

---

13 9-12

14 corn] "Applied collectively to the cereal plants while growing, or, while still containing the grain" (*OED*).

mals.

> Not being with civil forms confirmed and bounded,
> For human dignities and comforts founded,
> But loose and secret all their glories hide.
> Fear fills the chamber; darkness decks the bride.[15]   50.

In his "Introduction to Shakespeare's Sonnets," W.H. Auden writes:

> In this century we have reacquired a taste for the conceit,[16] as we have for baroque architecture, and no longer think that artifice is incompatible with passion.[17]

When he mentions our rediscovered "taste for the conceit," I wish he would have given examples, because I cannot begin to guess what he has in mind. That artifice is not incompatible with passion is true enough. Chapman, however, takes it one step further: you can't have real passion without artifice.

----

15 105-154

16 conceit] In poetry, "conceit" refers to a complex system of metaphor.

17 Reprinted as an Appendix to Sylvan Barnet's edition of *The Sonnets and Narrative Poems*. Everyman's Library, 1992, p. 234.

NINETEEN

"OFT CRUEL FIGHTS WELL PICTURED FORTH DO PLEASE"

S IR PHILIP SIDNEY'S *Astrophel and Stella* would be considered the best sonnet sequence of the Elizabethan age, but for the pesky fact that William Shakespeare existed, and wrote sonnets. Even excellence, when compared to Shakespeare, can seem like *mere* excellence.

Here's Sonnet 34. Since it's an internal dialogue, I've formatted it accordingly.

VOICE 1. Come, let me write.

VOICE 2. *And to what end?[1]*

VOICE 1.   To ease
          A burdened heart.

VOICE 2. *How can words ease, which are*
          The glasses[2] of thy daily vexing care?[3]

VOICE 1. Oft cruel fights well pictured forth do please.

VOICE 2. *Art not ashamed to publish thy disease?*

---

1 And to what end?] For what purpose?
2 glasses] Mirrors.
3 care] Anxiety.

VOICE 1.   Nay, that may breed my fame, it is so rare.

VOICE 2.   *But will not wise men think thy words fond* [4]
ware?[5]

VOICE 1.   Then be they close, and so none shall dis-
please.

VOICE 2.   *What idler thing than speak and not be*
heard?

VOICE 1.   What harder thing than smart and not to
speak?
Peace, foolish wit; with wit my wit is marred.
Thus write I while I doubt to write, and wreak
My harms in ink's poor loss; perhaps some
find
Stella's great powers, that so confuse my mind.

Let's recross the terrain—this time, a little more carefully.
I'll comment between the lines.

VOICE 1.   Come, let me write.

A simple human impulse, this.

VOICE 2.   *And to what end?*

The question has a lovely simplicity—the simplicity of a
young child's "why?"

VOICE 1.   To ease
A burdened heart.

---

4 fond]   Foolish, silly.

5 ware]   Merchandise.

The poem hasn't yet been proposed as something that others might be invited to read. The easing of a burdened heart is a private enterprise.

VOICE 2. *How can words ease, which are*
The glasses of thy daily vexing care?

Good question. Perhaps a suffering soul might find relief by writing a detective story or anything else that's conspicuously imaginative. But VOICE 1 proposes to write about his own misery. The better the poet, the better his ability to make language accurately reflect his feelings, and these are the very feelings from which the sufferer wants to escape. The competent poet will become ensnared in his unhappiness in direct proportion as he attempts to escape from it.

This is ahead of its time, anticipating T.S. Eliot's "The Love Song of J. Alfred Prufrock," which is a poem about the impossibility of communication—a poem about the existential booby-traps scattered throughout communication itself.

VOICE 1. Oft cruel fights well pictured forth do please.

People are entertained by disorders and tensions that are so volatile that they can't be counterpoised against each other. It's only here that the poem is proposed as a public phenomenon. If a martyrdom occurs in a forest, and there's no one there to hear it, it doesn't quite make a noise.

VOICE 2. *Art not ashamed to publish thy disease?*

In other words, isn't this exhibitionism just a little unmanly?

VOICE 1. Nay, that may breed my fame, it is so rare.

VOICE 1 proposes that a romantic hurricane within the heart is a precious commodity. Simply to "spill your guts" is downright common, but to show an audience the battle between the need for catharsis and its tragic impossibility—this is "rare."

Sonnet 34 was written in the 1580s, and it isn't until 1615 that we find the first recorded use of "rare" referring to lightly cooked meat. If this usage was in circulation, it would add an extra strata of meaning to the poem, making verse-writing seem like the gladiatorial games, where public excitement was stimulated by the spectacle of bloody meat.

> VOICE 2.   *But will not wise men think thy words fond*
>   *ware?*

The implication is that foolish men might be entertained, but that "wise men" will think you're behaving like a jackass.

> VOICE 1.   Then be they close, and so none shall dis-
>   please.

It's unclear what "they" refers to: "wise men" or "thy words." It's even knottier because "close" has a range of meanings. If we assume that "they" refers to "thy words," then we can find clarity in one of the more peripheral definitions of "close:" "Not open to public access or competition; confined or restricted to a privileged few" (*OED*). The "privileged few" would be those who aren't wise, upending the hierarchy as Jesus does when he says that "the meek will inherit the Earth."

> VOICE 2.   *What idler thing than speak and not be*
>   *heard?*

VOICE 2 ends up exactly where it began, wondering about what the point is.

> VOICE 1.   What harder thing than smart and not to
>   speak?
>   Peace, foolish wit; with wit my wit is marred.
>   Thus write I while I doubt to write, and wreak

> My harms in ink's poor loss; perhaps some
>> find
> Stella's great powers, that so confuse my mind.

The tensions go largely unresolved. The couplet, which in a sonnet, typically brings closure, is teetering here on the crumbly edge of a "perhaps." Such resolution as the poem affords is generated not in what is said, but in *how* it's said: firmly within the conventions of the English sonnet. The dialectical confusion of the "content" is offset by the certainty of the form.

TWENTY

"CRÆFT"

C YNEWULF, THE nineth-century Anglo-Saxon poet, writes in "The Ascension:"

> The one in whom the craft of
> Wisdom is entrusted in the heart can sing and tell
> Very many things.[1]

According to *Bosworth-Toller's Anglo-Saxon Dictionary*, "cræft" means "power, might, strength as of body"—a nimbus of meaning that's backlit by another sense of "cræft:" a kind of ship, "a machine, instrument, engine."

In the entry for "*hearpe-streng*" [harp string], we find the illustrative quote:

> *Hé ða hearpestrengas mid cræfte ástirian ongan.*
> [He began to move the strings of the harp skillfully.]

This reminds me of a line from "Andreas," a Christian epic poem preserved in the so-called the Vercelli Book:

> [Matthew] was the first among the Jews to write the

---

1 Robert E. Bjork, trans. *The Old English Poems of Cynewulf*. Harvard University Press, 2013, p. 17.

gospel in words with wonderful skill [*wundor-cræfte*].[2]

We haven't lost the sense that craft can be exercised in the arrangement of words; we all know that politicians and advertisers exercise tremendous craft. What we've lost, however, is any sense that craft can enable us to arrange words into things of Goodness, Truth, and Beauty. We've ceded craft to bad people.

Poets need it back.

---

2 Mary Clayton, trans. *Old English Poems of Christ and His Saints*. Harvard University Press, 2013, p. 184.

TWENTY-ONE

"MATERIALS FOR AN ART"

I N HIS PREFACE to *The Picture of Dorian Gray*, Oscar Wilde writes:

> Thought and language are to the artist instruments of an art. Vice and virtue are to the artist materials for an art.

This reminds me of great luthiers I've met. They'll discover a marvelous piece of wood, something with a vivid and unusual character, and they'll store it away for some unknown future use. The piece of wood isn't good or bad. It's better than good: it's *interesting*, and it might spend a decade in a climate-controlled room until the wood declares itself perfect for this guitar neck or that fretboard. Destiny summons the wood from storage when it becomes clear that a particular project cannot be completed without it, and that, in being so used, the wood's unique dignity will be recognized. The craftsman knows how to hear Destiny.

As the luthier is to wood, the poet is to vice and virtue.

TWENTY-TWO

THE POINT OF POINTLESSNESS

" 'A CHIEVEMENT' IS THE 'diabolical' element in human life," writes English philosopher Michael Oakeshott, "and the symbol of our vulgarization of human life is our near exclusive concern with achievement." He elaborates:

> Not scientific thinking, but the "gifts" of "science"; the motor car, the telephone, radar, getting to the moon, antibiotics, penicillin, the bomb. Whereas the only human value lies in the adventure and the excitement of discovery. Not standing on the top of Everest, but getting there. Not the "conquests" but the battles; not the "victory" but the "play." It is our non-recognition of this, or our rejection of it, which makes our civilization a non-religious civilization. At least, non-Christian: Christianity is the religion of "non-achievement."[1]

In *The Quest for Community*, Robert Nisbet addresses a different dimension of the same fundamental problem when he observes that "[f]unction and meaning tend to become dramatically fused in time of war."[2]

Oakeshott and Nisbet agree that, in a healthy society, some things should be permitted to exist for their own sake.

---

1 Quoted by Paul Franco in *Michael Oakeshott: An Introduction*. Yale University Press, 2004, p. 38.

2 ISI Books, 1990, p. 32.

On my weekly supermarket run, the Ocean Spray cranberry juice bottle informs me that "[e]ach 8oz glass is equal to 1 cup of fruit," and that the USDA "recommends a daily intake of 2 cups of fruit for a 2,000 calorie diet." I don't know what sort of liability they're skirting by providing the raw materials of a syllogism rather than just saying that two glasses of the stuff will satisfy your USDA recommendation.

Major Premise: Each 8oz glass is equal to 1 cup of fruit.
Minor Premise: The USDA recommends a daily intake of 2 cups of fruit.
Ergo: Two tumblers should do the trick.

(This, however, is said outright: "Consuming one serving [8 oz] each day [...] may help reduce the risk of recurrent urinary tract infection [UTI] in healthy women." It's good to know, though personally irrelevant: I'm neither a woman nor healthy.)

Quaker Oats Old-Fashioned Oatmeal, God bless them, also gives me an opportunity to use my training in formal logic:

Major Premise: "3 grams of soluble fiber from oatmeal daily in a diet low in saturated fat and cholesterol may reduce the risk of heart disease."
Minor Premise: "This cereal has 2 grams [of soluble fiber] per serving."
Ergo: Have a little over one portion, and you're in business.

The dominant advertising strategy nowadays is to frame a food as if it were a "delivery system" for this or that salubrious chemical. Food is rhetorically proposed as a type of medicine; indeed, a company responsible for a particularly good ginger tea is even more forthright, taking as its name "Traditional Medicinals." I've always found it mystifying how American parents can criticize youngsters for drinking "just to get drunk" (in other words, for instrumentalizing booze), while many of these parents have scarcely ever regarded a foodstuff as worthwhile for its own sake.

This mindset produces all sorts of perversions, like the concept of "wasted calories"—the idea being that each calorie should be pulling its own weight in the health-giving department, and that any unemployed calorie is like an unemployed worker: a cumbersome burden that should be deeply ashamed of itself.

Some of us, however, have a different relationship with food: we eat for pleasure. What's the *function* of a bacon cheeseburger? It has none, and that's the point. The function of a bacon cheeseburger *is to be a bacon cheeseburger.*

A motley band of troublemakers imagines the "uses" of poetry just as Ocean Spray imagines the "uses" of cranberry juice. Postmodernists regard poetry as a delivery system for beliefs. A certain kind of conservative regards poetry as a delivery system for moral instruction. The conjurers of standardized tests (may they come down with chlamydia) regard individual lines of poetry as delivery systems for "information" which can somehow be abstracted from the text, and then paraphrased. They regard the analysis of literature as a means of separating those fools who aren't bound for academic distinction from those fools who *are.*

(By the way, the very idea of "analyzing" literature is insulting and ridiculous. Does one "analyze" a *pain au chocolat?*— perhaps, if a traumatic brain injury has left you incapable of experiencing pleasure. For literature, we need to borrow the language of connoisseurship.)

When I took the absurd "Praxis" exam to earn my teaching licensure, there was a line from T.S. Eliot's "The Love Song of J. Alfred Prufrock," followed by a multiple-choice question about its "purpose." I forget what the options were, but the "right" answer was: "To show the narrator's regret about the past." It's like saying that the "purpose" of *King Lear* is to warn of the consequences of inept parenting.

Let's be done with this reductive nonsense. The purpose of a poem is to be a poem.

TWENTY-THREE

THE DECLINE OF POETRY'S RESPECTABILITY

T HE 1960S COMES IN for an awful lot of blame, and I hate to add to it. The '60s can seem like the Jew among decades: a wretched, all-purpose scapegoat. However, the cultural trends that destroyed poetry's respectability came to fruition during that unfortunate decade.

I was a kid, not during the '60s, but during the '80s and '90s, which was the golden age of basketball. I was lucky enough to see Michael Jordan play. He inspired awe because everyone agreed on what it meant to play basketball well. No one could do what he did, and everyone knew it. It's thrilling to see anything done masterfully. It doesn't matter if it's a rancher lassoing a steer, a stonemason working his marble into a church's balustrade, or a luthier counterpoising the tensions in a weightless-seeming mandolin. Excellence is mesmerizing.

It was during the 1960s that poetry became democratized; when something is democratized, excellence is superseded by participation. Beat icon Allen Ginsberg achieved titanic fame, not only for his indecency, but for his gospel that anyone could write poetry. He frankly disdained craft, preaching "First Thought, Best Thought." Therefore, if your first thought is about pederasty (and Ginsberg's sometimes were), then—presto!—you're in business.[1] If your first thought is unintelligible,

---

1 Ginsberg served as a semiofficial spokesman for the North American Man-Boy Love Association (NAMBLA).

do commit it to paper; its very unintelligibility indicates a poetic voice unmediated by that inner censor stationed there by a puritanical values system to smother spontaneous thought and speech.[2]

Ginsberg's mantra was later intellectualized into the slogan "Poetry is a process, not a product." This negates even the *possibility* of craft, since craft implies a product. The idea of poetry as a process is what sponsors some of the antics one finds in the world of "experimental" poetry—the sickly conceptual crap that's invaded every other area of highbrow culture. One notable avant-garde poet "explains" himself thusly:

> Opems [*sic*] are my pomes [*sic*], a forms of improvisational manuscript poeming [*sic*] with variable entry points and without time restriction or bondage that calls for a concentration of performed poetic trajectories as they originate via the keys with any opem [*sic*]. Make them umbleuttphabite [*sic*] and others.[3]

How edifying.

And then came "identity politics" to piss on the ruins, further alienating poetry from craft by asserting that a poet's demographic profile trumps absolutely everything.

Twentieth-century disorientation estranged poetry from craft; trends in pedagogy finalized the divorce. It's common nowadays to hear people, even fairly literate people, echo what

---

2 As on so much else, Leonard Cohen was wise on the topic of "First Thought, Best Thought:"

> You know that first-thought, best-thought promotional activity of the writing Jewish Buddhists. This idea that it's all just there, just say it. That's never worked for me. My first thoughts are dull, are prejudiced, are poisonous. [...] [V]ery few things that you love are spontaneous and visceral. I think right now what the age seems to demand is a much more modest approach to our psyches.

> (Jeff Burger, ed. *Leonard Cohen on Leonard Cohen: Interviews and Encounters*. Chicago Review Press, 2014, pp. 340-341.)

3 Michael Basinski, Artist statement for "soundvision / visionsound III," a group exhibition / reading at Nave Gallery, 2005.

they've learned in school, that poetry is purely subjective, and that its meaning (to the extent that it can be said to have one) depends upon what the reader "brings to it." The implication is that poetry is only slightly less legible than tea leaves. Few are taught that the best poetry is the least ambiguous, and that a good poem is like a precisely designed, expertly machined piece of artillery.

I recite a great deal of poetry when I teach.

"What does this passage *mean*?" I'll ask.

The respondent will often preface his answer with:

"Well, what *I* got out of it was…"

And I'll find myself recalling a particularly tense tutorial I had over twenty years ago at Oxford, where I was an exchange student. My tutor was vivisecting the essay I'd submitted that week. His exasperation with my writing wasn't exceeding normal bounds—until he arrived at a phrase that shifted him to an even severer pitch of (perfectly justified) highbrow English disapproval:

"*It seems to me that…*"

"Mr. Burghauser," he enunciated painfully, "it is of very little consequence to me, or to anybody else, how *it* 'seems' to *you*."

Students have grown so sensitive recently. Any criticism of their writing must now be translated into a vaguely aethereal sort of suasion. This can be frustrating.

"Mr. Smith," I want to insist, "it is of very little consequence to me, or to anybody else, what *you* 'got' out of *it*."

If I've succeeded in the classroom, it's because I teach literature via a simplified version of the method that the rabbis used when teaching me Scripture. Rabbinical exegesis recognizes two levels on which a text may be understood. The first is called *p'shat*,[4] which involves the literal meaning of the text; the second, *d'rash*,[5] involves everything else, including a more rigorous variant of "what I got out of it."

---

4 Literally "straight."

5 Literally "enquire."

Here's an example. Christopher Marlowe's *Doctor Faustus* is about a scholar pining for unlimited knowledge, to which Man isn't entitled. The literary record argues that Man has a designated place, and that he ought to be a good sport about it.

Faustus will have none of it, contracting an agreement with the demon Mephistopheles that, in exchange for 25 years of omniscience, Faustus will thereafter relinquish himself to the eternal torments of Hell. The play is especially wise about the nature of these types of transgressions: Faustus ends up using his powers not for the public good, and not even for private enrichment or personal vengeance, but to play practical jokes and to serve as a court magician.

This sense of waste backlights the soliloquy that Faustus delivers an hour before the devil collects his due. These 61 lines constitute one of the most gripping episodes in English literature.

> [*The clock strikes eleven.*]
> Ah, Faustus,
> Now hast thou but one bare hour to live,
> And then thou must be damned perpetually.
> Stand still, you ever-moving spheres of heaven,
> That time may cease, and midnight never come.   5.
> Fair Nature's eye, rise, rise again, and make
> Perpetual day, or let this hour be but
> A year, a month, a week, a natural day,
> That Faustus may repent and save his soul.
> O *lente, lente currite noctis equi!*   10.
> The stars move still, time runs, the clock will strike,
> The devil will come, and Faustus must be damned.
> O I'll leap up to my God! Who pulls me down?
> See, see where Christ's blood streams in the firmament!
> One drop would save my soul, half a drop: ah my
>   Christ—   15.
> Ah, rend not my heart, for naming of my Christ;
> Yet will I call on Him—O spare me, Lucifer!
> Where is it now? 'Tis gone: and see where God

Stretcheth out his arm, and bends his ireful brows!
Mountains and hills, come, come and fall on me,   20.
And hide me from the heavy wrath of God.
No, no?
Then will I headlong run into the earth:
Earth, gape! O no, it will not harbor me.
You stars that reigned at my nativity,   25.
Whose influence hath allotted death and hell,
Now draw up Faustus like a foggy mist
Into the entrails of yon laboring cloud,
That when you vomit forth into the air
My limbs may issue from your smokey mouths,   30.
So that my soul may but ascend to heaven.
                              [*The clock strikes.*]
Ah, half the hour is past: 'twill all be past anon.
O God, if thou wilt not have mercy on my soul,
Yet for Christ's sake, whose blood hath ransomed me, 35.
Impose some end to my incessant pain:
Let Faustus live in hell a thousand years,
A hundred thousand, and at last be saved.
O no end is limited to damnèd souls!
Why wert thou not a creature wanting soul?   40.
Or why is this immortal that thou hast?
Ah, Pythagoras' metempsychosis—were it true,
This soul should fly from me, and I be changed
Unto some brutish beast:
All beasts are happy, for when they die,   45.
Their souls are soon dissolved in elements;
But mine must live still to be plagued in hell.
Cursed be the parents that engendered me!
No, Faustus, curse thyself, curse Lucifer,
That hath deprived thee of the joys of heaven.   50.
                              [*The clock strikes twelve.*]
O it strikes, it strikes! Now body, turn to air,
Or Lucifer will bear thee quick to hell.
                              [*Thunder and lightning.*]
O soul, be changed into little water drops   55.

And fall into the ocean, ne'er be found.
My God, My God, look not so fierce on me!
                    [*Enter DEVILS.*]
Adders and serpents, let me breathe awhile!
Ugly hell gape not! Come not, Lucifer!   60.
I'll burn my books—ah, Mephistopheles!
                    [*Exeunt with him.*]

Let's cut this steak into smaller bites; we'll sample a few. For each, I'll provide the *p'shat* (which, for convenience, I'll call "Level A") and *d'rash,* "Level B."

Lines 1 – 3
                    Ah, Faustus,
Now hast thou but one bare hour to live,
And then thou must be damned perpetually.

A. Faustus acknowledges that the end has come; he has one hour to live before an eternity in Hell.

B. The remaining hour is described as "bare." In addition to the usual definitions, the *OED* gives us:
    1. "Of natural objects, as earth, heavens, trees: without such coverings as they have at other times, e.g. without vegetation, clouds, bark, foliage, etc.";
    2. "Without armor or weapons, unarmed."

For an hour to be "bare," therefore, is to have its very essence on display; this is terrifying. The only reason we're usually able to function is that hours extend us the common courtesy of covering themselves up. In "An Essay on Man," Alexander Pope writes:

The hour concealed, and so remote the fear,
Death still draws nearer, never seeming near.
Great standing miracle! That Heaven assigned

Its only thinking thing this turn of mind.[6]

Here, Faustus is doubly screwed: first, he must confront raw Time, but then he must be absorbed into the only thing that's scarier—Timelessness.

The undressed truth is awful. We value concealment. The first act of human culture described in Genesis is Adam and Eve weaving fig leaves into clothing to cover their just-discovered nakedness, and thereby to mitigate nakedness's faithful attendant: Shame. Nudity is a curse. "The Revelation," shorthand for the End of the World, is a "revealing," a shedding of illusion. For Faustus, Time is no longer concealing her reality.

> Lines 4 – 9
> Stand still, you ever-moving spheres of heaven,
> That time may cease, and midnight never come.
> Fair Nature's eye, rise, rise again, and make
> Perpetual day, or let this hour be but
> A year, a month, a week, a natural day,
> That Faustus may repent and save his soul.

A. Faustus wants Time to stop so that he might survive. Failing that, Faustus wants Time to be flexible enough that it might somehow accommodate his salvation.

B. Faustus may be a fool, but he's no idiot. He knows astronomy. Although he understands that the "spheres of heaven" are "ever-moving," he cries for them to "stand still." He's sacrificed his soul for knowledge; that very knowledge includes the impossibility of his salvation. Quite the existential predicament, this.

Conceding that Time advances inexorably, Faustus offers a more nuanced proposal: let Time advance, but let Faustus' experience of Time somehow slow down. This recalls "The Secret Miracle" by Jorge Luis Borges, which concerns a Jewish writer, Jaromir Hladik, who is to be executed by a Nazi firing squad.

---

6 3.75-78

Locked in his cell, he prays for the gift of one year, so that he might finish his play, "The Enemies." On the appointed morning in the grim courtyard, "[t]he sergeant called out the final order." And then: "The physical universe stopped."

> He had asked God for an entire year in which to finish his work: God in His omnipotence had granted him a year. God had performed for him a secret miracle: the German bullet would kill him, at the determined hour, but in Hladik's mind a year would pass between the order to fire and the discharge of the rifles. From perplexity Hladik moved to stupor, from stupor to resignation, from resignation to sudden gratitude.[7]

But Hladik and Faustus are not birds of a feather. Hladik speaks of "The Enemies" as something whose completion would justify his own existence, and also reflect God's glory. Faustus' thoughts are elsewhere.

In his Conclusion to *The Renaissance: Studies in Art and Literature*, Walter Pater argues that you don't need magic or grace to make Time feel like it's mercifully slowing down; rather, you need Beauty:

> As Victor Hugo says: we are all under sentence of death but with a sort of indefinite reprieve[.] [...] [W]e have an interval, and then our place knows us no more. Some spend this interval in listlessness, some in high passions, the wisest, at least among "the children of this world," in art and song. For our one chance lies in expanding that interval, in getting as many pulsations as possible into the given time.

According to neuroscientist David Eagleman, it isn't cramming the mind with Beauty that makes life seem to slow down, but cramming the mind with quotidian details when under the influence of terror. National Public Radio reports:

---

7 Andrew Hurley, trans. *Collected Fictions*. Penguin Books, 1999, pp. 161-162.

According to David, it's all about memory, not turbo perception. "Normally, our memories are like sieves," he says. "We're not writing down most of what's passing through our system." Think about walking down a crowded street: You see a lot of faces, street signs, all kinds of stimuli. Most of this, though, never becomes a part of your memory. But if a car suddenly swerves and heads straight for you, your memory shifts gears. Now it's writing down everything—every cloud, every piece of dirt, every little fleeting thought, anything that might be useful.

Because of this, David believes, you accumulate a tremendous amount of memory in an unusually short amount of time. The slow-motion effect may be your brain's way of making sense of all this extra information. "When you read that back out," David says, "the experience feels like it must have taken a very long time." But really, in a crisis situation, you're getting a peek into all the pictures and smells and thoughts that usually just pass through your brain and float away, forgotten forever.[8]

Faustus is experiencing plenty of terror. Time isn't slowing down, however: it's actually accelerating. In the time it takes to recite 31 lines, 30 minutes have passed.

Line 10: *O lente, lente currite noctis equi!*

A. The quote comes from Ovid's *Amores* (1.12.40): "Slowly, slowly run, O horses of the night!"

B. "*O lente currite noctis equi!* O softly run, nightmares!"[9] This is uttered by Humbert Humbert, the narrator of Vladimir Nabokov's *Lolita*, as he and his young captive make their way across America, and Humbert comes to suspect that they're being followed.

In Marlowe's own translation of *Amores*, he limits himself

---

8   Jad Abumrad, "Why A Brush With Death Triggers The Slow-Mo Effect." Broadcast August 17, 2010.

9   Knopf Doubleday, 1989, p. 219.

to giving only the general idea expressed in the line.

Lines 11 – 14
The stars move still, time runs, the clock will strike,
The devil will come, and Faustus must be damned.
O I'll leap up to my God! Who pulls me down?
See, see where Christ's blood streams in the firmament!

A. Faustus recognizes the inevitability of his damnation. Although he vows to repent, he's somehow restrained.

B. Back when stage effects were primitive, you had to have the actor describe the scene. In *Hamlet*, Horatio needs to observe:

But, look, the morn, in russet mantle clad
Walks o'er the dew of yon high eastward hill.[10]

Nowadays, dawn would be indicated with stage lighting. Hence Faustus' "See, see where Christ's blood streams in the firmament!"

"Firmament" and "sky" are different. While "sky" (a humble Anglo-Saxon word) is a straightforward label for, well, the sky, "firmament" suggests wonder, the divine, and the domain of stars whose immutable arrangement decides our destiny. It would be arresting enough if Christ's blood streamed in the sky; that it streams in the firmament, however, suggests a redemptive force that's capable of encompassing Reality itself—Reality, with its splendors, miseries, and riddles.

When Faustus says "See, see where Christ's blood streams in the firmament!" he's describing a redemption that, while active on the grandest scale, would seem to exclude him alone. Such is the extent of Faustus' alienation.

Lines 15 – 19
One drop would save my soul, half a drop: ah my Christ—

---

10   1.1.166-167.

Ah, rend not my heart, for naming of my Christ;
Yet will I call on Him—O spare me, Lucifer!
Where is it now? 'Tis gone: and see where God
Stretcheth out his arm, and bends his ireful brows!

A. Faustus yearns for Christ's salvation but feels himself restrained by Lucifer's influence. He then has a powerful, if ambiguous, vision of the divine.

B. "An outstretched arm" symbolizes salvation in the Hebrew Bible. Indeed, religious Jews continue to recall how their ancestors were delivered from Egyptian bondage "with a mighty hand and an outstretched arm."

"Ireful brows," however, suggests condemnation. The fact that God "bends" his "ireful brows" is even more mysterious. God is so overwhelming that Man cannot engage in a reciprocal relationship with Him. In Christianity, this problem is solved by what's termed "condescension:" in the form of Jesus Christ, God stoops so that we might see Him at work on the human scale. In Marlowe's play, God is "bending"—but bending in rage rather than mercy. This extends the motif established in line 14. Christ's blood may grant salvation, but here it remains sublimely inaccessible.

Faustus' disorientation is deeper still. "Ah, rend not my heart, for naming of my Christ; / Yet will I call on Him—O spare me, Lucifer!" While Faustus utters these lines, we note that the devils aren't even on-stage yet. In his delirium, Faustus' mind, the source of his grief, is devouring itself.

Lines 20 – 24
Mountains and hills, come, come and fall on me,
And hide me from the heavy wrath of God.
No, no?
Then will I headlong run into the earth:
Earth, gape! O no, it will not harbor me.

A. Faustus begs mountains and hills to bury him, believing that this will protect him from God's anger. The mountains and hills refuse. Faustus then vows to bury himself, but the soil somehow rejects him.

B.   Faustus apparently believes that hiding his physical body will save him from God's wrath. When someone dies, we achieve the first stages of "closure" by burying him. Ruins of defunct civilizations are covered in earth; they're normally invisible to us, so that finding ruins is often a great surprise. Out of sight, out of mind.

But here, Faustus presents himself in a position that's rather analogous to that of a child playing hide-and-go-seek, who, in closing his eyes, believes himself invisible.

Lines 25 – 31
You stars that reigned at my nativity,
Whose influence hath allotted death and hell,
Now draw up Faustus like a foggy mist
Into the entrails of yon laboring cloud,
That when you vomit forth into the air
My limbs may issue from your smokey mouths,
So that my soul may but ascend to heaven.

A.   Faustus asks Destiny (symbolized by the stars that were visible at the time of his birth) to demand that the atmosphere gather up his body as if it were water vapor, and to scatter it as if it were rain.

B.   Astrology was then considered trustworthy. As far as the average educated Elizabethan was concerned, the "stars" "reigned" indeed. Astrology was rooted in the belief that the celestial world was unchangeable and, therefore, an eternal point of reference. Stars were seen as having the power to "[allot] death and hell." Faustus, on some level, must know perfectly well that *he* allotted *himself* death and hell. Perhaps, however, we might excuse his inconsistency; after all, he's delirious with fear, and that state of mind isn't famously conducive to systematic thought.

In his hysterical way, Faustus is attempting to strike a deal. "If I'm going to be subject to nature in one respect, the stars," he seems to be saying, "let me also be subject to the natural cycle of evaporation and condensation."

Faustus doesn't understand, however, that eternal torment strikes not the body, but the soul. And therefore he regards his body as the problem. If the rain cycle can disperse it, Faustus believes, his "soul may but ascend to heaven."

> Lines 48 – 50
> Cursed be the parents that engendered me!
> No, Faustus, curse thyself, curse Lucifer,
> That hath deprived thee of the joys of heaven.

A. Faustus first curses his parents for ever having brought him into the world; he then changes his mind, and curses Lucifer.

B. If you want to see how polluted we are by Freudian psychoanalysis, observe that here, over 250 years before Freud's birth, it takes Faustus 48 lines before blaming his parents. And Faustus spins away from it almost immediately.

But he isn't kvetching about specific decisions his parents made (or didn't make); his criticism is far more grittily existential, and even less fair on Mom and Dad than Freudian balderdash tends to be. Faustus' parents represent an entire way of life.

The socioeconomic class into which Faustus is born (and his triumph over it) is an issue lurking in the play's background. We learn in the very Prologue that Faustus' family is poor. The opening Chorus sings:

> Not marching in the fields of Trasimene
> Where Mars did mate the warlike Carthagens,
> Nor sporting in the dalliance of love
> In courts of kings where state is overturned,
> Nor in the pomp of proud audacious deeds   5.

Intends our muse to vaunt his heavenly verse:
Only this, gentles—we must now perform
The form of Faustus' fortunes, good or bad:
And now to patient judgements we appeal,
And speak for Faustus in his infancy.   10.
Now is he born, of parents base of stock,
In Germany, within a town called Rhode[.]

"Now is he born, of parents base of stock." In addition to
the usual, current definitions of "base," the *OED* offers:
1. "Occupying a low position; situated lower down than
neighboring parts, low-lying; situated not far above the
ground or other reference point;"
2. "Law (now chiefly historical). In the feudal system: en-
tirely subject to the jurisdiction of a lord or a manorial
court; not free;"
3. "Low in the social scale; not noble, low-born; relating
or belonging to the lower social classes;"
4. "Of language: not classical, regarded as less refined than
at an earlier stage of development. Also: not elevated,
straightforward in expression, linguistically or rhetorical-
ly unsophisticated;"
5. "Alloyed with less valuable metal; debased, counterfeit;"
6. "Of comparatively little value, esp. monetary value;
worthless. Also in figurative contexts, esp. relating to al-
chemy or refining of metals;"
7. "Illegitimate; born or occurring out of wedlock, bas-
tard."

Faustus' class identity isn't just one detail among others.
The play's first dozen lines constitute a disclaimer that the au-
dience shouldn't expect a tale of gods or Great Men—no, this is
a play about a peasant. The whole work may be read as a cau-
tionary tale about the destruction awaiting anyone who has the
temerity to believe that he can transcend his native class.
Faustus sometimes reveals himself to our Freud-contam-
inated minds. We see him, "bare" as the hour, when fellow col-

legians pay him a visit:

> Come, German Valdes and Cornelius,
> And make me blest with your sage conference.
> Valdes, sweet Valdes, and Cornelius,
> Know that your words have won me at the last
> To practice magic and concealed arts—   5.
> Yet not your words only, but mine own fantasy,
> That will receive no object, for my head
> But ruminates on necromantic skill.
> Philosophy is odious and obscure.
> Both law and physic[11] are for petty wits.   10.
> Divinity is basest of the three,
> Unpleasant, harsh, contemptible, and vile.
> 'Tis magic, magic, that hath ravished me.[12]

Faustus associates law, medicine, and theology with baseness. Magic alone makes Faustus feel capable of transcendence. It's ironic, then, that he aims to transcend his submission by submitting himself to magic, which has "ravished" him.

This dual interest in baseness and ravishing reappears when Faustus attempts to convince himself that, in signing away his soul, he's made a reasonable decision:

> Have not I made blind Homer sing to me
> Of Alexander's love and Oenon's death?
> And hath not he that built the walls of Thebes
> With ravishing sound of his melodious harp
> Made music with my Mephistopheles?   5.
> Why should I die, then, or basely despair?
> I am resolved Faustus shall not repent.—
> Come, Mephistopheles, let us dispute again,
> And reason of divine astrology.[13]

Despair is base; it's expected somehow to be dissipated by

---

11   physic] Medicine.

12   1.1. 125-137.

13   2.2. 596-604.

the experience of ravishment—in this case, by the music played for him by Amphion, whose virtuosity at the lyre lightened the load when Zethus was building Thebes's walls.

> Lines 59 - 61   [*Enter DEVILS.*]
> Adders and serpents, let me breathe awhile!
> Ugly hell gape not! Come not, Lucifer!
> I'll burn my books—ah, Mephistopheles!

A. Although Faustus begs for clemency, he is dragged to hell.

B. Human intelligence is a problem: we're smart enough to change the world, but stupid enough that such changes are seldom for the better. Recall the cliché that most of the evil in this world is done by people with good intentions. It's actually much worse than that: most of the evil in this world is done by people who actually think they're producing good results. And we continue to believe in the goodness of those results, even as those results are making life a misery.

In *Memoirs of a Superfluous Man*, Albert Jay Nock confesses his misgivings about universal literacy, which, he insists, helps businesses...

> ...by extending the reach of advertising and increasing its force; and also in other ways. Beyond that I see nothing on the credit side. On the debit side, it enables scoundrels to beset, dishevel and debauch such intelligence as is in the power of the vast majority of mankind to exercise.[14]

The "intelligence [that's] in the power of the vast majority of mankind to exercise" is often denigrated, while its more respectable, collegiate alternative is overrated. A.E. Housman is on to something in *A Shropshire Lad*, XLIX:

> Think no more, lad; laugh, be jolly:

---

14 Harper & Brothers, 1943, p. 49.

Why should men make haste to die?
Empty heads and tongues a-talking
Make the rough road easy walking,
And the feather pate of folly   5.
Bears the falling sky.

Oh, 'tis jesting, dancing, drinking
Spins the heavy world around.
If young hearts were not so clever,
Oh, they would be young forever: 10.
Think no more; 'tis only thinking
Lays lads underground.

Housman stylishly revisits his thesis in *A Shropshire Lad*,
LXII:

And malt does more than Milton can
To justify God's ways to man.
Ale, man, ale's the stuff to drink
For fellows whom it hurts to think.[15]

This sentiment has a distinguished pedigree. In his *Meditations*, Marcus Aurelius urges: "But put away your thirst for books, so that you may not die murmuring, but truly reconciled and grateful from your heart to the gods."

This perspective may seem wrongheaded. From infancy, we absorb the cliché that "Knowledge is Power;" unlike so many other clichés, this one isn't even true. Knowledge is often much more frustrating than ignorance, for knowledge must include the knowledge of one's powerlessness. As Eric Jarosinski puts it: "Anxiety: Fear of the unknown. (Depression: Fear of the known.)"[16]

In this famous passage in *Narrative of the Life of Frederick Douglass*, the former slave recalls the unexpected consequences of literacy. He describes reading anti-slavery tracts, which...

---

15 21-24.
16 *Nein: A Manifesto*. Black Cat, 2015, p.117.

...enabled me to utter my thoughts, and to meet the argu-
ments brought forward to sustain slavery. But while they
relieved me of one difficulty, they brought on another
even more painful than the one of which I was relieved.
[…] As I writhed under it, I would at times feel that learn-
ing to read had been a curse rather than a blessing. It had
given me a view of my wretched condition, without the
remedy. It opened my eyes to the horrible pit, but to no
ladder upon which to get out. In moments of agony, I
envied my fellow-slaves for their stupidity. I have often
wished myself a beast. I preferred the condition of the
meanest reptile to my own. Anything, no matter what, to
get rid of thinking!

In vowing to burn his books, Faustus reveals the shallow-
ness of his human understanding—a shallowness which can
easily coexist with formidable erudition. The desperation of his
vow (suggested by the fact that he saves it for the very end—a
last ditch gambit) emphasizes the extent to which his identity is
derived from his facility with books, even though these are the
very books that have gotten him into this fix in the first place.

Books don't just mislead; they may also weaken you. In
The Anatomy of Melancholy, the awesomely learned Robert Bur-
ton writes:

For (as [Machiavelli] holds) study weakens their bodies,
dulls the spirits, abates their strength and courage. And
good scholars are never good soldiers, which a certain
Goth well perceived, for when his countrymen came into
Greece, and would have burned all their books, he cried
out against it, by all means they should not do it: "Leave
them that plague, which in time will consume all their
vigour, and martial spirits."

The anonymous author of this medieval poem has a nice
chuckle:

I ought not to dig, because I am a scholar,
Born from a line of knights who know how to fight.

> But because the work of a knight terrified me,
> I preferred to follow Virgil than you, Paris.[17]

And here's Alexander Pushkin, in the verse novel *Eugene Onegin*:

> To live and think is to be daunted,
> To feel contempt for other men.
> To feel is to be hurt, and haunted
> By days that will not come again,
> With a lost sense of charm and wonder,   5.
> And memory to suffer under—
> The stinging serpent of remorse.[18]

"The stinging serpent of remorse" can't help but remind us of the "adders and serpents" by which Faustus, in his final moments, is being strangled.

If ignorance is untenable and if knowledge can be lethal, what might we strive for? As he often does, Petrarch comes to the rescue:

> It is clear that we cannot know everything, or even know many things. [...] Let us then be content to know what suffices for our salvation.[19]

Of course, it isn't reasonable to expect the average student to be able to field-strip an Elizabethan soliloquy on this level. But it isn't insane to suggest that students may benefit from literary instruction rooted in the following maxims:

---

17 David A. Traill, trans. *Carmina Burana*. Harvard University Press, 2018, p. 365.
18 Anthony Briggs, trans. Pushkin Press, 2016, p. 73.
19 David Marsh, trans. *Invectives*. Harvard University Press, 2003. p. 353.

1. A real poem is about something particular.
2. That thing can be identified and discussed objectively.
3. Although we can think adventurously about that thing, we don't have unlimited license; it's possible to be wrong even when thinking creatively.

When we demand the same rigor in English that we do in math or science, the idea will gain currency that verse can be done well. And people are thrilled to see anything done well.

TWENTY-FOUR

THREE ADDITIONAL QUOTES ON THE HAZARDS OF KNOWING

"Oh, blindness to the future, kindly given,
That each may fill the circle marked by Heaven."[1]
  —Alexander Pope, "An Essay on Man"

"Gavest thou the goodly wings unto the peacocks? or wings and feathers unto the ostrich, which leaveth her eggs in the earth, and warmeth them in dust, and forgetteth that the foot may crush them, or that the wild beast may break them? She is hardened against her young ones, as though they were not hers. Her labor is in vain without fear, because God hath deprived her of wisdom, neither hath he imparted to her understanding."
  —The Book of Job 39:13-17

"Like Mr. Jefferson, I have always been content to 'repose my head on that pillow of ignorance which a benevolent Creator has made so soft for us, knowing how much we should be forced to use it.'"[2]
  —Albert Jay Nock, *Memoirs of a Superfluous Man*

---

1 1.85-86.
2 pp. 9-10.

TWENTY-FIVE

(THE DECLINE OF POETRY'S RESPECTABILITY, CONTINUED) ACADEMIC SOPHISTICATION

I T ISN'T JUST ignorance that's dethroned poetry; there's a certain type of academic sophistication whose effects seem just as pernicious.

It wasn't until I arrived at college that I heard people speaking the language of literary criticism. They would say things like: "Smith's poems are interested in questions about the interplay of marginalized sexual identities and ornamental Etruscan metalwork"—or some such garbage. Since I wanted to write, I began asking myself about what my poems would be "interested in."

It took me longer than it should have to realize that poems aren't "interested" in abstract issues. A poem is a discrete object crafted by an individual person; this individual's mind contains the idiosyncratic blend of knowledge, prejudice, and priority that he develops during a life.

TWENTY-SIX

(THE DECLINE OF POETRY'S RESPECTABILITY, CONTINUED) NAUGHTY BOY

E ARLIER, I DISCUSSED the sad legacy of the 1960s, and what it meant for poetry's respectability. Perhaps that very same decade offers a model for a possible resurgence. Perhaps poetry can become respectable via its very lack of respectability. In *Tobacco: A Cultural History of How an Exotic Plant Seduced Civilization*, Ian Gately writes:

> [T]he release of statistical proof that smokers were more likely to die of lung cancer than nonsmokers coincided with explosive growth in the youth market, to whose icons the proven danger of smoking was an attraction, and the nascent, youth-oriented antismoking program something else to rebel against.[1]

Read real poetry. Write real poetry. It's naughty.

---

1 Grove Press, 2001, p. 299.

TWENTY-SEVEN

AUTHENTICITY

"His appearance was certainly that of a hairdresser's dummy; but in the great demoralization of the land, he kept up his appearance."

—Joseph Conrad, *Heart of Darkness*

"What is a highbrow? Someone who is not passive to his experience, but who tries to organize, explain and alter it—someone, in fact, who tries to influence his history. A man struggling for life in the water is for the time being a highbrow."[1]

—W.H. Auden

I NEVER LOOK FORWARD to writing prose. The problem has something to do with my dislike of the sound of my own voice; prose writing requires that you spend a good deal of time listening to yourself. Poetry-writing, however, is lovely— likely because it's not my own voice.

I was educated in the late 1990s and early 2000s by erudite, well-meaning professors who believed in a kind of radical "localist" sincerity. If you grew up in, say, Harlem, you were expected to feel comfortable in your "authentic" language. Someone like Henry Wadsworth Longfellow was beneath seri-

---

1 Quoted by Ian Sansom in *"September 1, 1939": a Biography of a Poem*. 4th Estate, 2019, p. 99.

ous consideration because he was seen as having disowned his "local" idiom in favor of the "Man of Letters register." Indeed, Robert Creeley (my teacher at the SUNY-Buffalo) loved telling the story of Louis Zukofsky, who, as a street kid, having been cornered by Irish thugs, would face a stark choice: either get pummeled, or recite from memory bits of the Yiddish translation of Longfellow's *The Song of Hiawatha*.[2] It was almost as if Zukofsky's inevitable recitation was, for Creeley, the only plausible means by which Longfellow might be redeemed. After all, Yiddish was *someone's* native language—a claim that couldn't be made for Longfellow's "unnatural" register.

These prejudices (innocent as prejudices go—but prejudices all the same) inhibit our understanding of many things. T.S. Eliot, for example, was born in America, but decided to become an English aristocrat. When I was an undergraduate, the "party line" grievance against Eliot surpassed the mere fact of his expatriation; the professors seemed especially hung-up on the detail that Eliot wasn't just an American, but a Missourian, as if, barring the corrosive dream of becoming the 4th Earl of God-Knows-What, little Tommy Eliot's life would have been an Ozark idyll of banjo-plucking, frog-gigging, ballad-singing, and relaxed, townie egalitarianism.

I wonder how many of Eliot's detractors have ever visited the places associated with his St. Louis upbringing. Eliot's childhood home is a posh red-brick edifice in the Federal style. William Greenleaf Eliot, the poet's grandfather, founded nearby Washington University. There's a broad, handsome medallion devoted to his memory set into the flagstone beneath the university's main archway. Standing at the medallion, you can peer east, across the landscape over which the university lords, quasi-Acropolis-like; peer to the west, and there's an academic quad as austerely gothic as anything in Europe. And in terms of "bloodline," Eliot was a thoroughbred New England Brahmin.

I can scarcely imagine anything more appropriate than T.S. Eliot's move to England.

---

2 Likely the 1910 translation by Yehoash (the pen name of Solomon Blumgarten).

The "rules" of authenticity are confusing. Eliot was as often the author of this confusion as he was the casualty of it. In "A Note on the Verse of Milton," he famously observes: "Milton writes English like a dead language."[3] But Eliot is forgetting two essential facts:

Firstly, in Milton's milieu, Latin and Greek were far from dead. Indeed, Latin was (in a very real sense) Milton's mother tongue; there was an extensive range of thought and feeling that would have felt most natural to express in a "dead language."

Secondly, when Eliot accuses Milton of writing English like a "dead language," he's implying that the poetry is unnatural by being an "academic exercise." If this is true, however, the "taint" of self-conscious experimentation and cerebral artifice can be found (if anywhere) not in Milton's syntax and diction, but in those very aspects of his poetry which Eliot might find most natural. Nobody before Milton had managed successfully to write an epic, vernacular theodicy.[4] Those on the lookout for calculated, intellectualized oddness might begin with this.

While Eliot's move to England was perfectly authentic, it remains to be explained why, exactly, authenticity is better than affectation. I question those who inveigh against the traditional forms of authority that Eliot can be seen to represent: should someone like Eliot move into the Ozarks and "go native," even at the risk of inauthenticity?

The issue's perimeters announce themselves when we take a more comprehensive view of what constitutes a tradition. Racism, for instance, which is reinforced by a hairballishly convolved, inherited perplexity of cultural, social, religious, historical, and economic assumptions, constitutes an unmistakable tradition. Racism can be as traditional as Yorkshire pudding.

Racism and Yorkshire pudding, however, are different in

---

3 T.S. Eliot's thoughts on Milton are nuanced and fascinating. What I offer here is a simplification. Anyone serious about poetry would profit by reading the entire essay.

4 theodicy] A tale that, in Milton's words, is meant to "justify the ways of God to Man."

one crucial respect: the former is a nasty vice, while the latter is a pastry. Is it "cultural appropriation" to affect an egalitarianism into which you haven't been born? And (come to that) who is really "born" into *any* type of egalitarianism?

Authenticity can be wicked; more frequently, however, it's just boring. When I found myself teaching a high school song-writing class a few years ago, I made the mistake of giving my students *carte blanche* to write whatever came naturally. What "came naturally" (it transpired) was cliché suburban angst, self-pity, and down-market Romanticism. I would have been much more effective had I demanded that my students write only songs that came *un*naturally. After all, what really "comes naturally" to a teenager in Central Ohio? What are the indigenous riches of which they're supposed to avail themselves?

Down with authenticity.

TWENTY-EIGHT

SHLOMO CARLEBACH AND A.E. HOUSMAN

O BSERVANT JEWS are often surprised to learn that their favorite devotional melodies weren't written in seventeenth-century Romania, but rather, in the 1960s or '70s by a rabbi / minstrel named Shlomo Carlebach (1925 – 1994). This surprise was mentioned repeatedly in his obituaries. Carlebach lived in the tradition, and the tradition lived in him. He was an active creator, but also a mysteriously passive conduit—an Aeolian harp, to use a Romantic metaphor for the creative process. Here was an individual of such consummate talent that he achieved the nearly unachievable: sublime anonymity.

A.E. Housman achieved the poetic analogue to Carlebach's musical anonymity. His collection, *A Shropshire Lad,* seems to come out of no place, and no time. Here's poem LVII:

> You smile upon your friend today;
> Today, his ills are over.
> You hearken to the lover's say,
> And happy is the lover.

> 'Tis late to hearken, late to smile, 5.
> But better late than never:
> I shall have lived a little while
> Before I die forever.

This could plausibly have been written at any point in the

past few centuries, and it carries the stylistic fingerprint of nobody in particular. This "planned timelessness" (the opposite of "planned obsolescence") is among poetry's goals.

Earlier, I discussed my difficulties in teaching a songwriting class—the difficulties that came of letting students write whatever "came naturally." My songwriting students were hardly unique. Most people, if they don't take special and sustained care, will waddle through a perfectly adequate life without ever crossing paths with an interesting idea. What I'll term the "World of Serious Things" (WOST)—of art, philosophy, real religion, music, and poetry—is very seldom inherited nowadays; it must be chosen. Few have properly inhabited the WOST (as I—the product of the late '80s and early '90s—inhabit the world of *Sesame Street*, Steven Spielberg, *Seinfeld*, Nirvana, hamburgers, and whimsically soundtracked YouTube videos of rental trucks being blithely driven toward not-quite-high-enough overpasses) since the early twentieth century.

What, then, is the WOST? I can't do better than to compare it to the computer system known as "the Cloud:" a non-local place (pardon the oxymoron), a capacity, a power, an intelligence, which can be harnessed so as to sponsor your everyday life. *You* act within *it*, wherever you are; *it* acts within *you*, and is nowhere. It's both a collective memory and a collective possibility. It's both the thing via which a thing occurs and the Thing Itself. You don't really know who's hooked up to it. You don't really know if *you* are—or *if* you are, to what extent? Where's the border between Me and Out There? Nobody knows, and the question approaches irrelevance.

Although the Cloud wasn't around during my childhood in the suburban "shtetl" of northern New Jersey, I had intimations of certain patterns and archetypes. There was a bus stop across from the synagogue by means of which commuters, having finished morning prayers, could commute into Manhattan. The transition fascinated me: the man who'd just participated in the quorum carefully folds his prayer shawl, crosses the street, steps into the plexiglass hutch, and waits for the 114. Although he's crammed in with everyone else, he carries his universe inside of himself (a universe of language, literature, memory, tribal identity, and metaphysical commitment), and he lives on its behalf. Those who try to reduce Judaism to folkways, or to a community, or even to a system of "belief," miss, if not the whole point, then certainly a big part of it. Real Judaism is a spirit which moves the individual through reality; it's a spirit which (in turn) he drives.

The WOST represents a similar spirit.

Perhaps my Cloud metaphor is too remote, and too strange. Perhaps the truth is far more straightforward. Perhaps the WOST is like a tune you get stuck in your head.

Oscar Wilde was friends with Laurence Housman, brother of the poet. In a letter dated August 22, 1897, Wilde comments on one of A.E.'s detractors, who cannot "see the wonderful strangeness of simple things in art and life[.]"[1] "[T]he wonderful strangeness of simple things" is a beautiful phrase; it should be used as the title for something. It applies to A.E. Housman and Shlomo Carlebach equally.

The musical mode in which Carlebach specialized is called the "*niggun*" (plural, *niggunim*), which means, simply, "tune." The *niggun* is a folk genre and is meant to be performed not by trained singers, but by men at the table, usually on the Sabbath, especially after the slivovitz bottle has made its rounds. Although *niggunim* are wordless, biblical verses may be grafted on, assuming the verse is metrically suitable. They often have an A part and B part, each of which is sung twice before the whole thing starts up again; a particular *niggun* can be sung for a long time indeed, and, when there are a few dozen men singing, the effect can be captivating.

Different Hassidic dynasties have their own *niggunim*, which evolved and were cherished by that group. Shlomo Carlebach was a one-man dynasty.

---

1 *The Complete Letters of Oscar Wilde*. Fourth Estate, 2000, p. 928.

7. MIZMOR L'DOVID (HOVU L'HASHEM)

Mizmor L'David © Rabbi Shlomo Carlebach, BMI. Used with the permission of the Estate of Rabbi Shlomo Carlebach.

One of the most stubborn preoccupations of the poet is the immortality he expects to achieve. It's a meta-element that should be more striking than it is, like rappers' preoccupation with their own talent, indicated by their tendency to rap about how well they're rapping. Robert Herrick is far from unusual when he writes:

Trust to good verses, then;
They only will aspire,
When pyramids, as men,
Are lost i' th' funeral fire.

And when all bodies meet,   5.
In Lethe[2] to be drowned,
Then only numbers[3] sweet
With endless life are crowned.[4]

Robert Graves disliked this entire business, outlining his
reasons in "To Evoke Posterity:"

To evoke posterity
Is to weep on your own grave,
Ventriloquizing for the unborn:
"Would you were present in flesh, hero!
What wreaths and junketings!"[5]   5.

And the punishment is fixed:
To be found fully ancestral,
To be cast in bronze for a city square,
To dribble green in times of rain
And stain the pedestal.   10.

Spiders in the spread beard;
A life proverbial
On clergy lips a-cackle;
Eponymous institutes,
Their luckless architecture.   15.

Two more dates of life and birth
For the hour of special study

---

2   Lethe] The river of forgetfulness in the Greek underworld.
3   numbers] Poems.
4   "Live Merrily, and Trust to Good Verses," 45-52.
5   junketings] In this context, delicacies, and lavish gifts.

From which all boys and girls of mettle
Twice a week play truant
And worn excuses try.   20.

Alive, you have abhorred
The crowds on holiday
Jostling and whistling — yet would you air
Your death-mask, smoothly lidded
Along the promenade?   25.

In the early twentieth century, when this was written, I imagine it seemed cynical and pessimistic. Nowadays, however, it seems perversely hopeful, for it assumes that there will *be* a future. Just as liberals have become the puritan killjoys, they (and not the Christian preachers) are now the ones standing on the proverbial street corner, puffing and snorting about the End Times.

In *Manhood for Amateurs: The Pleasures and Regrets of a Husband, Father, and Son*,[6] Michael Chabon reflects on the pop culture of his childhood, which agreed that the future would be a wonderland of convenience and possibility; Chabon compares this to the tendency (which has only strengthened since the book's 2009 publication) for children to believe that (a) the world is about to end, and (b) that the human race has somehow forfeited its very right to a future. The message is: "The world is ending; it's your fault." And the children, heartbreakingly, say: "Amen."

Suddenly, "To be cast in bronze for a city square, / To dribble green in times of rain / And stain the pedestal" is looking a lot more attractive.

Folks believe in imminent apocalypse. It shouldn't surprise us that they act like it. On March 14, 2022, *The Guardian* published Kari Paul's article entitled: "Slobbing Out and Giving Up: Why Are So Many People Going 'Goblin Mode'?." We learn the following:

---

6 Harper, 2009.

The term embraces the comforts of depravity: spending the day in bed watching *90 Day Fiancé* on mute while scrolling endlessly through social media, pouring the end of a bag of chips in your mouth;[7] downing Eggo toaster oven waffles with hot sauce over the sink because you can't be bothered to put them on a plate. Leaving the house in your pajamas and socks, only to get a single Diet Coke from the bodega. [...] On TikTok, #GoblinMode is affixed to videos of everything from "smoking weed alone and getting scared," to "not taking your meds," and "hoarding weird shit just in case you run out." In other videos, it is associated with women wearing no makeup and mismatched sweat suits, speaking confessional-style into the camera. [...] Though they do not explicitly use the term "goblin mode," videos expressing similar ideologies have been rising in popularity. "My body is a garbage can with an expiration date and I got no time for healthy shit," one with 90,000 views says. "I love barely holding on to my sanity and making awful selfish choices and participating in unhealthy habits and coping mechanisms," said another with 325,000 views.

Needless to say, Ms. Paul doesn't frame this as a crisis requiring the most urgent attention; rather, "goblin mode" is presented as one lifestyle choice among many. Some prefer boxers; others, briefs. Some prefer non-stick pans; others, cast-iron. Some prefer a life of meaning and redemptive toil; others, a suicidal hedonism lacking the only thing that makes hedonism worthwhile: fun.

It might seem odd to attack nihilism and, in the same breath, laud A.E. Housman, who was a gloomy, tortured atheist. We're talking about someone who once wrote:

[I]n other times and countries, women have been ravished by half-a-dozen dragoons,[8] and taken it less to heart. It

---

7 pouring the...your mouth] I hate to be a pedant (Do I, really?), but it isn't the end of the bag that's being poured; rather, the end of the bag is the means by which the chips are poured.

8 dragoons] Soldiers.

looks to me as if the state of mankind always had been, and always would be, a state of just-tolerable discomfort.[9]

The *Mister Rogers'* theme song, this is not.

Carlebach's music recognizes this element of pain that runs through everything. Like most Ashkenazi music, it's in a minor key, overlaying joy with an excruciating awareness of that darkness which can be but imperfectly kept at bay. His is the musical tradition that created the *krekhts*, which is among the defining features of Ashkenazi music—a melodic ornament imitating a sob, which appears even in celebratory tunes. What Edgar Allan Poe writes in "The Poetry Principle" applies equally to this type of music:

> And thus, when by poetry [...], we find ourselves melted into tears, we weep [...], not [...] through excess of pleasure, but through a certain, petulant, impatient sorrow at our inability to grasp now, wholly, here on earth, at once and forever, those divine and rapturous joys of which, through the poem, [...] we attain to but brief and indeterminate glimpses.

We can weep for sorrow. But we can also weep in frustration at our inability to comprehend the forces moving our joy.

When, recalling my songwriting students, and trying to determine why their songs were so terrible, it occurs to me that their sorrows weren't contextualized in any understanding of human nature, of history, of the transcendent, and (most importantly) of a tradition of expression. Without the guidance supplied by these, sorrow is demoted from a human tragedy and becomes indistinguishable from the plight of a Boston terrier that's lost its favorite ball beneath the sofa.

Though obviously different in so many ways, Shlomo Carlebach and A.E. Housman share a sublime awareness of the internal world in which real art is created, and in which it must exist.

---

9 Quoted by Richard Perceval Graves. *A.E. Housman: The Scholar-Poet.* Charles Scribner's Sons, 1979, p. 94.

And that's why their works are immortal.

TWENTY-NINE

POWER

I T MAY SURPRISE you to learn that poetry was once considered manly. Poetry was a classier age's analogue to country club golf: a social necessity for serious, ambitious men. There was a group of seventeenth-century poets that congregated around Ben Jonson, a poet and dramatist whose name you'd certainly know, had Shakespeare never existed.[1] This band of poets, called "The Tribe of Ben," met in bars, got roaring drunk, roistered on a grand scale—and read poetry.

More than a few English poets knew something about manliness. Jonson himself was a bricklayer, and once killed a man. Sir Philip Sidney was a soldier and, apparently, an able jouster. Lord Byron was famously described as "mad, bad, and dangerous to know."[2] Dylan Thomas made Mick Jagger look chaste. And as for John Wilmot, the 2nd Earl of Rochester, don't get me started.

None of this is relevant, of course. It's the poem that matters, not the poet. I give these examples only to establish that poetry-writing wasn't always seen as preempting any claim to swaggering virility. Poets are men of power.

---

1   In a sense Shakespeare never *did* exist; the works attributed to him were likely penned by Edward de Vere, 17th Earl of Oxford. During the Covid-19 lockdowns of 2020, when the civilized world went mad with cabin fever, some came to believe that the world was dominated by a secret cabal of billionaire cannibals; I came to believe in Oxfordianism. I think I got off easy.

2   This remark is attributed to Lady Caroline Lamb, one of Byron's lovers.

Nobody has a good thing to say about power nowadays. When we hear the word, we often think of subjugation, exploitation, and abuse—nasty things, all. But power can be virtuous. And to write poetry is to exercise virtuous power. The poet is a linguistic sorcerer. He aspires to a mastery of language that reminds us of J.S. Bach's mastery of the keyboard. He aspires to a manly grace that recalls the most transcendent feats of athleticism.

In the following pages, I'll discuss three kinds of power that poetry can demonstrate:
1. The Power of Rhyme,
2. The Power of Wit, and
3. The Power of Truth.

THIRTY

THE POWER OF RHYME

IT DOESN'T REQUIRE any particular skill to throw balls into the air. To catch them, however, is a different story. Not only does the proficient juggler catch them; he catches them with apparently effortless panache.

The dramatic tension is engendered by three elements:

1. The playful abandon with which he launches the balls.
2. The length of their flight, during which they seem somehow beyond the scope of his concern, and
3. Our confidence that he'll catch them, oddly coexisting with the anxiety that he won't.

The only thing more satisfying than watching the juggler catch balls is hearing the poet rhyming well. Here's a relatively straightforward example: a quatrain from *In Memoriam*, a book-length elegy by Alfred, Lord Tennyson:

> I sometimes hold it half a sin
> To put in words the grief I feel;
> For words, like Nature, half reveal
> And half conceal the Soul within.[1]

When he ends the first line with "sin," he tosses a ball into the air, which he catches when ending the fourth line "with-

---

1 Section 5, 1-4.

in." After the "-in" is launched, we lose track of it, since Tennyson has diverted our attention with a couplet ("feel" / "reveal") which gives us a more immediate (though milder) thrill, since that ball isn't airborne for very long at all.

And another thing: "sin" is monosyllabic; "within," bisyllabic. When rhymed words differ in syllable count, the shorter word should always come first, as it does here. The "caught" rhyme tends to arrive as a happier surprise when things are thus arranged. Many of our greatest poets, sadly, fail to observe this "best practice;" every time a longer word is rhymed with a shorter, aesthetic energy is lost.

Here's another (highly idiosyncratic) "best practice:" two words shouldn't be rhymed if they share too many "syllable sounds," or if one word "contains" the other. Here's an example from *The Rape of Lucrece* by Shakespeare, who wasn't above mishandling the occasional line. In this scene, Lucrece is pleading with the villainous Tarquin to leave her alone. She cries:

> To thee, to thee, my heaved-up hands appeal
> Not to seducing lust, thy rash relier.
> I sue for exiled magisty's repeal:
> Let him return, and flatt'ring thoughts retire.

"Appeal" and "repeal" are basically the same word, but with different prefixes.

If you pay close attention, you'll find that many rhyming words that seem distinct are musically (and sometimes even lexically) pretty much the same. Words like "yak," "kayak," "cardiac," "maniac," "ammoniac," and "ileac" are essentially musical variations on what, in the International Phonetic Alphabet (IPA) notation, would be written /jæk/. Accordingly, they shouldn't be rhymed with each other.

If you need to rhyme something with "back," for instance, I suggest that you list all viable candidates, and then cluster them according to "root sound:"

Yak, Kayak, Cardiac, Maniac, Ammoniac, Iliac	Tack, Attack	Lack, Shellac
Paperback, Piggyback	Knack, Almanac, Pasternak	Rack, Wrack
Jack, Lumberjack	Pack, Unpack	Whack, Bivouac, Kerouac

The remainder of our eligible words ("Thwack," "Hack," "Black," "Clack," "Plaque," "Flak," "Slack," "Mac," "Smack," "Snack," "Quack," "Crack," "Track," "Sack," "Shack," "Stack") avoid stepping on each other's toes. Where clusters exist, make sure not to use more than one word per cluster.

Another rhyme-related fumble is when two words that are meant to rhyme don't end up quite rhyming. Here's Shakespeare again, this time from Sonnet 77:

> The wrinkles which thy glass[2] will truly show
> Of mouthéd graves will give thee memory;
> Thou by thy dial's shady stealth mayst know
> Time's thievish progress to eternity.[3]

"Memory" and "eternity"? Really? Do try harder next time, young William.

It's important to use rhyme with scrupulous care, since it can be powerful—and power is what we're after. Here's an example from "An Epithalamion, or Marriage Song on the Lady Elizabeth and Count Palatine, Being Married on St. Valentine's Day." The poet is John Donne, and an Epithalamion is a poem celebrating a marriage. It often describes the entire wedding,

---

2 glass] Mirror.

3 5-8.

from before the church service all the way to the wedding night. We seldom speak nowadays of a marriage's "consummation," since premarital canoodling is nearly universal. And when we do speak of it, it's seldom without wink-winking, nudge-nudging, and ribald euphemism.

Donne, however, has no such squeamishness. Stanza six contains some of the sexiest lines of poetry in the English language. In full, it reads:

> They did, and night is come; and yet we see
> Formalities retarding thee.
> What mean these ladies, which (as though
> They were to take a clock in pieces) go
> So nicely about the bride?   5.
> A bride, before a "Goodnight" could be said,
> Should vanish from her clothes into her bed,
> As souls from bodies steal, and are not spied.
> But now she's laid; what though she be?
> Yet there are more delays, for where is he?   10.
> He comes, and passeth through sphere after sphere:
> First her sheets, then her arms, then anywhere.
> Let not this day, then, but this night be thine;
> Thy day was but the eve to this, O Valentine.

Man, that's good. I sometimes pump my fist in the air when I read something so perfect, which has been known to stimulate the worried attention of security personnel when I find such passages while sitting in a library.

Lines 11 through 12 constitute a symphony in twenty syllables, a triumph of sound and sense, of rhyme and prosody:

> [*Inhale*] He cómes [*pause*] and pásseth through sphére
>   after sphére [*Inhale*]
> Fírst her shéets [*pause*] thén her árms [*longer pause*]
>   then ánywhere.

And that "anywhere" sprawls forth, each of its three syllables fully articulating itself, suggesting an almost carnal opulence that amplifies the line's literal meaning. The lines produce an aesthetic consummation reflecting the nuptial consummation being described. And the effect is heightened when you realize that, in the seventeenth century, "sphere" and "anywhere" constituted a tighter rhyme.

After such a release of power, there's nothing to be done but to slide into lines thirteen and fourteen—the refrain, which, in kaleidoscopically shifting versions, concludes each stanza.

The power of well-executed rhyme is so vivid that its absence is something we actually feel, rather than acknowledge abstractly. There are more than a few reasons why modern pop music is bad, but one of them is the total perversion of rhyme. This negligence is so widespread that even someone like country singer Brad Paisley, who's otherwise a scrupulous songwriter (or hires scrupulous songwriters), stumbles into it. He proves himself so sloppy in the rhyme department, that, if only in this respect, he seldom rises above hit-parade drivel.

See, for instance, "I'm Still a Guy:"

> I can hear you now talking to your friends,
> Saying, "Yeah, girls, he's come a long way
> From dragging his knuckles and carrying a club
> And building a fire in a cave."
> But when you say a backrub means only a backrub,   5.
> Then you swat my hand when I try,
> Well, now what can I say? At the end of the day,
> Honey, I'm still a guy.

While "friends" isn't supposed to rhyme with anything, "way" is meant in some vague, wishful way to rhyme with "cave"—which it doesn't. I count seven pseudo-rhymes in the song as a whole. Compare this mess of sub-poetic corner-cutting to stanzas three and six of Hank Williams' "Settin' the Woods on Fire:"

I don't care who thinks we're silly.
You'll be daffy; I'll be dilly.
We'll order up two bowls of chili.
Settin' the woods on fire...

[...]

You clap hands and I'll start bowin'.
We'll do all the law's allowin'.
Tomorrow I'll be right back plowin'.
Settin' the woods on fire...

The most conspicuous reason why "Settin' the Woods on Fire" is so much more charming than "I'm Still a Guy" is that the latter is half-assed about rhyme, while the former is committed to precision. Charm isn't just a function of what you say, but of the lyrical firepower brought to bear in the saying of it.

Using rhyme badly is like an archer aiming not at the target, but pointing his weapon in the target's general direction.

THIRTY-ONE

THE POWER OF WIT

NOWADAYS, WE USE the word "wit" to refer either to intelligent humor, or to someone who specializes in it. According to the dictionary, however, "wit" can also refer to "astuteness of perception or judgment." We can speak of "gentle wit" (P.G. Wodehouse comes to mind) or of "venomous wit" (one thinks of Evelyn Waugh).

Being the spiritually mutilated product of a deeply dysfunctional family, I prefer wit mobilized in the service of indignation or disapproval. The classic specimen is an essay called "The Fleshly School of Poetry: Mr. D. G. Rossetti" by Robert Buchanan, published from behind the crenelated battlements of a *nom de plume*, Thomas Maitland. Its incandescence is available to everyone, even those who've never heard of Dante Gabriel Rossetti. All you need to know is that he was an English poet and painter belonging to the so-called Pre-Raphaelite Brotherhood, a circle of artists that, uncommonly for Victorians, depicted *all* of life, even those carnal recreations whose merest prospect is the sole reason that men bathe, and own a toothbrush. Here's the crescendo:

> Passages like these are the common stock of the walking gentlemen of the fleshly school. We cannot forbear expressing our wonder, by the way, at the kind of women whom it seems the unhappy lot of these gentlemen to encounter. We have lived as long in the world as they have, but never yet came across persons of the other sex who

conduct themselves in the manner described. Females who bite, scratch, scream, bubble, munch, sweat, writhe, twist, wriggle, foam, and in a general way slaver over their lovers, must surely possess some extraordinary qualities to counteract their otherwise most offensive mode of conducting themselves.

Historian Edward Gibbon packs an impressive quantity of venom into a single sentence about Empress Julia Domna, the wife of Septimius Severus: "Chastity was very far from being the most conspicuous virtue of the Empress Julia." Here's Gibbon on the ancient Hungarians: "[I]f they have emerged from heresy, it is only because they are too illiterate to remember a metaphysical creed."

To bring things into the late 1990s, here's how American critic Roger Kimball begins a book review: "Anyone seeking a vivid illustration of the proposition that an expensive education is no barrier to stupidity will wish to consult John Carey's new book, *The Intellectuals and the Masses: Pride and Prejudice Among the Literary Intelligentsia, 1880 – 1939*."

While Hitler's *Mein Kampf* is a work of linguistic violence, it doesn't hold a candle to William S. Schlamm's review of the 1943 English translation, which begins:

Though we have been recently warned, on highest authority, to go easy on heads of foreign states, professional integrity compels this reviewer to inform you that Adolf Hitler is a poor writer. Such literary criticism will give but little comfort to the little children of Warsaw. Still, what has been printed black on white, put between covers and copyrighted in Washington, constitutes a book, even if it is *Mein Kampf*. So here it is, "the definitive new translation," selling for $3.50,[1] which is quite a lot of money for a bad book, but far less than what it is going to cost the Germans.[2]

---

1 Over $50 in 2022 dollars.

2 Published in *The New York Times*; republished on the *Times'* website, March 24, 2020.

Here's the money shot from William Logan's much-quoted review of Philip Levine's *The Mercy*:

> Levine is an old, accomplished artisan. You trust the leathery tone, the rueful air, the sly jokes at his own expense. He long ago learned how to shape a sentence, and sometimes you can almost see him measure one by eye and plane it with his hands. I once saw a glassblower in Venice with such hands. He took the glaring bulb of glass from the furnace with his glassblower's pipe, and blew it and shaped it as it glowed. At each step it was a thing of extraordinary beauty, a bow toward the antique arts. In the end he gave a deft twist, a knowing knock, then held it out—and *Ecco!*, it was an ashtray.[3]

And we can be assured that the art of vituperation is alive and well in the twenty-first century if Tibor Fischer can be thus provoked by a Martin Amis novel:

> *Yellow Dog* isn't bad as in not very good or slightly disappointing. It's not-knowing-where-to-look bad. I was reading my copy on the Tube and I was terrified someone would look over my shoulder (not only because of the embargo, but because someone might think I was enjoying what was on the page). It's like your favourite uncle being caught in a school playground, masturbating.[4]

The operative force in these specimens is disciplined compression. The writer has been confronted by something he thoroughly dislikes, and his impulse is to twitch, and then to snarl an obscenity. But he doesn't, opting instead to pressurize his rage in the carbon steel cylinder of civilized language. Our delight when encountering a piece of witty rage is a function of the tension between language and sentiment.

If disciplined compression is of the essence, then poetry (which is all about compression) must afford the writer enor-

---

3 *The Undiscovered Country: Poetry in the Age of Tin*. Columbia University Press, 2008, p. 105.

4 *London Daily Telegraph*. 4 August 2003.

mous scope for witty rage. Not only is language compressed, but meaning is, too. You want to call your adversary a "jackass" but can't, because the word required for that slot has got to rhyme with "Ahmadinejad." The assorted lines of tension within a poem can be so violent that the whole thing pulses, its continued existence the proof of an indefinite stalemate.

"The Hashish" by John Greenleaf Whittier is a thing of exquisite compression:

> Of all that Orient lands can vaunt
> Of marvels with our own competing,
> The strangest is the hashish plant,
> And what will follow on its eating.
>
> What pictures to the taster rise,   5.
> Of dervish[5] or of *almeh*[6] dances!
> Of Eblis[7] or of Paradise,
> Set all aglow with *houri*[8] glances!
>
> The poppy visions of Cathay,[9]
> The heavy beer-trance of the Swabian,[10]   10.
> The wizard lights and demon play
> Of nights Walpurgis[11] and Arabian!
>
> The mullah[12] and the Christian dog
> Change place in mad metempsychosis;[13]

---

5 dervish] Sufi mystic.

6 almeh] Egyptian courtesan.

7 Eblis] A particular devil in Islamic mythology.

8 Houri] In Islamic mythology, a woman who will accompany believers in heaven.

9 Cathay] A poetic name for China.

10 Swabian] Relating to Swabia, a region in Germany.

11 Walpurgis] A Christian feast involving bonfires.

12 mullah] A Muslim religious scholar.

13 metempsychosis] A type of reincarnation.

The muezzin[14] climbs the synagogue,   15.
The rabbi shakes his beard at Moses!

The Arab by his desert well
Sits choosing from some caliph's[15] daughters,
And hears his single camel's bell
Sound welcome to his regal quarters.   20.

The Koran's reader makes complaint
Of Shitan[16] dancing on and off it;
The robber offers alms, the saint
Drinks tokay[17] and blasphemes the Prophet.

Such scenes that Eastern plant awakes.   25.
But we have one ordained to beat it:
The hashish of the West, which makes
Or fools or knaves of all who eat it.

The preacher eats, and straight appears
His Bible in a new translation;   30.
Its angels, negro overseers,
And Heaven itself a snug plantation!

The man of peace, about whose dreams
The sweet millennial[18] angels cluster,
Tastes the mad weed, and plots and schemes—   35.
A raving Cuban filibuster![19]

The noisiest Democrat, with ease,

---

14 muezzin] In Islam, the singer who issues the call to prayer; he doesn't climb a synagogue, of course, but the minaret of a mosque.

15 caliph] A Muslim ruler.

16 Shitan] Satan.

17 tokay] A type of wine.

18 millennial] Relating to the "millennium;" a period discussed in Christian eschatology that will be characterized by peace.

19 filibuster] Irregular soldier.

It turns to Slavery's parish beadle;[20]
The shrewdest statesman eats and sees
Due southward point the polar needle.   40.

The judge partakes, and sits erelong
Upon his bench a railing blackguard;
Decides off-hand that right is wrong,
And reads the Ten Commandments backward.

O potent plant! so rare a taste   45.
Has never Turk or Gentoo[21] gotten.
The hempen hashish of the East
Is powerless to our Western cotton!

The poem has the structure of a joke, and a punchline
which feels, well, rather like an actual punch. It needs more
than a literary scholar to comprehend such a poem; it needs a
ballistics expert.

---

20 beadle] Church caretaker.
21 Gentoo] Heathen.

THIRTY-TWO

AN ADDENDUM ON WIT

W HILE IT'S FUN to aim your wit at others, it's vital, also, to direct it toward yourself. Sir Roger Scruton writes in "Defending the West:"

> If I were to venture a definition of this virtue, I would describe it as a habit of acknowledging the otherness of everything, including oneself. However convinced you are of the rightness of your actions and the truth of your views, look on them as the actions and views of someone else, and rephrase them accordingly. So defined, irony is quite distinct from sarcasm: it is a mode of acceptance rather than a mode of rejection. And it points both ways: through irony I learn to accept both the other on whom I turn my gaze, and also myself, the one who is gazing. Irony is not free from judgment: it simply recognizes that the one who judges is also judged, and judged by himself.[1]

Literal-minded people aren't just boring; they're also potentially dangerous. And a whole civilization devoid of irony is bound to do some serious damage. In *The Monument: Art, Vulgarity and Responsibility in Iraq*, Samir al-Khalil writes:

> Platonic irony in the sense of a journey into the unknown, even the unknowable—the humbling experience

---

1 In *Confessions of a Heretic: Selected Essays.* Notting Hill Editions, 2017, p. 185.

of knowing how little one knows—is itself unknown in Arabic culture; it is impossible for the traditional or classically formed Arab mind to conceive of irony even as an abstract idea.[2]

Eighteenth-century British politician Charles James Fox makes this more explicit, writing:

> The only foundation for toleration is a degree of skepticism; and without it there can be none. For if a man believes in the saving of souls, he must soon think about the means; and if, by cutting off one generation, he can save many future ones from Hellfire, it is his duty to do it.[3]

Irony is incompatible with the belief that it's praiseworthy to detonate an explosive vest inside an Israeli discotheque. The 9/11 attacks were perpetrated by 19 hijackers. I'll bet that not one of them could take a joke.

On January 26, 2003, a Palestinian terrorist strapped explosives to his donkey, and then tried to cajole it into charging at a packed Israeli bus—donkeys being famed both for their speed and their responsiveness to human commands. As with 9/11, nobody involved in this masterpiece of military cunning could possibly have possessed the ability to laugh at himself.

You'll be shocked to learn that the plot failed; the donkey exploded prematurely. No Israelis were injured, unless you count the passengers who had to be rushed to hospital in shock, having just witnessed what appeared to be a heavily burdened donkey spontaneously combust.

But the tale gets better still. The most vehement outcry came from one Ingrid Newkirk, who represented an organization which is famously impaired in the irony department: People for the Ethical Treatment of Animals. Her open letter to Yasser Arafat dated February 3, 2003 demonstrates a level of mirthlessness that's nearly frightening. Her *cri de cœur* is worth

---

2 University of California Press, 1991, p. 132.

3 Quoted in Samuel Rogers: *Table-Talk & Recollections*. Ed. Christopher Ricks. Notting Hill Editions Ltd., 2011, p. 14.

quoting at length:

> I am writing from an organization dedicated to fighting animal abuse around the world. We have received many calls and letters from people shocked at the bombing in Jerusalem on January 26 in which a donkey, laden with explosives, was intentionally blown up. [...] All nations behave abominably in many ways when they are fighting their enemies, and animals are always caught in the crossfire. [...] We watched on television as stray cats in your own compound fled as best they could from the Israeli bulldozers. [...] If you have the opportunity, will you please add to your burdens my request that you appeal to all those who listen to you to leave the animals out of this conflict?[4]

This was during a war (the "Second Intifada") that killed thousands. Ms. Newkirk looked on while the television news broadcasted footage of the Israeli Defense Forces besieging the *"Mukata'a"* (Arafat's compound). And amid the images of stuttering machine guns, tanks, bulletproof bulldozers, fireballs, and thick columns of smoke, Ms. Newkirk saw...fleeing cats.

Ms. Newkirk's letter is funny, but it's also diabolical; it represents a kind of evil to which we're all susceptible when we misplace our sense of irony.

Irony is virtuous.

The ability to laugh at yourself isn't a sign of weakness; indeed, it can be used as a vehicle for boasting, and can therefore be especially manly. Here are the first five stanzas from Ben Jonson's "My Answer: The Poet to the Painter:"

> Why, though I seem of a prodigious waist,
> I am not so voluminous and vast
> But there are lines wherewith I might be embraced.

---

4 Quoted by Wesley J. Smith, "Terrorists Blow Up Donkey—PETA's Past Protest." *National Review Online*. May 26, 2010.

'Tis true: as my womb swells, so my back stoops,
And the whole lump grows round, deformed, and
    droops.   5.
But yet the Tun at Heidelberg[5] had hoops.

You were not tied by any painter's law
To square my circle, I confess, but draw
My superficies.[6] That was all you saw,

Which, if in compass of no art it came   10.
To be described but by a monogram,[7]
With one great blot, you had formed me as I am.

But whilst you curious were to have it be
An archetype[8] for all the world to see,
You made it a brave[9] piece, but not like me.   15.

In the Western tradition, obesity has long been associated with sexual immorality. John Wilmot, the 2nd Earl of Rochester, however, seems eager to bypass the symbolism, and to describe his predilections with a candor that remains shocking. The poem is called "*Régime de Vivre*" ("A System of Life").

Buckle your seatbelt, dear Reader. We're in for some rough language.

I rise at eleven. I dine about two.
I get drunk before seven. And the next thing I do,
I send for my whore, when, for fear of a clap,[10]

---

5 Tun at Heidelberg] The Tun [wine barrel] at Heidelberg was an immense wine vat installed in Heidelberg Castle.

6 superficies] Full dimensions.

7 monogram] A simple line drawing.

8 archetype] According to the *OED*, the relevant sense of this word comes from comparative anatomy: "An assumed ideal pattern of the fundamental structure of each great division of organized beings, of which the various species are considered as modifications."

9 brave] Excellent.

10 clap] Gonorrhea.

I spend[11] in her hand, and I spew[12] in her lap.
Then we quarrel and scold 'till I fall fast asleep...   5.
When the bitch, growing bold, to my pocket does
     creep.
Then slyly she leaves me, and, to revenge the
     affront,
At once she bereaves me of money and cunt.
If by chance then I wake, hot-headed and drunk,
What a coil[13] do I make for the loss of my punk![14]   10.
I storm and I roar, and I fall in a rage,
And, missing my whore, I bugger my page.[15]
Then, crop-sick[16] all morning, I rail at my men,
And in bed I lie yawning 'till eleven again.

This isn't an approach to life that I'd recommend. However, I do have a nagging respect for those who take a thing to its natural conclusion; and, criticize the earl as you like, but he can't be accused of going in for half measures. Nor can he be accused of being a sissy.

I quote the entire poem because it perfectly illustrates my point about wit and irony. While the narrator of such a poem might spread more than his share of venereal disease, ruin the bed linen, debauch your daughter, and puke on the pavement, he's extremely unlikely to burn anyone at the stake for heresy.

---

11   spend] Disburse money into.

12   spew] Ejaculate.

13   coil] A noisy disturbance.

14   punk] Prostitute.

15   page] A serving boy.

16   crop-sick] "[D]isordered in stomach" (*OED*), especially because of intemperance.

THIRTY-THREE

THE POWER OF TRUTH

"A straightforward answer is like a kiss on the lips."
—Proverbs 24:26

M ANY OF OUR generation's worst problems originate from our inability to distinguish the Plausible from the True. This confusion began in academic humanities departments, and then metastasized. It's *plausible*, for instance, that Joseph Conrad is engaged in "discursive violence" in his depiction of Africans; it's *plausible*, but (contrary to the claims of aspiring academics who'd otherwise have nothing to write about) it isn't *true*.

Once one becomes comfortable blurring these lines in the interests of what's come to be denominated "scholarship," it's perilously easy to broaden one's scope. It's *plausible* that Western police forces evolved from bands of slave-catchers; it's *plausible*, but it isn't *true*. And some Conservatives have learned from the Left. It's *plausible* that reptilian plutocrats meet every Passover in a hollowed-out mountain to advance their plans to undermine Civilization; it's *plausible*, but it isn't *true*.

In poetry, there's always a temptation to privilege the Plausible over the True. In the Author's Forward to his *Collected Shorter Poems, 1927 – 1957*, W.H. Auden writes, "A dishonest poem is one which expresses, no matter how well, feelings or beliefs which its author never felt or entertained."[1]

In *Infernal Library: On Dictators, the Books They Wrote, and Other Catastrophes of Literacy*, Daniel Kalder makes an astute observation about Mussolini and prose that applies to dictators and writing in general:

> Had he not confused his gift for words with a superhuman ability to transform the course of history, thus misidentifying his true vocation as dictator instead of writer, the world would most likely have been a less awful place in the twentieth century. Alas, as a writer, Mussolini was subject to the same vanity and delusions of grandeur that afflict many born to the calling—and in particularly extreme form: instead of merely hurting his own family and loved ones and seething against critics, he managed to wreak havoc upon two continents.[2]

The type of insincerity for which Auden apologizes is close indeed to the totalitarian impulse. To manipulate people as one might manipulate language and ideas can lead only to hell. But Kalder's implicit criticism of writing as such (that it's an anarchic zone where the writer's whim dominates) is unfair. Kalder forgets about the obligation that a writer has to tell the truth. The writer doesn't enjoy *total* freedom—if he's a real writer, in any case. Great writing is great because it says true things, and does so in a way that's decorous, thoughtful, and orderly. After reading only a few lines of a great work, we know instinctively that we're in the presence of Truth. And we know with equal certainty that Truth is good.

Contrary to the trendy academic drivel, something like universal human nature absolutely exists. Most disbelievers in human nature conduct their actual lives in ways presupposing that we're fundamentally knowable—that (in other words) we have a nature. There are, to be sure, those who are alienated from human norms; they're called "psychopaths."

---

1 Reprinted in *Collected Poems*. Vintage International, 1991, pp. xxv – xxvi.
2 Henry Holt and Company, 2018, p. 113.

Whenever you encounter an article exploring how this or that "cutting-edge"[3] technology will change "what it means to be human," you know you're in the presence of Dangerous Bullshit. Technology doesn't change human nature; it simply makes us happier or sadder, according to eternal, basic needs. Dishwashers, vaccines, and safety glass cheer and encourage us, for they make it easier to be a person; social media, iPhones, earbuds, 3D printing, and internet pornography depress and harry us, for they make it harder to be a person. It's really that simple.

Poetry is the ideal "venue" for Truth because it asks to be judged by eternal standards.

To make truthful poems, you'll need to acquire the usual experiences of adulthood. If you live only among books, you'll turn into Ezra Pound. Read a few pages of his and you'll discover why that's a bad thing.

Don't imagine yourself some sort of lofty exception to the normal human rules. Live a real life in the real world. Existence is a problem. Submit yourself to it. There are many reasons why T.S. Eliot was a better poet than Ezra Pound, but the most conspicuous reason was that Eliot knew more than his mentor did about life. W.H. Auden was a better poet than Eliot for the same reason. And one of the reasons why Shakespeare is godlike is his uncanny understanding of so many different human classes and conditions. It's obvious that Shakespeare lived a full, intense, and various life.

A poet's obligation to tell the truth isn't limited to the "big things;" he must tell the truth about the "little things," too. Here's a dishonest poem by William Blake, entitled "Infant Joys:"

"I have no name:
I am but two days old."
What shall I call thee?
"I happy am,

---

3 Although something with a "cutting edge" may help you to sever a piece of rope, it's just as capable of slitting your throat.

Joy is my name."   5.
Sweet joy befall thee.

Pretty joy!
Sweet joy but two days old.
Sweet joy I call thee.
Thou dost smile;   10.
I sing the while
Sweet joy befall thee.

Could it be clearer that William Blake never spent any meaningful time with a newborn? At two days old, a baby cannot experience joy or sweetness. A newborn resembles a pancreas. It cannot lift its head. And if it could, it wouldn't be able to see anything more than six inches from its gargoylish face.

"Infant Joy" appears in *Songs of Innocence*, each constituent lyric of which has its "minor key" counterpart in *Songs of Experience*. The poem's evil twin is entitled "Infant Sorrow:"

My mother groaned! My father wept.
Into the dangerous world I leapt
Helpless, naked, piping loud,
Like a fiend hid in a cloud.

Struggling in my father's hands,   5.
Striving against my swaddling bands,
Bound and weary, I thought best
To sulk upon my mother's breast.

This, too, is dishonest, imputing to a newborn an impressive range of volition: it "leaps," "strives," and "struggles." A newborn's sob in no way recalls "a fiend hid in a cloud." What's really so harrowing about a newborn is its somehow confrontational passivity.

Sometimes the truth that a poet tells can leave you breathless, and then haunt you forever. The reader feels the sense of absolute recognition—that another person has accessed the essence of something, and then fixed it in time and space, so that it's like Keats' Grecian urn, which we can circumambulate, and see from every angle. We sense that, no matter how outlandish the subject matter, the writer has experienced it personally. This greatness of experience is fused with greatness of understanding, greatness of empathy, and then embodied in excellent language.

A writer is blessed if he can manage this a half-dozen times in his career. Shakespeare's ability to do it frequently is among the things that make him downright superhuman. Recall *Macbeth* 4.3, where we meet Lady Macduff. She doesn't understand that her castle shall soon be the scene of a massacre. The exchange between her and her young son is handled with heartbreaking delicacy. The boy has been encouraged to believe that his father is dead. Although he doesn't buy it, the boy nevertheless refers to his father in the past tense.

> SON: Was my father a traitor, mother?

> LADY MACDUFF: Ay, that he was.

> SON: What is a traitor?

> LADY MACDUFF: Why, one that swears and lies.

> SON: And be all traitors that do so?

> LADY MACDUFF: Every one that does so is a traitor, and must be hanged.

> SON: And must they all be hanged that swear and lie?

> LADY MACDUFF: Every one.

> SON: Who must hang them?

LADY MACDUFF: Why, the honest men.

SON: Then the liars and swearers are fools, for there are
        liars and swearers enough to beat the honest men, and
        hang up them.

LADY MACDUFF: Now God help thee, poor monkey!
        But how wilt thou do for a father?

SON: If he were dead, you'd weep for him. If you would
        not, it were a good sign that I should quickly have a
        new father.

LADY MACDUFF: Poor prattler, how thou talk'st!

A messenger rushes in to urge Lady Macduff to flee with
her family immediately. Her purehearted perplexity is wrench-
ing when she replies:

> Whither should I fly?
> I have done no harm.

Then she muses:

>   But I remember now
> I am in this earthly world, where to do harm
> Is often laudable, to do good sometime
> Accounted dangerous folly. Why then, alas,
> Do I put up that womanly defense
> To say I have done no harm?

The murderer enters, and calls the absent Macduff a trai-
tor. The son, who has clearly had difficulty with the concept of
treason, will nevertheless not abide such an insult to his father.
He cries:

Thou liest, thou shag-eared villain!

And then the child is murdered.

The Bible also offers Truth. And if this is a truth that can enable us to live forever, then lesser gradations of truth, such as those we might aspire to in our own poems, must, at the very least, be powerful indeed.

THIRTY-FOUR

ELABORATION

MORE THAN A FEW people I've known over the years have regarded me as a jerk. Shocking, I know. Since we derive our sense of self from those around us, I came to believe that, indeed, I must be a jerk.

Actually, come to think of it, not all of us derive our sense of self from those around us; psychopaths don't, and, although I might be a jerk, I'm no psychopath. Thank heavens for small mercies.

It turns out that those quirks that were getting me into so much trouble were actually symptoms of prosopagnosia, otherwise known as face blindness. Although my case seems to be relatively moderate, people do have the bewildering tendency to blur into one person. Faces can seem as indistinguishable to me as polka songs to someone who doesn't know the first thing about polka. I'll enter a multiplex cinema, see someone just behind me on the box office queue, and then, see what appears to be that very same person leaving a theater where a film has just concluded. And then they'll sell me popcorn.

Although this is occasionally frightening, it's mostly a giant pain in the ass, and, not infrequently, the engine of a great deal of embarrassment. Reflecting on a years-old office blunder of uncommon gravity, I wrote the following lines:

While there was a man I thought was my boss,
In point of fact, there wasn't one, but three

Distinct persons my mind had synthesized
Into one. I'd start a conversation
With the first, finish it with the second,   5.
And reference it when chatting with the third.

The stanza vexed me for two reasons:

1. It didn't rhyme;
2. Although the lines were syllabically consistent (10 per line) there wasn't any metrical regularity.

The stanza begged to be edited into something else, but any change I made only diminished it. The stanza was far more deranged than me: I have prosopagnosia, but the stanza had dissociative identity disorder. It wanted simultaneously to be something else and to remain exactly what it was.

I soon realized my luck, however: what I had on my hands was a sestet—a stanza of six lines. This made it eligible for elaboration by means of a poetic form called a sestina, which relies not on rhyme, but on the choreographed repetition of end words. When coerced into a table, it looks like this:

Stanza One:	(1)	(2)	(3)	(4)	(5)	(6)
Stanza Two:	(6)	(1)	(5)	(2)	(4)	(3)
Stanza Three:	(3)	(6)	(4)	(1)	(2)	(5)
Stanza Four:	(5)	(3)	(2)	(6)	(1)	(4)
Stanza Five:	(4)	(5)	(1)	(3)	(6)	(2)
Stanza Six:	(2)	(4)	(6)	(5)	(3)	(1)

If I took my sestet and used it as a sestina's opening stanza, my template would look like this:

Stanza One

1. While there was a man I thought was my boss,
2. In point of fact, there wasn't one, but three
3. Distinct persons my mind had synthesized
4. Into one. I'd start a conversation
5. With the first, finish it with the second,
6. And reference it when chatting with the third.

Stanza Two

1. _____ third
2. _____ boss
3. _____ second
4. _____ three
5. _____conversation
6. _____synthesized

Stanza Three

1. _____synthesized
2. _____ third
3. _____conversation
4. _____ boss
5. _____ three
6. _____ second

Stanza Four

1. _____ second
2. _____synthesized
3. _____ three
4. _____ third
5. _____ boss
6. _____conversation

Stanza Five

1. _____conversation
2. _____ second
3. _____ boss

4. _____synthesized
5. _____ third
6. _____ three

Stanza Six

1. _____ three
2. _____conversation
3. _____ third
4. _____ second
5. _____synthesized
6. _____ boss

I entitled the resulting poem "Identity Crisis:"[1]

While there was a man I thought was my boss,
In point of fact, there wasn't one, but three
Distinct persons my mind had synthesized
Into one. I'd start a conversation
With the first, finish it with the second,   5.
And reference it when chatting with the third.

And neither the first, nor second, nor third
Knew they were thus unselved into "The Boss"
As far as my mind (scarcely a second-
Rate instrument) was concerned. Behold three   10.
Faces, bodies, modes of conversation:
Added, divided by three, synthesized.

And, notwithstanding what I'd synthesized,
It gets even worse: for neither the third,
Second, nor first pleasant, conversation-   15.
Ready hominid was my actual boss.
He was quite distinct from the other three,
Plainly unlike the first, third, or second.

But I wouldn't have waited a second

---

1 First published in *New English Review*, April 2022.

In affirming I was liked…synthesized,   20.
As this opinion was, of nearly three
Months—or two? One?—at the job. On the third
Day of work, I discovered that "The Boss"
Was always up for a conversation.

To Him-Them, the earnest conversation   25.
Sounded quite like this:—*scarcely a second—*
And neither the first, nor—my actual boss—
Distinct persons my—what I'd synthesized—
In point of fact, there—second, nor third—
Plainly unlike the—concerned. Behold three.   30.

Although I can make one man out of three,
I can't do the reverse. Conversation
With my absurd psychiatrist (my third
In as many years) takes a mere second
Showing that everyone is synthesized   35.
Of many. To ourselves, we're all "The Boss."

I'd stumbled into a rare, felicitous sort of success: I'd made
a poem where the form and content exactly reflected each other.
The poem is about stasis, and the sestina form *enacts* it, advanc-
ing without advancing, grinding its gears, and running in place.

In order to understand the procedure whereby a fragment
of verse is developed into a proper poem, the concept of "*elab-
oratio*" will come in handy. In his *Music in the Castle of Heaven:
A Portrait of Johann Sebastian Bach*, John Eliot Gardiner calls
"*elaboratio:*"

> [T]he second stage in the fleshing out of a musical com-
> position as defined by Christoph Bernhard. In his *Tracta-
> tus compositionis augmentatus* (c. 1657), widely circulated
> in manuscript during the second half of the seventeenth
> century, Bernhard brought Cicero's five divisions of rhet-
> oric up to date, and, in applying them to music, reduced
> them to three: *inventio, elaboratio,* and *executio.* First,

Bach crafts a workable idea (*inventio*), one that opens the door to creative embellishment (*elaboratio*), and then puts it to the test in performance (*executio*). These concepts are complementary and vital.[2]

Elaboration is about understanding what a particular idea or fragment is pregnant with. A great artist will find shocking potentialities within relatively simple ideas. Beethoven's Fifth Symphony exemplifies this. The unassuming four-note opening motif is a shallow pit out of which Beethoven manages to haul an entire universe.

For a poetic example, let's examine the seventh stanza of Robert Browning's "Childe Roland to the Dark Tower Came"—a 204-line fever dream about an Arthurian knight's nightmare odyssey in search of the "Dark Tower," a place of ambiguous (though somehow decisive) significance. The stanza reads:

> Thus, I had so long suffered in this quest,
> Heard failure prophesied so oft, been writ
> So many times among "The Band"—to wit,
> The knights who to the Dark Tower's search addressed
> Their steps—that just to fail as they, seemed best.   5.
> And all the doubt was now—should I be fit?[3]

While Browning's intentions obviously cannot be as knowable as our own, they can be deduced. We can imaginatively reverse-engineer the stanza, and determine what was elaborated out of what, and how.

The stanza's kernel is:

> Thus, I had so long suffered in this quest,
> Heard failure prophesied so oft, been writ
> So many times among "The Band" [...]

An unrhymed couplet is a low-pressure way to begin a

---

2 Penguin Books, 2014, p. 214.

3 38-43.

stanza. You can launch those two balls with abandon, comforted by the knowledge that some time will pass before you must worry about how they'll be caught. Since the beginning of line three is syntactically integral with the two preceding lines, it's plausible that Browning began with iambic prose ("Thus, I had so long suffered in this quest, heard failure prophesied so oft, been writ so many times among 'The Band'") and inserted the line breaks later.

Again, here's the complete stanza:

Thus, I had so long suffered in this quest,
Heard failure prophesied so oft, been writ
So many times among "The Band"—to wit,
The knights who to the Dark Tower's search addressed
Their steps—that just to fail as they, seemed best.   5.
And all the doubt was now—should I be fit?

The phrases "seemed best" and "to wit" are so anemic that their appearance must indicate a compromise. Browning needed to catch the balls thrown up by "quest" and "writ."

Sometimes, however, a great poet can find aesthetic potential even in a compromise. This is exactly what Browning accomplishes with "The knights who to the Dark Tower's search addressed / Their steps[.]" You wouldn't write like this unless you were confined by formal strictures. The line is like a bonsai tree; it's Nature operating under discipline. Nobody talks like that; you'd say that you "went" to the Dark Tower, or that you "travelled toward" it, or something similar. Browning needs to catch the ball thrown up by "quest," and ends up with "The knights who to the Dark Tower's search addressed[.]"

Correspondents "address" letters; orators "address" an audience. The word suggests a certain formality. The poem is about a disoriented man wandering through a hellscape. Of all the phenomena on offer, which one seems least to merit the verb "address?" Why, of course: the wanderer's footsteps. There's a wonderful perversity in it.

To make it even sweeter, to end a line with "addressed"

allows Browning to generate tension over what the word will ultimately refer to. "The knights who to the Dark Tower's search addressed"—what, exactly?—"Their steps." Ah!

THIRTY-FIVE

LOVE POEMS

DISCLAIMERS:
[1] I have no expertise in the romance department. If you take even a quick look at my author photo, this will cease to be a mystery. I'm a sloppy heap of bewilderment, gracelessness, embarrassment, shame, and piercing regret at past screwups. I'll leave it at this, dear Reader: you'd never want to be flown by a pilot who had the same experience level in his vocation as I do in the art of love.

[2] The following chapters say some discouraging things about love poems. Please note that I'm speaking specifically about the deployment of love poems during a relationship's initial stages. When you're established in a relationship based on trust, a well-written love poem can be a singular gift. I never gave much thought to love poems as a genre until I started teaching, and I discovered how alarming so many of my female students found the classic love poems. My suspicion of the genre was stimulated by these classroom experiences.

There are exceptions, of course. A love poem might do the trick. Just be mindful, dear Reader, of the risks involved.

Most contemporary poetry is so terrible because it isn't written for real people to read. Poetry is a form of communication, and, in a world where few people read poetry, that entire mode of expression becomes perverted. Language doesn't flourish in solitary confinement.[1]

It's ironic, then, that the one genre of poetry which is unambiguously a form of communication is so disaster-prone. It's upsetting, and even deranging, to be a misunderstood or ignored poet. But to be the author of a love poem that's gone amiss with its intended audience is a special kind of hell. And a love poem is much more likely to explode in your face than it is to whisk your beloved into a Swiss meringue of awakened longing, or to reduce her to a jelly of carnal submission.

Although the reasons for this are complex, they all concern the basic human fact that it's unpleasant to be scrutinized. The only people who enjoy being stared at are psychopaths: actors and politicians. Normal people squirm.

The love poet is obsessed with his beloved, and romanticizes her into quasi-angelic status. She moves with otherworldly grace. Her posture and luminosity recall Renaissance painting. The birds burst into song at her approach.

None of this could be farther from your beloved's actual experience of herself, however. She's got her own terrestrial concerns. She's studying for an exam. She's worrying about when she'll have the time to get that blasted CHECK ENGINE light looked at. She's just trying to get through the surreal horror show that is a human life.

And then...you show up—or rather, your surrogate, the poem you've foolishly deputized to speak on your behalf. And she discovers that, while she was eating a salad or lugubriously wondering how to mend her relationship with her mother, you were (metaphorically, at least) crouching behind a shrubbery, squinting at her, and hyperventilating.

This is not sexy or endearing. It's scarcely sane.

---

1   In *Samuel Johnson, and the Life of Writing*, Paul Fussell observes: "Elegance is, [Johnson] finds, a function of benevolence, that benevolence that loves the audience enough to aim at transmitting matter in a delightful way. Obscurity and clumsiness in prose are here associated with fraud and vanity." (W.W. Norton & Co., 1986, p. 105.)

And it gets worse. A good poem (regardless of the genre) is a well-crafted poem. Craft takes time and meticulous attention. The best poet working at the height of his powers can craft a poem so well that it doesn't seem to be crafted at all—it simply *is*. In *Modern Painters*, John Ruskin writes:

> Nature is always mysterious and secret in her use of means; and art is always likest her when it is most inexplicable. That execution which is least comprehensible, and which therefore defies imitation, (other qualities being supposed alike), is the best.[2]

But few of us are capable of being so magically fluent, and those who are cannot be so perpetually. The fruit of hard work will look, frankly, like the fruit of hard work. So now, your beloved isn't just disturbed by the idea that you've been sitting at your desk, scrutinizing your mental image of her; her disturbance is amplified by the knowledge that you've spent an awfully long time at that desk. She hardly knows that you exist, and you've been sitting in your workshop with your 35-watt soldering iron and lighted magnifying glass, designing an entire metaphysical outlook that has her as its center.

And therefore, in a sense, your beloved will find the poem unsettling in direct proportion to its quality. If it's a bad poem, she'll find it creepy; if it's a good poem, she'll find it even creepier.

In *A Portrait of the Artist as a Young Man*, James Joyce has his protagonist consider sending a love poem to his muse, speculating that, if he went through with it, her family would read it aloud "at breakfast amid the tapping of eggshells." He concludes:

> Folly indeed! Her brothers would laugh and try to wrest the page from each other with their strong hard fingers. The suave priest, her uncle, seated in his armchair, would hold the page at arm's length, read it smiling, and approve

---

2 Vol. I. Smith, Elder and Co., 1873, p. 36.

of the literary form.[3]

Nowadays, they'd take out a restraining order.

This development in social mores doesn't necessarily reflect cultural degeneration. In our egalitarian age, women have grown unaccustomed to being regarded as angels or commodities, and it's difficult to regret this change. Nobody wants to be otherworldly if it involves relinquishing your stake in *this* world, where life actually occurs.

---

3 B. W. Huebsch, 1922, p. 261.

THIRTY-SIX

(LOVE POEMS, CONTINUED)
A LYRIC BY CAMPION

T HE DELUSIONS involved in love poetry are demonstrat-
ed by this lyric (2.4) from Thomas Campion's *Book of
Ayres*:

Fain[1] would I my love disclose,
Ask what honor might deny.
But both love and her I lose
From my motion if she fly.
Worse than pain is fear to me;   5.
Then hold in fancy[2] though it burn.
If not happy, safe I'll be,
And to my cloistered cares return.

Yet, O yet, in vain I strive
To repress my schooled desire.   10.
More and more the flames revive;
I consume[3] in mine own fire.
She would pity, might she know
The harms that I for her endure.
Speak then, and get comfort so.   15.
A wound long hid grows past recure.

---

1 fain] Gladly.
2 fancy] Imagination.
3 consume] Am consumed.

Wise she is, and needs must know
All the attempts that beauty moves.
Fair she is, and honored so
That she, sure, hath tried some loves.   20.
If with love I tempt her then,
'Tis but her due to be desired.
What would women think of men
If their deserts[4] were not admired?

Women, courted, have the hand   25.
To discard what they distaste;
But those dames whom none demand
Want[5] oft what their wills embraced.
Could their firmness iron excel,
As they are fair, they should be sought.   30.
When true thieves use falsehood well,
As they are wise, they will be caught.

Here's the poem again, this time with my annotations, stanza by stanza:

Stanza 1:
    Fain would I my love disclose,
Ask what honor might deny.
But both love and her I lose
From my motion if she fly.
Worse than pain is fear to me;   5.
Then hold in fancy though it burn.
If not happy, safe I'll be,
And to my cloistered cares return.

1.5-8: "Worse than pain…cloistered cares return."
Male lust is inherently possessive. The narrator is less concerned with failing to win his beloved than he is with the prospect of their relationship being at all ambiguous. He wants

---

4 deserts] That which is deserved.

5 want] Lack.

binary clarity. In *Othello*, Shakespeare demonstrates some of the dangers involved in indulging this instinct. We know we're headed hellward when the Moor laments:

> O curse of marriage,
> That we can call these delicate creatures ours
> And not their appetites! I had rather be a toad
> And live upon the vapor of a dungeon
> Than keep a corner in the thing I love
> For others' uses (3.3.309-314).

Stanza 2:
>   Yet, O yet, in vain I strive
> To repress my schooled desire.
> More and more the flames revive;
> I consume in mine own fire.
> She would pity, might she know   5.
> The harms that I for her endure.
> Speak then, and get comfort so.
> A wound long hid grows past recure.

2.2: "schooled desire"

"Schooled [trained] desire" is an oxymoron. Desire is anarchic.

2.5-6: "She would pity…her endure."

Firstly, the narrator hasn't done anything for her. Believing that he has, he will regard her coldness as ingratitude. His understanding of the situation is so deranged that anything he says or does in response will be deranged.

Secondly, we must explore the implications of the word "pity." Nowadays, "pity" refers to a condescending disgust, such as you might experience if you ever saw me attempt yoga. But the *OED* offers us two additional, relevant senses:

1. "The disposition to mercy or compassion; clemency, mercy, mildness, tenderness."

2. "Tenderness and concern aroused by the suffering, distress, or misfortune of another, and prompting a desire for its relief."

Perhaps a woman will lovingly "pity" a man if his "suffering, distress, or misfortune" resulted from some noble, chivalrous deed—or a deed of any kind. But, again, Campion's narrator hasn't done much. A cycle of misunderstanding is thus established: the more he feels entitled to his lady's love the less he'll deserve it.

2.8: "A wound...recure"

I hate to quibble, but in the late 1500s, a wound long exposed was just as likely to "grow past recure" as a wound long hid.

Stanza 3:
> Wise she is, and needs must know
> All the attempts that beauty moves.
> Fair she is, and honored so
> That she, sure, hath tried some loves.
> If with love I tempt her then,   5.
> 'Tis but her due to be desired.
> What would women think of men
> If their deserts were not admired?

3.1-2: "Wise she is...beauty moves"

Not really, no. Men see provocation in female beauty; they're so thoroughly conquered by it that they assume that women must understand the effect they're having. But it isn't so. And much dangerous male resentment is fueled by the failure of men to recognize that, by and large, women "know not what they do" when it comes to the inflammation of male ardor.

3.5-6: "If with love…to be desired."

The word "due" gives the game away. He feels that she's "earned" his love, and that to deprive her of it would be to violate her dignity.

3.7-8: "What would women…not admired?"

What would women think of men if men didn't ogle women? Their lives would be unchanged, but for the relief they'd enjoy of no longer being the subjects of poems like this one.

Stanza 4:
>   Women, courted, have the hand
> To discard what they distaste;
> But those dames whom none demand
> Want oft what their wills embraced.
> Could their firmness iron excel,   5.
> As they are fair, they should be sought.
> When true thieves use falsehood well,
> As they are wise, they will be caught.

4.1-2: "Women, courted…they distaste"

In other words, a woman being courted by a man holds all the cards and can discard those she dislikes.

4.3-6: "But those dames…be sought"

Undesired women cannot satisfy their own desires; they cannot make men court them no matter how strong their wills may be, but those who are fair, should be sought after.

4.7-8: "When true thieves…will be caught"

A woman courted is likely to pretend indifference. She is like a thief who has stolen a man's heart, but denies it. In the end, she allows herself to be caught.

THIRTY-SEVEN

(LOVE POEMS, CONTINUED)
NEED

W E'VE CONSIDERED A few lenses through which the poetically minded man might regard a woman. They've all presupposed that he's actually interested in her response— that there are two human beings involved, however misaligned their priorities.

There is, however, an especially degrading mindset that experiences a woman as an entirely aesthetic phenomenon. This mindset is embodied in a vulgar line that male movie characters (and not especially evil characters, either) would deploy up until recently—something to the effect of: "God, you're pretty when you're angry."

There are intellectualized versions of this—intellectualized, but no less depraved. Søren Kierkegaard offers one such version in *The Seducer's Diary*:

> All opposition enhances a person's beauty. Every young girl ought to fall in love with a zephyr,[1] for no man knows how to heighten her beauty the way it does when it skirmishes with her.[2]

Not only is this perspective unwholesome; it can lead to

---

1 zephyr] The west wind.

2 Translated by Howard V. Hong, et al. Princeton University Press, 2003, p. 77.

horror. In *Lolita*, Humbert Humbert's central mistake is believing that his love for Lolita can breach the wall surrounding the aesthetic imagination, and step into Reality. Humbert's most substantial pro-pedophilic arguments come from art. And that's exactly where nympholepsy should remain.

Although this "aestheticized" engagement with women is less acceptable than it was, I wonder if it risks returning. We appreciate each other's humanity in many ways. One of them emerges when we realize that we need each other. In *Wystan and Chester: A Personal Memoir of W.H. Auden and Chester Kallman*, Thekla Clark recalls:

> Wystan [once] said that to him the most difficult commandment to obey was "Love thy neighbor." This started a lengthy discussion involving tradition, literary sources, and history until I asked, "Wystan, just who is your neighbor?" Everyone had an answer to that question, and we had arrived at "all humanity" when Wystan answered, "Anyone who needs you."[3]

Need is crucial, and ours is (increasingly) a world in which women *qua* women don't need men *qua* men. Women outperform men. Fathers are seen as inessential. Women no longer acquire social legitimacy from marriage. And as for sex, men have always been laughable; today, however, they aren't even needed for insemination. It's now thought to be doubtful whether a woman benefits in any substantial way from a lifelong attachment to a man. Women know this. Men know this. And each knows that the other knows this.

The apparent problem, however, is that men still seem to need women. I suspect that the resulting imbalances and spiritual perversions must play some role in the deepening misogyny that curdles online. The heart hardens when faced with a person, a profession, a church, even a nation, that makes demands on you, but doesn't need you.

And when the heart hardens, people become things. It's a

---

3 Columbia University Press, 1995, p. 37.

sad irony that feminism, which ostensibly aims at asserting human dignity, should have this effect. There is no more sublime partnership on earth than that between man and woman. In making this partnership harder to achieve, feminism has alienated us from one of our most reliable sources of meaning.

THIRTY-EIGHT

(LOVE POEMS, CONTINUED) QUICHE

W HEN I WAS A younger chap, I once tried to impress a woman with my cooking. The only thing that I knew about her culinary tastes was that she liked quiche. This intelligence was the canvas upon which I'd paint my masterpiece.

Seafood seemed just the thing, for two reasons, the first being deduced by means of a rather shaky syllogism:

Major Premise: Girls like expensive things.
Minor Premise: Seafood is expensive.
Ergo: Girls like seafood.

The second reason was subconscious. Seafood had, for religious reasons, been forbidden to me during my childhood. Once I left home, however, I began eating it by the net-load, and seafood still retained for me something of its transgressive magic. On some level, I still felt that seafood was associated with every kind of dark, brooding, cultivated depravity, and I was eager to cut a vaguely Byronic figure.

If a single type of seafood was good, then many types of seafood must, I reasoned, be better still. In addition to a pre-made quiche crust, I bought shrimp, squid, prawns—perhaps even some crab meat, if I remember aright. It wasn't inexpensive; we were 955 miles away from the nearest body of salt water—or 998 miles, if you want to avoid tolls.

The question now turned to seasoning, a topic on which I was even more clueless than I was about the secrets of a woman's heart. I'd consumed gallons of mint tea while living in Israel. It was good—indeed, very good—and I figured that any spice that made a cup of tea come so splendidly to life must certainly have a similar effect on a seafood quiche.

Ah, and did I mention that this was my beloved's birthday?

I shall describe neither the quiche nor my belle's reaction to it. It's perfectly sufficient to repurpose a line from *Macbeth*, uttered by the Thane of Fife under slightly different circumstances:

"Confusion now hath made his masterpiece!"[1]

If I fell significantly in my lady's esteem, I must somehow have regained lost ground, for she consented to have two children with me. To have one child by a man might be the result of a mistake; to have two suggests volition. But this redounds more to God's grace in softening the hearts of those who have every reason to reject us than it does with such virtues as I may possess—such virtues that might compensate for my culinary ineptitude.

Dear Reader: allow me to propose that a love poem is often like a mint seafood quiche made specially (and at great expense) for one's girlfriend's birthday. If she loves you back, it won't be because of the poem, but very much *despite* it.

---

1   2.3.838.

THIRTY-NINE

(LOVE POEMS, CONTINUED)
"RUDE AM I IN MY SPEECH"

H AVING BEEN CALLED upon to explain how he won Desdemona's heart, Othello prefaces his remarks thusly:

> [...] Rude[1] am I in my speech,
> And little blessed with the soft phrase of peace:
> For since these arms of mine had seven years' pith,
> Till now some nine moons wasted, they have used
> Their dearest action in the tented field,   5.
> And little of this great world can I speak,
> More than pertains to feats of broil and battle,
> And therefore little shall I grace my cause
> In speaking for myself. [...][2]

And soon, he gets down to business. His speech is worth reproducing in full:

> Her father loved me, oft invited me,
> Still questioned me the story of my life
> From year to year: the battles, sieges, fortunes
> That I have passed.
> I ran it through, even from my boyish days,   5.

---

1 rude] Unsophisticated.

2 1.3. 421-429.

To the very moment that he bade me tell it,
Wherein I spake of most disastrous chances,
Of moving accidents by flood and field,
Of hair-breadth scapes i' the imminent deadly breach,
Of being taken by the insolent foe   10.
And sold to slavery, of my redemption[3] thence
And portance in my travels' history;
Wherein of antres[4] vast and deserts idle,
Rough quarries, rocks and hills whose heads touch
  heaven
It was my hint to speak, (such was the process),   15.
And of the cannibals that each other eat,
The Anthropophagi[5] and men whose heads
Do grow beneath their shoulders. This to hear
Would Desdemona seriously incline.
But still the house-affairs would draw her thence,   20.
Whichever as she could with haste dispatch,
She'd come again, and with a greedy ear
Devour up my discourse; which, I observing,
Took once a pliant hour, and found good means
To draw from her a prayer of earnest heart   25.
That I would all my pilgrimage dilate,
Whereof by parcels she had something heard,
But not intentively.[6] I did consent,
And often did beguile her of her tears,
When I did speak of some distressful stroke   30.
That my youth suffered. My story being done,
She gave me for my pains a world of sighs.
She swore, in faith, 'twas strange, 'twas passing strange;
'Twas pitiful, 'twas wondrous pitiful.
She wished she had not heard it, yet she wished   35.
That heaven had made her such a man. She thanked me,
And bade me, if I had a friend that loved her,

---

3 redemption] Liberation.

4 antres] Caves.

5 Anthropophagi] Mythical race of cannibals.

6 intentively] Heedfully.

I should but teach him how to tell my story,
And that would woo her. Upon this hint I spake.
She loved me for the dangers I had passed,   40.
And I loved her that she did pity them.
This only is the witchcraft I have used.[7]

And the Duke of Venice, who is among the audience, observes: "I think this tale would win my daughter, too."[8]

Damn straight, as they say.

Othello's account has much to tell us. Firstly, he's careful to admit that he's "rude" (unsophisticated) in speech. This isn't just meant to preempt any snide remarks from his audience; it serves to assure them that, in wooing Desdemona, he never had recourse to the poetic language that they might have considered a form of witchcraft.

But his proviso isn't just defensive; it can also be interpreted as something of a boast. After all, sophistication in speech isn't always a good thing. Indeed, the word is associated with "sophist," which refers to the type of classical rhetorician that today we'd call "a bullshit artist." Turning to the *OED*'s entry on "sophistication," we notice that the definitions are overwhelmingly negative:

1. "Mixed with some foreign substance; adulterated; not pure or genuine."
2. "Altered from, deprived of, primitive simplicity or naturalness. Of a literary text: altered in the course of being copied or printed."
3. "Falsified in a greater or lesser degree; not plain, honest, or straightforward."
4. "Of a printed book, containing alterations in content, binding, etc. which are intended to deceive."

Incredibly enough, "sophisticated" doesn't apparently appear as a term of praise until 1895.

To be "rude" in speech might very well be a virtue. In

---

7   473-514.

8   518.

Hamlet, the two most ridiculous characters are the most verbally facile.

First, we have Polonius. Once Hamlet accidentally slays him in Gertrude's private quarters, the Prince of Denmark regards the corpse, sneering:

> I'll lug the guts into the neighbor room.
> Mother, good night. Indeed, this counsellor
> Is now most still, most secret, and most grave,
> Who was in life a foolish, prating knave.[9]

A foolish, *prating* knave; his silver tongue was not among his selling points.

And then there's Osric, the courtier who's so eloquent that nobody can understand a word he's saying. He arrives to tell Hamlet that he (Hamlet) has been challenged to a duel with Laertes, who's

> ...an absolute gentleman, full of most excellent differences, of very soft society and great showing: indeed, to speak feelingly of him, he is the card or calendar of gentry, for you shall find in him the continent of what part a gentleman would see.[10]

Hamlet responds mockingly, trying to out-Osric Osric:

> Sir, his definement suffers no perdition in you; though, I know, to divide him inventorially would dizzy the arithmetic of memory, and yet but yaw neither, in respect of his quick sail. But, in the verity of extolment, I take him to be a soul of great article; and his infusion of such dearth and rareness, as, to make true diction of him, his semblable is his mirror; and who else would trace him, his umbrage, nothing more.[11]

---

9 3.4.338.

10 5.2.119-124.

11 119-124.

Osric replies, "Your lordship speaks most infallibly of him." Once Osric can no longer hide his confusion, Horatio observes, "His purse is empty already; all's golden words are spent."[12] And after Osric has taken his leave, Hamlet explains:

> He did comply with his dug, before he sucked it. Thus has he—and many more of the same bevy that I know the dressy age dotes on—only got the tune of the time and outward habit of encounter; a kind of yeasty collection, which carries them through and through the most fond and winnowed opinions; and do but blow them to their trial, the bubbles are out.[13]

If, in matters of love, eloquence is sometimes like an open mineshaft, how should the young lover use language? Honestly. Unostentatiously. Precisely. Don't use language to conceal who you are; use it to reveal yourself. Remember the line attributed to Socrates: "Speak, my lad, so that I can see you." Be mindful of what your beloved will see when you speak. Make sure that what she sees is worth seeing.

12 143-144.

13 5.2.125-133.

FORTY

RHYMING DICTIONARIES

Y OU WOULD HAVE to be a fool to reject on principle the aid of a rhyming dictionary. Xerox machines are better than ink-stained monks. An ammunition cartridge is better than a lead ball and a powder horn. Anesthesia is better than a slug of brandy and a stick to bite down on. Rhyming dictionaries exist, and they are unequivocally better than any alternative. I only regret that my weapon of choice (Rosalind Fergusson's *Penguin Rhyming Dictionary*) isn't currently available as a smartphone app.

The website RhymeZone.com can be useful in a pinch, but it's like showing up at a gunfight with a single-action .22 when something rather more substantial is called for. Let's say you're looking for rhymes for "dude." RhymeZone will give you the usual suspects ("brood," "crude," "food," "feud," "lewd," "prude," "nude," "rood," "rude," "shrewd," etc.), but there's a whole category of words largely excluded: "-oo" words set in the past tense ("brewed," "cued," "glued," "hewed," "queued," "stewed," "viewed," etc.). Although my dear *Penguin Rhyming Dictionary* won't mix those two rhyme families, it will inform you that "-ood" words can be made by adding an "ed" to "-oo" words. That's helpful.

I wrote a poem a few years ago entitled "Elaborations on a Line by Blake;" my habit at the time was to write stanzas backward. After all, the worst place for a technical compromise is in the very place where you want the greatest punch. I realized that I had much more flexibility in the lead-up. My prosody / rhyme scheme was:

1. A.   / u u / u u / u
2. B.   / u u / u u /
3. A.   / u u / u u / u
4. B.   / u u / u u /
5. C.   / u u / u u / u
6. D.   / u u / u u /

[Lines 7 and 8—taken from William Blake's *The Marriage of Heaven and Hell*—constituted a refrain]

7. C.   Man wears the fell[1] of the lion;
8. D.   Woman, the fleece of the sheep.

I started with this:

1. A.   / u u / u u / u
2. B.   / u u / u u /
3. A.   Herding flocks frantic to get at
4. B.   Clover mislaid in the turf—
5. C.   / u u / u u / u
6. D.   / u u / u u /
7. C.   Man wears the fell of the lion;
8. D.   Woman, the fleece of the sheep.

Quite the challenge. It's difficult to use end-rhyme when the lines end with unstressed syllables. For instance, a rhyme like "candor / encore" lacks umph. Normally, rhyme is most effective when the rhyme coincides with a stressed syllable.

It makes most sense, therefore, to craft what's called a "feminine rhyme"—this is where the penultimate syllable rhymes, and the terminal syllable is the same for each line. For example: "—fuse my / —abuse my" might be anatomized thusly:

---

1 fell] Skin.

Syllable #	1.	2.	3.
Stress	u	/	u
		FUSE	MY
	A—	BUSE	MY

Back to my poem, what can be made to rhyme with "get at?" We need an "-et" rhyme where the stress falls, after which will appear "at," as in "baguette at," "barrette at," "beget at," "brunet at," "cadet at," "coquette at," "forget at," "gazette at," "regret at," "Tibet at," "upset at," "alphabet at," "bayonet at," "bassinet at," "cigarette at," etc.

None of them quite worked. The music worked, certainly. But a poem must be more than music: it needs to actually make sense, and none of these options could graft themselves onto the two lines I'd already written.

And then, I realized: I'm not limited by the need for "-et" rhymes, the stock of which was ample. No. My stanza was getting clotted because of the need to end the line with the word "at." What if I found a trisyllabic word, where the first syllable was both unstressed and began with the letters "a-t"? The two remaining syllables would need the stress pattern / u. That way, I could break the word after the first syllable, and then slot the remainder into the beginning of the following line without interrupting the metrical scheme.

The word would need to be structured as follows:

Syllable 1	Syllable 2	Syllable 3
"-at" Rhyme	No Rhyme	No Rhyme
Unstressed	Stressed	Unstressed

And this, gentlemen, is where my secret weapon was readied for use: the Scrabble Word Finder at www.WordFinder.com. The search page looks like this:

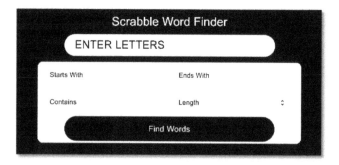

I'd simply need to search for a word beginning with "at," and select the candidates that fit my metrical criteria. "Atoning?" "Atomic?" "Ataxia?" I test-drove a few. But none quite worked. Recall that the second syllable of my ultimate choice would constitute the opening syllable of the following line, and I thought it might be crisper for that line to begin with a clean vowel. But most of the candidates involved a double-T: "Attorney;" "Attire;" "Attuning." Something seemed intriguing about "attires:"

1.	A.	/ u u / u u /	at-
2.	B.	Tires u / u u /	
3.	A.	Herding flocks frantic to get at	
4.	B.	Clover mislaid in the turf—	

What "-et" rhyme to precede "at?" Something seemed right about "Antionette:"

1.	A.	/ u u /	Antionette at-
2.	B.	Tires u / u u /	
3.	A.	Herding flocks frantic to get at	
4.	B.	Clover mislaid in the turf—	

And who did she attire?

1.	A.	/ u u /	Antionette at-
2.	B.	Tires herself u u /	

3. A.   Herding flocks frantic to get at
4. B.   Clover mislaid in the turf—

The rest of the stanza wrote itself:

> Gentle Marie Antoinette at-
> Tíres herself like a serf
> Herding flocks frantic to get at
> Clover mislaid in the turf—
> Foolery placing Versailles on   5.
> Intimate terms with the Deep.
> *Man wears the fell of the lion;*
> *Woman, the fleece of the sheep.*

And here's the final product:

ELABORATIONS ON A LINE BY BLAKE[2]
after A.C. Swinburne & Leonard Cohen

> Lovers perform a ballet, a
> Drama enacting the old
> Prophecy dazing Isaiah
> There in the beryl & gold
> Garden inside of the Zion   5.
> Trapped in an hour of sleep:
> *Man wears the fell of the lion;*
> *Woman, the fleece of the sheep.*
>
> Donning these sodden & tattered
> Skins will diminish the hard   10.
> Worry of being the battered
> Thing of another's regard.
> Thanatos fastens his eye on
> What he endeavors to keep.
> *Man wears the fell of the lion;*   15.
> *Woman, the fleece of the sheep.*

---

2 First published in *New English Review*, February 2021.

Gentle Marie Antoinette at-
Tires herself like a serf
Herding flocks frantic to get at
Clover mislaid in the turf—   20.
Foolery placing Versailles on
Intimate terms with the Deep.
Man wears the fell of the lion;
Woman, the fleece of the sheep.

Soldiers uncaged by the Tsar in-   25.
Dignantly pant in the hay,
Hunting for women (…who are, in
General, ready to say
Something engagingly wry on
Orders announced from a jeep.)   30.
Man wears the fell of the lion;
Woman, the fleece of the sheep.

Naked & freezing, he kneels. Of
Course all the national news
Packages fulsome appeals of   35.
Tailors & seamstresses whose
Robes of defeat you can buy on
Credit; they never were cheap.
Man wears the fell of the lion;
Woman, the fleece of the sheep.   40.

Everything's going to hell, or
Hell is advancing to us.
Echoes at odds in a shell or
Vault of the sunset discuss
Why the white hand of Orion   45.
Clenches a pelt. And we weep:
"Man wears the fell of the lion;
Woman, the fleece of the sheep."

"Tell us," the supplicants chanted,
"Who can subsist from within   50.
Genuine, Providence-granted
Eyes & original skin!"—
Devils ordaining we die on
Mellowing slopes of a heap.
Man wears the fell of the lion;   55.
Woman, the fleece of the sheep.

Man wears the fell of the lion;
Woman, the fleece of the sheep.
Lye is the caustic they ply on
Both when their carcasses seep.   60.
Grace (like a vest) is awry on
Mortals who cower & creep.
Man wears the fell of the lion;
Woman, the fleece of the sheep.

FORTY-ONE

CHEATING

W HEN I WAS A COLLEGIAN, I interned at a Manhattan literary agency. I recall one of the books they'd hustled into print, a reference work for writers. Let's say you were writing fiction about 1920s Chicago mobsters, and your hitman is about to ply his trade. What type of gun might he be carrying? Consult the reference book, and you'll find a long, detailed list of firearms, each with a small picture, and just enough information for the writer to make a thoughtful choice.

Indeed, the entire book was nothing but lists: lists of getaway vehicles, lists of foods that one might order in an expensive restaurant, lists of important Moscow streets, lists of ballet moves (nearly every name wearing a headdress of diacritics), lists of different types of stone, etc.

While the internet certainly existed, it didn't have much to offer the writer looking for the appearance of erudition. Today, I can Google "What kind of gun did Al Capone use?" and within 0.49 seconds, learn that it was a Colt Model 1911 .45-caliber pistol, which, in 2021, sold at auction for $1 million.[1]

This information about Capone's firearm preference is a little frustrating, truth be told. Like most people, I associate mobsters of the period with the iconic Thompson submachine

---

1 Inflation is running so badly amok, that, were it sold only ten months later, the price would have spiked to over $1,117,000. This, according to www.USDebtCalculator.com, yet another high-tech shortcut for folks who want to seem as though they know what they're talking about.

gun—the "Tommy gun." The idea of Scarface wielding that tasteful little pistol with the staghorn handles seems just a little…well, inauthentic.

The question for all creative writers in this Information Technology environment becomes: now that our most fundamental imaginative processes are interwoven with cyberspace, what does it mean for learning to be "fairly" or "genuinely" acquired? What does it mean to know something? When reading *Moby-Dick*, we sense that we're experiencing an authorial presence that really knows something about whaling. What cues are we picking up on?

It would be tidy if we could say simply that material learned from books can be used without anxiety, but that to demonstrate knowledge of anything experienced purely online is affectation.

But that feels…*off*. I indulge some of my most nourishing obsessions largely online: traditional Appalachian music, Near Eastern bagpipes, rimfire pistols, and so much else besides. Is my knowledge of rimfire pistols somehow "validated" by the fact that I own such a pistol, and know how to shoot it? What if I only knew about rimfire pistols from the internet? Would I be entitled to use one as the basis of a poetic conceit? What if I only knew about rimfire pistols from books? Why does www.wood-database.com[2] feel like a vaguely disreputable place to harvest material for poems, while a rhyming dictionary seems perfectly acceptable?

The poet who's committed to being truthful must grapple with these questions.

---

2 The database attempts to catalogue every wood known to man. For each, a dizzying range of information is supplied: Common Name, Scientific Name, Geographical Distribution, Tree Size, Average Dried Weight, Specific Gravity, Janka Hardness, Modulus of Rupture [which should be the title of the next James Bond movie], Elastic Modulus, Crushing Strength, Shrinkage, Color/Appearance, Grain/Texture, Rot Resistance, Workability, Odor, Allergies/Toxicity, Pricing/Availability, Sustainability, and Common Uses.

FORTY-TWO

THE COMMONPLACE BOOK

B EFORE PHOTOCOPIERS, serious readers kept a so-called "commonplace book:" a notebook filled with interesting quotes harvested over years in the library. Despite all our technology, it remains a good idea. A quote that's obviously brilliant or useful may be remembered easily. But what about those little literary discoveries that are striking, even though you can't tell why? These are often the most fruitful kernels for future poems. And, while I'd be flattered to have you believe that I possess a photographic memory, I wouldn't have been able to write this volume without the use of my own commonplace books.

A quote might stand out for several reasons.

i. ARRESTING TABLEAU

According to *The Patria: Accounts of Medieval Constantinople*:

> In olden times, there were trumpets on top of the walls. Underneath, the wall was hollow like a cistern, and when a heavy south or north wind blew, strong currents of air came up as the waves of the sea were repulsed from the walls, and a melody of the sirens was heard, and the tower opposite responded. When the Roman fleet was ready to depart, it assembled there, and the ships sounded together with the sound of the towers, and departed.[1]

---

1 Albrecht Berger, trans. Harvard University Press, 2013, p. 163.

From George Bryan's *Chelsea, In the Olden and Present Times*, concerning the execution of some Jewish convicts:

> These men, as was customary formerly in cases of murder, were tried on a Friday, and on the following day (the Jewish Sabbath) they were anathematized in the Synagogue.

> As their execution was to take place on the following Monday, one of the Rabbis went to them in the pressroom of Newgate, and delivered to each of them a Hebrew book, but declined attending them to the place of death, nor even prayed with them, at the time of his visit. Their wives and children were admitted to take their leave of them before they set out for Tyburn, where executions took place. An immense number of people attended the execution.

> They prayed together, sung an hymn in the Hebrew language, and soon afterwards were launched into eternity.[2]

The Scots Magazine added a macabre detail:

> After they had hung for the usual time, their bodies were taken down, and carried to Surgeon's Hall for dissection. Levi Weil [...] is to be anatomized, and hung up in Surgeon's Hall.[3]

Here's a passage I've been schlepping around the world with me ever since discovering it over twenty years ago in the Brotherton Library at the University of Leeds. It's from William Hickling Prescott's *History of the Reign of Philip the Second, King of Spain* (Vol. III) and concerns the building of El Escorial, a Renaissance compound hosting a royal palace, a church, a monastery, a college, and a library:

> A violent thunderstorm was raging in the mountains, and the lightning struck one of the great towers of the monastery. In a short time the upper portion of the building

---

2 Published by the author, 1869, pp. 158-159.

3 Vol. XXXIII., A. Murray and J. Cochran, 1771, p. 704.

was in a blaze. So much of it, fortunately, was of solid materials that the fire made slow progress. But the difficulty of bringing water to bear on it was extreme. It was eleven o'clock at night when the fire broke out, and in the orderly household of Philip all had retired to rest. They were soon roused by the noise. The king took his station on the opposite tower, and watched with deep anxiety the progress of the flames. The Duke of Alva was one among the guests. Though sorely afflicted with the gout at the time, he wrapped his dressing-gown about him and climbed to a spot which afforded a still nearer view of the conflagration. Here the "good duke" at once assumed the command, and gave his orders with as much promptness and decision as on the field of battle.

All the workmen, as well as the neighboring peasantry, were assembled there. The men showed the same spirit of subordination which they had shown throughout the erection of the building. The Duke's orders were implicitly obeyed; and more than one instance is recorded of daring self-devotion among the workmen, who toiled as if conscious they were under the eye of their sovereign.

The tower trembled under the fury of the flames; and the upper portion of it threatened every moment to fall in ruins. Great fears were entertained that it would crush the hospital, situated in that part of the monastery. Fortunately, it fell in an opposite direction, carrying with it a splendid chime of bells that was lodged in it, but doing no injury to the spectators.[4]

From Nancy Isenberg's *White Trash: The 400-Year Untold History of Class in America*:

The most lavish destruction occurred in Columbia, South Carolina, the fire-eaters' capital, where the most conspicuous planter oligarchy held court. In tiny Barnwell, sixty miles south of Columbia, Brevet Major General Hugh Judson Kilpatrick of New Jersey staged what he called a

---

4 J.B. Lippincott, 1875, pp. 418-419.

"Nero's ball," forcing the southern belles of the town to attend and dance with Union officers while the town burned to the ground.[5]

In his *Ecclesiastical History*, the Venerable Bede describes Saint Augustine's[6] visit to bring the Gospel to Æthelberht, King of Wessex:

> Within therefore some days hereof, the king came unto the island, and, sitting in an open place, he bid Augustine with his fellows to come to commune with him therein. For he would not, by reason of an old superstition, suffer him to come unto him in any house, least, if they were skillful in sorcery, they might the rather by surprise deceive him and prevail against him.[7]

ॐ

ii. A PUZZLING IDEA

From Jennifer Michael Hecht's *Stay: A History of Suicide and the Philosophies Against It*:

> Jansson tells us that, for men, an alternative path to indirect suicide was to falsely confess to bestiality; in the sixteenth and seventeenth centuries, at least six hundred people were executed in Sweden for this crime. A considerable number of men apparently confessed without having been accused, and while some may have done so out of guilty feelings for having actually committed the act, others were surely seeking death.[8]

And it turns out that the internet wasn't the first technological innovation immediately put to prurient or crass uses. According to *Graffiti in the Athenian Agora*:

---

5 Viking, 2016, p. 171.

6 Augustine of Canterbury, not of Hippo.

7 J.E. King, trans. Harvard University Press, 1930, p. 111.

8 Yale University Press, 2013, p. 88.

One of the very earliest uses to which the art of writing was put, along with alphabetic exercises and marks of ownership, was sexual insult and obscenity.[9]

This, from the diary of Abraham Lincoln's assassin, John Wilkes Booth, scribbled on April 22, 1865:

I have too great a soul to die like a criminal.[10]

I've been mulling over this quote for nearly a decade, and I'm no closer to understanding what it might mean.

❧

iii. A CLUSTER OF THEMATICALLY RELATED TEXTS
From Girolamo Fracastoro's *Carmina*:

That man alone is worthless who lives neither for others nor for himself.[11]

This reminded me of something I'd stumbled upon in Hesiod's *Works and Days*:

The man who thinks of everything by himself, considering what will be better, later and in the end—this man is the best of all. That man is fine too, the one who is persuaded by someone who speaks well. But whoever neither thinks by himself nor pays heed to what someone else says and lays it to his heart—that man is good for nothing.[12]

This, in turn, reminded me of a passage from Michel Houellebecq's *Submission*:

---

9 American School of Classical Studies, 1988, p. 5.

10 Harold Holzer, ed. *President Lincoln Assassinated! The Firsthand Story of the Murder, Manhunt, Trial and Mourning.* Library of America, 2014, p. 71.

11 James Gardner, trans. *Latin Poetry.* Harvard University Press, 2013, pp. 344-345.

12 Glenn W. Most, trans. Harvard University Press, Loeb, 2018, p .111.

The mere will to live was clearly no match for the pains and aggravations that punctuate the life of the average Western man. I was incapable of living for myself, and who else did I have to live for? Humanity didn't interest me—it disgusted me, actually. I didn't think of human beings as my brothers, especially when I looked at some particular subset of human beings, such as the French, or my former colleagues.[13]

This brought me to C.S. Lewis's *The Screwtape Letters*:

You can make him waste his time not only in conversation he enjoys with people whom he likes, but in conversation with those he cares nothing about on subjects that bore him. You can make him do nothing at all for long periods. You can keep him up late at night, not roistering, but staring at a dead fire in a cold room. All the healthy and outgoing activities which we want him to avoid can be inhibited and nothing given in return, so that at least he may say, as one of my own patients said on his arrival down here, "I now see that I spent most of my life in doing neither what I ought nor what I liked." The Christians describe the Enemy as one "without whom Nothing is strong." And Nothing is very strong: strong enough to steal away a man's best years not in sweet sins but in a dreary flickering of the mind over it knows not what and knows not why, in the gratification of curiosities so feeble that the man is only half aware of them, in drumming of fingers and kicking of heels, in whistling tunes that he does not like, or in the long, dim labyrinth of reveries that have not even lust or ambition to give them relish, but which, once chance association has started them, the creature is too weak and fuddled to shake off.[14]

---

13 Lorin Stein, trans. Farrar, Straus and Giroux, 2015, pp. 168-169.
14 The Folio Society, 2008. pp. 49-50.

iv. INHERENTLY INTERESTING TIDBITS

From Kevin Tuite's "The Autocrat of the Banquet Table: the Political and Social Significance of the Georgian Supra:"

As I mentioned earlier, the Georgian banquet is an arena of competition among the men at the table. Descriptions of the supra tend to foreground what I will call "positive agonism", that is, the competitive display of quantity. This is most notoriously expressed through the amount and quality of the food and drink laid out before the guests (cp. "four-story banquets", with trays of food piled so high on the table that the guests cannot see the fellow partiers seated across from them, lampooned in one of the Niangi cartoons exhibited by Manning 2003); the dozen or more glassfuls, hornfuls—and even flower-vase-fuls—of wine chugged down by each drinker in the course of an evening. Positive agonism is also expressed verbally, in the form of lengthy, elaborate toasts, sometimes accompanied by the recitation of poetry or quotations from Georgian literature.

Less often remarked upon, but of equal importance if one is to understand many otherwise puzzling aspects of traditional Caucasian behavior, is "negative agonism", by which I mean the competitive display of restraint and self-control. If one is to believe the accounts of ethnographers, seconded by the vivid descriptions of highland morality contained in Grigol Robakidze's short story Engadi, the Xevsur mountaineers made self-control (*tav-šek'aveba*) into something of a cult. True self-mastery was manifested by controlling your sword strokes in a duel so as to only lightly wound your opponent; to control your passions so as to pass the night caressing a friend of the opposite sex (*sc'orperi*) without consummating the relationship; to bear the excruciating pain of traditional surgical interventions (including trepanation), or the agony of a difficult childbirth, without crying out. At the banquet, negative agonism is directly joined to the excessive consumption just described. The ideal drinker not only ingests as much or more than his fellow banqueters, but at the same time he manifests no significant impairment of his alertness, eloquence, singing or dancing ability. The fame of the 17th-century champion drinker Č'iladze depended as much on the latter as on the former talent. In at least some regions of the Caucasus, there was a negative counterpart to the positive-agonistic display of hostly generosity as well: Seated at a table piled high with food, the ideal guest, according to an Ossetian proverb, leaves it untouched "even though hungry cats be clawing at his stomach."[15]

Regarding *scʼorperi*, here's a song stanza quoted in Kevin Tuite's "'Anti-Marriage' in Georgian Society:"

> Or may I be a golden cup,
> That I be filled with wine for you.
> May I be tinted in red,
> Drink me — I will refresh you.
> May I be a silken shirt,
> That I might melt on your heart.[16]

Tuite elaborates:

> Whenever a group of people from different households gathers together—hay-mowing, harvesting, wool-carding, weddings and even funerals—there is an opportunity for *scʼorproba*. Should a boy or girl wish to lie with someone who is not a fairly close relative, an "envoy" is asked to ascertain if the other party is receptive to the idea, and then to escort the boy or girl to the upper floor (*čʼerxo*), or wherever the two plan to spend the night. [...] In contrast to the love poetry inspired by *cʼacʼloba*, the rare mentions of husband-wife relations in Georgian poetry tend to be ironic or sarcastic in nature. [...] It was common in earlier times for couples to pair up for *cʼacʼloba* while camping

15 *Language, History and Cultural Identities in the Caucasus*. Papers from the conference, June 17-19, 2005. Malmö: Dept. of International Migration and Ethnic Relations, Malmö University, pp. 9–35.

16 *Anthropological Linguistics* 42 #1: 37-60.

out near the major Pshav shrines.[17]

v. A COMMONPLACE SENTIMENT, WEIRDLY PHRASED
James Boswell admitting he's a virgin, quoted in John B. Radner's *Johnson and Boswell: A Biography of a Friendship*:

> I have not yet had an opportunity of indulging my amorous genius, but I have hopes.[18]

---

17 Ibid.
18 Yale University Press, 2012, p. 39.

FORTY-THREE

POETRY AS PROCESS AND PRODUCT

E ARLIER, I MENTIONED banjo luthier Bill Rickard, who, after misplacing both legs and his left arm in a motorcycle accident, designed equipment enabling him to build world-class instruments using his right arm alone. I assume that Mr. Rickard's banjos would be fundamentally the same if he were able-bodied.

Sometimes, however, the "process" really does dictate certain aspects of the "product." Take, for example, Raymond Carver, who's known for his short, simple stories rendered in short, simple sentences. This is his aesthetic signature, and one might expect that this was a conscious aesthetic strategy.

Not so, we learn. In "Fires," he writes:

I have to say that the single greatest influence on my life, and on my writing, directly and indirectly, has been my two children. They were born before I was twenty, and from beginning to end of our habitation under the same roof—some nineteen years in all—there wasn't any area of my life where their heavy and often baleful influence didn't reach. [...] [T]he life I was in was vastly different than the lives of the writers I most admired. I understood writers to be people who didn't spend their Saturdays at the Laundromat and every waking hour subject to the needs and caprices of their children. [...] During these ferocious years of parenting, I usually didn't have the time, or the heart, to think about working on anything very lengthy. [...] The circumstances of my life with these

181

children dictated something else. They said if I wanted to write anything, and finish it, and if ever I wanted to take satisfaction out of finished work, I was going to have to stick to stories and poems. The short things I could sit down and, with any luck, write quickly and have done with. […] These circumstances dictated, to the fullest possible extent, the forms my writing could take.[1]

Process can dictate product. Likewise, in *The Art of Bible Translation*, Robert Alter writes:

It is remarkable—and, indeed, anomalous—that the narrative literature of ancient Israel was cast in prose, in contrast to the practice of other early cultures. […] What one can safely say is that the use of prose was obviously connected with the presence of literacy in this culture, as opposed to Homer's world, which did not know writing. Freed from the constraints of oral-formulaic composition in metrical lines, the Hebrew writers employed an impressive flexibility in how they could shape language.[2]

In other words, the biblical authors didn't select genres for abstract reasons. The processes of culture determined the nature of the product.

The decisive element of any public phenomenon is often something just this basic. Nations have made peace because their leaders liked each other. Groucho Marx's irritable demeanor was influenced by his gastrointestinal volatility. In *Moby-Dick*, Melville's narrator quips about the possible relationship between Queequeg's religious fasting and the general tenor of his spirit:

Besides, argued I, fasting makes the body cave in; hence the spirit caves in; and all thoughts born of a fast must necessarily be half-starved. This is the reason why most

---

1 *Collected Stories.* The Library of America, 2009, pp. 734 – 740.
2 Princeton University Press, 2020, p. 53.

dyspeptic[3] religionists cherish such melancholy notions about their hereafters. "In one word, Queequeg," said I, rather digressively, "hell is an idea first born on an un-digested apple dumpling, and since then perpetuated through the hereditary dyspepsias nurtured by Rama-dans."[4]

All the same, it's the end product that counts: the peace treaty, the one-liner, the religious system, and the literature. Were Carver's stories bad, they wouldn't be redeemed by any reference to his family life. This is one of the more conspicuous problems with "identity politics:" they focus on the process (the writer's biography), and not on the product (the art).

It's tempting to obsess about a writer's life. The constancy of W.H. Auden's love for Chester Kallman heartens me. That Oscar Wilde endured such hell gives me confidence that I'm tougher than I seem. When I feel like a failure, Gerard Manley Hopkins's difficulties reassure me, and make me feel that I'm in good company.

Perhaps it's only natural to indulge in this vice. But it remains a vice.

---

3   dyspeptic] Of or having indigestion, or, by figurative extension, depression or irritability.
4   Chapter XVII.

FORTY-FOUR

END-STOP AND ENJAMBMENT

A LINE OF POETRY will end in one of two ways: with an end-stop, or with enjambment.

An end-stopped line ends with a punctuation mark, and, accordingly, with a pause, whose duration will depend upon the punctuation mark.

An enjambed line doesn't end with any punctuation mark; the "measure" simply swings into the following line. For example, here's the first quatrain of Shakespeare's Sonnet 83:

> I never saw that you did painting need
> And therefore to your fair no painting set.
> I found, or thought I found, you did exceed
> The barren tender of a poet's debt.

Lines two and four are end-stopped; lines one and three, enjambed.

Most pop lyrics nowadays use only end-stopped lines. There's no reason for this beyond laziness and incompetence; the lyricist, in other words, has no particular effect in mind that only end-stopped lines can achieve. Since end-stops are easy and straightforward, they best accommodate simple thoughts. We find, therefore, a feedback loop: blunt thoughts inspire blunt technique, and blunt technique constrains the lyricist to blunt thoughts.

A quick visit to the *Billboard* Hot 100 website informed

me that, at the time of writing,[1] a song entitled "About Damn Time," by someone whose *nom de plume* is "Lizzo," was conquering the North American market. A jaunt to YouTube revealed that "Lizzo" is a morbidly obese strumpet resembling something made by an upholsterer whose cappuccino's been spiked with mescaline.

At first, I approved of her video, for it seemed clear that this must be a cautionary tale, intended for the young and impressionable, about the consequences of intemperance. I half-expected to see a caption below the frame, reading:

𝔉ollow 𝔑ot 𝔐y 𝔓ath.

Hogarth couldn't have done better.

What began as a distressing intuition, however, soon hardened into the certainty that one was expected to find this Gorgon glamorous, and, indeed, sexy.

Here's the opening stanza of "About Damn Time:"

It's bad bitch o'clock, yeah; it's thick-thirty.
I've been through a lot, but I'm still flirty.[2]
Is everybody back up in the buildin'?
It's been a minute; tell me how you're healin',
'Cause I'm about to get into my feelings.   5.
How you feelin'? How you feel right now?[3]

The first line is hard to parse. According to www.urban-dictionary.com, "thick" is:

a word used to describe a female who may be defined by health charts as "overweight," but still attracts mad[4] guys

---

1 May 28, 2022.

2 How very reassuring.

3 Transcribed from YouTube.

4 mad] According (again) to www.urbandictionary.com: "An adjective used to describe something that is of a large amount, or large quantity. Used most commonly in the New York area, meaning 'a lot' or 'lots of.'"

because the weight is in the right places (hips, buttocks, and breasts)[.] [A] female with too much weight in the wrong places (like a huge gut[,] stomach, or double/triple chins) would just be considered fat[.]

This didn't clarify much. While the music video established with little ambiguity that "Lizzo" has weight in the "hips, buttocks, and breasts," it also indicated that she had weight everywhere else, as well. We must sometimes be humble before such mysteries.

Whatever "It's bad bitch o'clock, yeah; it's thick-thirty" might conceivably mean, it doesn't require more than a single line to say it. Blunt thought; blunt technique.

Since it would be unjust (though obviously amusing) to compare "About Damn Time" to *Winterreise*, here's part of the chorus from another popular song, Anne Wilson's "My Jesus"—a formidable commercial success, nominated for a *Billboard* Music Award:

His love is strong and His grace is free,
And the good news is I know that He
Can do for you what He's done for me.
Let me tell you 'bout my Jesus.[5]

While the first thought takes only one line to express, the second needs some room to stretch, like a just-awoken cat. The second line cascades into the third, without any interruption to the natural syntax. This is enjambment used well.

---

5 Transcribed from YouTube.

FORTY-FIVE

"BEAD-BROWN EYES"

H ERE ARE THE opening lines of "The Keys of Morning" by Walter de la Mare, whose work is experiencing a wave of long-overdue interest:

> While at her bedroom window once,
> Learning her task for school,
> Little Louisa lonely sat
> In the morning clear and cool.
> She slanted her small bead-brown eyes   5.
> Across the empty street,
> And saw Death softly watching her
> In the sunshine pale and sweet.

"[B]ead-brown eyes:" lovely. Since "brown eyes" is cliché, the novice's temptation is to find a fancy synonym for "brown." *Thesaurus.com* supplies possibilities like "amber," "fawn," "chocolate," "auburn," "beige," "russet," "sepia," "tawney," "copper," "bronze," "mahogany," "tan," "chestnut," "ochre," and "umber." After searching for "shades of brown," *Wikipedia* yields such exotic offerings as "bone," "burgundy," "cordovan," "ecru," and "wheat."

But none quite does the trick: "Amber eyes?" "Auburn eyes?" "Beige eyes?" "Bone eyes?" "Bronze eyes?" "Burgundy eyes?" "Chestnut eyes?" "Chocolate eyes?" "Copper eyes?" "Cordovan eyes?" "Ecru eyes?" "Fawn eyes?" "Mahogany eyes?"

"Ochre eyes?" "Russet eyes?" "Sepia eyes?" "Tan eyes?" "Tawney eyes?" "Umber eyes?" "Wheat eyes?"

Although these words are certainly fancy, and not a few are musical ("mahogany eyes"), they fail to describe these brown eyes—or, indeed, any brown eyes. We'd be better off with a cliché, since a cliché at least has the benefit of a low-rent kind of clarity. Fancy words thrill nobody. We need something else. We need to describe these eyes. We aim at vividness, but vividness tempered by restraint, and obedient to the laws of proportion.

Hmm. How about this: if we're unlikely to make much headway with rough synonyms for "brown," let's compare the eyes to someTHING that's brown. Or, let's compare the eyes to something that can be (but isn't necessarily) brown. Then, that thing's ancillary qualities can be applied by implication to the eyes we're trying to describe.

"Bead" begins its life as a word for "prayer." According to the *OED*, it was in early Middle English when "[t]he name was transferred [...] to the small globular bodies used for 'telling beads,' i.e., counting prayers said, from which the other senses naturally followed." Also, there seems to be a filament associating "bead" with earth tones. "Bead-amber" (first used in 1611) refers to "ordinary yellow amber," which is sepia-brown. Many of the natural materials out of which beads were made tend in the direction of earth tones.

Eyes that are described as "bead-brown" will therefore be understood to possess a range of qualities exceeding mere brownness. Such eyes are precious, warm, associated with prayer, and (by extension) with love, devotion, mercy, gentleness, innocence, hope, faith, and childlike dependence.

∽

Exercise One
DESCRIBING A BODY PART

1. Name a body part: [*for example*] "face"
2. Describe it with an unexceptional adjective: "smooth face"
3. List objects that may be characterized by your adjective, but not necessarily so.

4. Try them out: "Amulet-smooth face;" "Bird-smooth face;" "Ice-smooth face;" "Stone-smooth face;" "Lute-smooth face;" "Flask-smooth face;" "Coffin-smooth face;" "Intaglio-smooth face."

FORTY-SIX

AFTER SAPPHO

T HERE'S A LOVELY fragment attributed to Sappho, which Willis Barnstone translates:

Far sweeter in sound than a lyre,
More golden than gold,
Far whiter than an egg.[1]

It's structured like a joke, with a twist at the end. The first comparison is straightforward, and (indeed) slightly cliché:

SWEETER SOUNDING → THAN → LYRE

The second is so severely straightforward as to be redundant, a tautology:

MORE GOLDEN → THAN → GOLD

This extremity having been achieved, Sappho swings around, and gives us a genuinely, concretely illustrative image:

WHITER → THAN → EGG

❧

---

1 *The Complete Poems of Sappho*. Shambhala Publications, 2009, p. 91.

Exercise Two
WRITE A THREE-PART SIMILE,
STRUCTURED AS FOLLOWS:

The topic of the simile: [*For example*]   "The night:"
Straightforward, nearly cliché: "Heavy like lead,"
Redundant: "Darker than darkness,"
Concrete: "Lethal as diamonds."

FORTY-SEVEN

DEFERRAL

Here is John Keats' famous sonnet "When I Have Fears That I May Cease to Be:"

When I have fears that I may cease to be
Before my pen has gleaned my teeming brain,
Before high-pilèd books, in charactery,[1]
Hold like rich garners the full ripened grain;
When I behold, upon the night's starred face,   5.
Huge cloudy symbols of a high romance,
And think that I may never live to trace
Their shadows with the magic hand of chance;
And when I feel, fair creature of an hour,
That I shall never look upon thee more,   10.
Never have relish in the faery power
Of unreflecting love—then on the shore
Of the wide world I stand alone, and think,
Till love and fame to nothingness do sink.

Let's ignore the "meaning" and focus on the syntactical structure. The poem is basically one long conditional sentence, where the "point" is withheld for 11.5 lines. Its structure can be expressed thusly:

---

1 charactery] "Expression of thought by symbols or characters; such characters or symbols collectively; a writing system" (*OED*).

WHEN _____   1.
_____   2.
_____   3.
_____;   4.
WHEN _____   5.
_____   6.
_____   7.
_____;   8.
AND WHEN _____   9.
_____   10.
_____   11.
_____; THEN_____   12.
_____   13.
_____ . 14.

∽

Exercise Three
WRITE A SENTENCE ORGANIZED LIKE KEATS' POEM:

"When X, when X, and when X, THEN X."
For example:

"When I got venereal disease, when my hydrangeas died, and when I lost my car keys, then I knew I'd received an awful lot of advice I should have listened to."

Elaborate that sentence into a poem.

FORTY-EIGHT

THREE RHETORICAL TEMPLATES FROM FULKE GREVILLE

I BECAME ENAMORED of Edgar Allan Poe when I was a kid, and I wanted to write prose that had that sound. So, I went to the Public Library, and asked the librarian if she could recommend a book that might teach me to write like that. Slightly flustered by my question, she suggested I consult a thesaurus and find an "old-fashioned" alternative for every "modern" word. This, she concluded, would make my writing feel like Poe's.

Although this seemed reasonable enough, when I tried it, the results didn't sound like Poe—they just sounded weird, and sometimes unintentionally funny. For instance, the exclamation "For the love of God, no!" became "For the adulation of our Splendiferous Adjudicator, no!"

Whenever a poetic "music" mesmerizes me, I'm curious about how that music is made. I've often wondered why Elizabethan poets "sound that way;" as with Poe, it's deeper than diction, or even the sentiments expressed. There must be something in the rhetoric itself that constitutes the poetic signature of that era.

The deliciously-named Fulke Greville provides an infinitely minable seam of Elizabethan rhetoric. Although many aspects of his poems can bring enormous pleasure, we're "on-duty" at the moment, and will therefore remain focused on rhetorical patterns.

EXHIBIT A:
CÆLICA, I., 1-4

Love, the delight of all well-thinking minds;
Delight, the fruit of virtue dearly loved;
Virtue, the highest good that Reason finds;
Reason, the fire wherein men's thoughts be proved[.]

What's going on here? Whatever it is, it must have some-
thing to do with those big, abstract "concept words" ("delight,"
"love," "virtue," and "reason"), and how they seem to cycle
through the quatrain. We can map it thusly:

STEP 1: *Locate the Key Words*

LOVE, the DELIGHT of all well-thinking minds;
DELIGHT, the fruit of VIRTUE dearly LOVED;
VIRTUE, the highest good that REASON finds;
REASON, the fire wherein men's thoughts be proved[.]

STEP 2: *Assign Each Key Word a Number*

LOVE (1), the DELIGHT (2) of all well-thinking minds;
DELIGHT (2), the fruit of VIRTUE (3) dearly LOVED
(1); VIRTUE (3), the highest good that REASON (4)
finds; REASON (4) , the fire wherein men's thoughts be
proved[.]

STEP 3: *Erase the Words*

1_____2_____
2_____3_____1
3_____4_____
4_____.

STEP 4: *Insert Your Own Key Words*

1. = "resentment" 2. = "disease" 3. = "gland" 4. = "doctor"

STEP 5: *Fill in the Blanks*

Resentment is the disease of a cramped memory.
Disease is the result of a gland when it's resentful.
A gland is the benthic thing a doctor finds.
The doctor is the only man we trust.

EXHIBIT B:
CÆLICA, LXXVIII, 1-2

The little hearts, where light-winged passion reigns,
Move easily upward, as all frailties do.

We have certain associations with "upward;" it's prover-bially a good direction in which to go. Prayers, virtuous souls, birds, and sunflowers all tend upward. But Greville surprises us with the reminder that Up = Good is cliché, and that other, less attractive things must also tend upward.

To appreciate how Greville's couplet works, we can make our own version, focusing on "downward."

The heavy hearts, where wingless passion reigns,
Move easily downward, as_____.

What are some situations where "Downward" is good?

EXHIBIT C:
CÆLICA, LXXIV, 1-6

In the window of a grange,[1]
Whence men's prospects[2] cannot range
Over groves and flowers growing,
Nature's wealth and pleasure showing;
But on graves where shepherds lie,   5.
That by Love or Sickness die.

Let's examine lines five through six:

But on graves where shepherds lie,
That by Love or Sickness die.

It might be useful to begin by untangling the inverted syntax:

But on graves where shepherds lie
That die by love or sickness.

That graves are filled with people who've died of sickness is hardly news; indeed, apart from violence, sickness is the only thing that can kill someone. To remark that graves are filled with folks who've died of sickness is like remarking that the fridge is full of food, that a bouquet is made up of flowers, or that a guitar has stretched strings.

Greville, however, fractures the commonplace, and then inserts a surprising word ("love") in the gap. The idea of love as a sickness is also cliché, of course. The tradition of chivalrous verse is dense with young men wheezing about having been "slain" by love. Greville is interrupting one cliché with another cliché but thereby producing something dynamic and beautiful.

---

1   grange] Barn or granary.
2   prospects] Views.

Let's craft our own poetic riffs according to Greville's structure. Begin with some obvious statements of fact:

1. "In a codex, the vellum is full of words."
2. "A neighborhood is made of houses lined up along a street."

Fracture each line just before the essential noun:

1. "In a codex, the vellum is full of [_____**and**] words."
2. "A neighborhood is made of [_____**and**] houses lined up along a street."

Visit www.RandomWordGenerator.com, search for words you can use as "surprise" nouns, and see what works:

1. "In a codex, the vellum is full of debts and words."
2. "A neighborhood is made of regrets and houses lined up along a street."

FORTY-NINE

IMPOSSIBLE THINGS

O<small>NE OF THE LYRICS</small> comprising the anthology we know as *Carmina Burana* offers a description of a topsy-turvy world in which:

> Featherless fledglings try to fly,
> Asses try to strike up the lyre,
> Oxen try to dance at court,
> And ploughshare loudmouths try to serve as knights.[1]

In his note on the poem, translator-editor David A. Traill observes: "The poem belongs to the 'World Upside-down' topos[2] [...], which leads into a list of *adynata* (impossible things)." [3]

According to the *Penguin Dictionary of Literary Terms and Literary Theory*, an *adynaton*, which means "not possible" in Greek, is "[a] form of hyperbole [...] which involves the magnification of an event by reference to the impossible."[4]

One of the most famous examples occurs in Andrew Marvell's "To His Coy Mistress," in which the sexually overheated narrator begins:

---

1 Vol. I., Harvard University Press, 2018, p. 17.

2 topos] A traditional theme.

3 p. 471.

4 John Anthony Cuddon. Penguin, 1998, p. 9.

Had we but world enough and time,
This coyness, lady, were no crime.
We would sit down, and think which way
To walk, and pass our long love's day.
Thou by the Indian Ganges' side   5.
Shouldst rubies find; I by the tide
Of Humber would complain.[5] I would
Love you ten years before the Flood,[6]
And you should, if you please, refuse
Till the conversion of the Jews.[7]   10.

Cuddon also cites Christ's statement: "It is easier for a camel to go through the eye of a needle, than for a rich man to enter into the kingdom of God."[8]

☙

Exercise Four

Let's make our own adynatons. List some phrases, each comprising a noun and a verb that, in regular usage, seems comfortable with that noun. For example: "Sponge absorbs;" "Dog fetches;" "Net catches;" "Bottle contains."

Now, prepare a list of random nouns, and try hitching them to the phrases you've already made, and see what happens. You might get things like: "The sponge absorbs nations;" "The dog fetches apologies;" "The net catches a word;" "The bottle contains a bed."

Now, find some interesting adjectives to modify the nouns,

---

5 Thou by the Indian…Humber would complain] The Ganges (a river in India, India at the time being shorthand for "very far away") and the Humber (an estuary in northern England) were on opposite sides of the known world.

6 before the Flood] The biblical flood that Noah and his family survived by means of the Ark they were instructed to build.

7 the conversion of the Jews] A herald of the End of Days.

8 Matthew 19:24.

and slot them in accordingly: "The sponge absorbs scummy nations;" "The dog fetches tardy apologies;" "The net catches a flailing word;" "The bottle contains a waterlogged bed."

And finally, you can try using these images to represent some kind of extremity:

• "My heart finds it harder to forgive than a sponge finds it to absorb scummy nations."

• "I'll love you until someone invents a net that can catch a flailing word."

• "You think that this construction project will be completed soon? Dogs will learn to fetch tardy apologies sooner."

• "The bottle is so full that it contains a waterlogged bed."

FIFTY

YOU CAN DO BETTER, THOMAS

I N "MY LIFE'S DELIGHT," Thomas Campion ends each of the two stanzas with a couplet. The first:

> O come, and take from me
> The pain of being deprived of thee![1]

And the second:

> Come, then, and make thy flight
> As swift to me, as heavenly light.[2]

The first couplet is brilliant. "The pain of being deprived of thee" is the pain of her absence; she can *take* the pain by *giving* her presence. Campion's muse subtracts pain by adding herself. The image is structured like a perfectly tied bow.

The old masters were extremely nimble in playing with binaries. John Donne has some fun with this in a six-line poem called "A Burnt Ship:"

> Out of a fired ship, which by no way
> But drowning could be rescued from the flame,
> Some men leaped forth, and ever as they came
> Near the foes' ships, did by their shot decay.

---

1   5-6.

2   11-12.

So all were lost, which in the ship were found,   5.
They in the sea being burnt, they in the burnt ship
        drowned.

The men "found" (i.e., discovered) in the ship were also "lost" (i.e., dead). In the water, there's burning; in the flames, drowning.

Campion's second couplet, ("Come, then, and make thy flight / As swift to me, as heavenly light.") misses an important opportunity. It presupposes (since it's based on an honest cliché) that "heavenly light" comes swiftly. Campion would have done well to work the conceit to subvert the cliché and make "heavenly light" move slowly.

FIFTY-ONE

INVERSION

"INVERSION" isn't just a Freudian euphemism for homosexuality; it's also the name of a poetic trick especially common in older poetry. Inversion occurs when a sentence's word-order is reshuffled to achieve a particular effect. There are two reasons to use inversion:

> 1. To withhold something until the end of a line for dramatic emphasis, or

> 2. To bully a line into rhyming that plainly wouldn't, were a more natural syntax preserved.

And sometimes, it's a combination of the two.

> Here's the first quatrain from Shakespeare's Sonnet 76:

> Why is my verse so barren of new pride,
> So far from variation or quick change?
> Why with the time do I not glance aside
> To newfound methods and to compounds strange?

It sounds perfectly natural to ask: "Why is my verse so barren of new pride, so far from variation or quick change?" That the first two lines have no inversion suggests that they were written first, when there wasn't yet any pressure to rhyme.

As for the next two lines, however, Shakespeare apparently wants to say: "Why do I not glance aside with the time to newfound methods and to strange compounds?" Since this obviously wouldn't do, he must get crafty. By using inversion, not only does he hit the rhymes, but he actually creates some drama: ending the final line with "compounds strange," he saves a surprising (and therefore pleasurable) adjective for the end. Its placement on the very edge of silence helps the stanza to resonate like one of those Tibetan singing bowls.

Poets sometimes write their stanzas backwards, since it allows for greater control of the "punchline." However, this often necessitates inversion in the lines leading up to it. Here, for example, is the third quatrain of Shakespeare's Sonnet 96:

How many lambs might the stern wolf betray
If like a lamb he could his looks translate!
How many gazers mightst thou lead away
If thou wouldst use the strength of all thy state!

The third and fourth lines are perfectly natural: "How many gazers mightst thou lead away if thou wouldst use the strength of all thy state!" It's the first and second lines that get contorted. Shakespeare wants to say: "How many lambs might be betrayed by the stern wolf if the wolf could translate his looks into those of the lamb!" But that won't do the trick.

Inversion can sometimes go very wrong indeed. In "Epithalamion," Edmund Spenser gets through three quarters of the following quatrain competently enough:

Ring ye the bells, ye young men of the town,
And leave your wonted labors for this day.
This day is holy. Do ye write it down,

Now, what he *wants* is: "That ye may remember it forever." Since this wouldn't satisfy any of the formal requirements, he produces one of the most wince-inducing lines in English verse:

That ye forever it remember may.[1]

There are few noteworthy poets nowadays who respect the old rules of poetic form. The consensus among such holdouts is that inversion is no longer acceptable. I agree. It's one of those few modern judgments that actually hold us to a higher aesthetic standard than whatever reigned before. Inversion is seen as sloppy, and, indeed, the modern ear (even the modern educated ear) revolts against old poetry that relies too much on it.

In his *Essay on Rime*, formalist poet Karl Shapiro defended inversion:

> Correctness dulls, precision often maims
> The poem; nor can the grammar rule the rime;
> It is the poem that sets the grammar right.[2]

I disagree. And I can disagree because I can easily understand what Shapiro is saying. And I can easily understand what Shapiro is saying because he doesn't use inversion.

---

1   261-264.
2   John Updike, ed. *Selected Poems*. The Library of America, 2003, p. 74.

FIFTY-TWO

A GAME OF CHICKEN

I N POETRY, cliché is sinful. And sin is inherently tempting. We like to flirt with sin; we like to see how close we can get to the edge, without tumbling in. It's like a game of chicken. For example, here's Robert Herrick's "Upon Julia's Voice:"

> So smooth, so sweet, so silvery is thy voice,
> As, could they hear, the damned would make no noise,
> But listen to thee, walking in thy chamber,
> Melting melodious words to lutes of amber.

The first line doesn't bode well. You can't get much more cliché than describing a pleasant voice as "smooth," "sweet," or "silvery." According to Google Books, the phrase "silvery voice" appears over 14,000 times in the nineteenth century alone.

We soon discover, however, that Herrick's apparent tailspin is actually a piece of daredevilry; he's created an opportunity to flaunt just how adeptly he can recover.

Let's talk the thing through, line by line:

Line 1: "So smooth, so sweet, so silvery is thy voice,"
    [*Again, pretty anodyne stuff.*]

Line 2: "As, could they hear,"
    [*Although we assume "they" must be her admirers, we*

learn it's]
"the damned"
   [*who*]
       "would make no noise."
[*Why are they silent? Wouldn't they be bewailing their
    isolation from this Beatrice-like muse?*]

Line 3: "But listen to thee,"
[*Ah; the spirits are silent because they're listening to Julia's
smooth, sweet, silvery voice. Although this would have been
sufficient, Herrick adds that Julia is*]

       "walking in her chamber."

[*The voice isn't public, then; it's the artless murmuring we
do when pacing alone where we feel safe—where we as-
sume that we cannot be overheard. It turns out, however,
that she has quite an audience—an audience captivated by
the sound of Julia, not speaking, and not even quite singing,
but*:]

Line 4: "Melting melodious words to lutes of amber."

[*A triumph, this. It makes no literal sense, of course: a lute
made of fossilized tree resin would sound awful. Herrick,
however, achieves a sort of poetical synesthesia. The lute
sounds just as amber would—if amber made its appeal not
to the eye but the ear. It reminds me of the Blandings Castle
novel where P.G. Wodehouse refers to a young lady with a
voice "like clotted cream, made audible." It recalls (more se-
riously) a one-line poem by Bill Knott: "Your nakedness: the
sound when I break an apple in half."[1]*]

The project of redeeming a cliché by a hair's breadth
sometimes amounts to little more than a slight recalibration of

---

1 "Poem" in *I Am Flying Into Myself: Selected Poems, 1960 – 2014*. Farrar,
Straus and Giroux, 2018, p. 71.

a stock phrase or image. Dylan Thomas wrote things like "once below a time." In "Laus Veneris," Algernon Charles Swinburne writes: "Their blood runs 'round the roots of time like rain."[2] The figurative nexus that equates blood with rain and bloodshed with agriculture is cliché. But here we have the surprise of "runs 'round." If it's the roots doing the work, we often think of them as "drinking;" if it's the blood doing the work, we often think of it as "soaking" the roots. The idea of blood running 'round the roots is just strange enough to make the line interesting. And among the artist's duties is to make the familiar strange; the strange, familiar.

Sometimes, you can redeem a cliché either by discovering what it's "pregnant" with or by following it to some unexpected conclusion. In "Before Dawn," Swinburne speaks of "Weaving the web Desire / To snare the bird Delight."[3] The figurative equation of desire with a snare is cliché. But Swinburne is curious enough to investigate where the cliché, if pursued, might lead to. His mental route seems to be something like this:

- A web catches things;
- Desire catches things;
- Desire is a web;
- Desire is a web that catches—what, exactly?
- Desire can't catch sexual partners; sexual partners aren't "caught," but seduced. Their consent is the whole point;
- How about Delight? You can delight in someone's charms even without seducing them;
- Delight is abstract, however;
- Ah, the "*bird* Delight!" Birds are delicate, they're full of life and color, they have flight, and they're hypervigilant. This avian anxiety is nearly counterbalanced by their confidence that they can fly away at any moment. Therefore, of all the animals to be caught in a web, the bird is most pathetic.

---

2   120.

3   47-48.

∽

Exercise Five

Make a list of clichés. For example, here are six specimens collected from "200 Common Clichés in Writing (and How to Avoid Them)," which appears on a website called Top Creative Writing Courses:

1. "…a clean slate;"
2. "…a loose cannon;"
3. "…a pain in the neck;"
4. "…bite the bullet;"
5. "…kid in a candy store;"
6. "…salt of the earth."

Explore each cliché, and discover where it "leads."

"…**a clean slate**" // You cannot clean a slate without water, and it's impossible to write on a slate while it's still wet. Since slate is porous, it's slow to dry, and may became stained.

"…**a loose cannon**" // The parts of a cannon that can be loose are:
1. The hinge connecting the barrel to the gun carriage;
2. The rigging that anchors the entire assembly to the embrasure or the gun port.

Since a cannon is inanimate, its looseness is the result of an individual person's incompetence. My neighbor gets furious that my dogs crap in his flowerbed; if I call him a "loose cannon," who (within the logic of the metaphor) am I alleging has failed to fasten him?

"…**a pain in the neck**" // Most neck pains are medically trivial and aren't amenable to any particular "cure;" you're told to take ibuprofen as needed and to get on with your life. Your wife calls you a "pain in the neck." Within the logic of the metaphor, she's stuck with you, as one might be stuck with neck pain. What's the metaphorical equivalent of ibuprofen? Also, the frustrating knowledge that your neck pain isn't such a big deal comes from the doctor—frustrating, because it certainly feels like a big deal indeed. Who delivers the analogous information to your wife? Who might a woman consult for marital advice who'd tell her "such is life," and then suggest that she'd be less miserable if she wasn't such a kvetch about it?

"…**bite the bullet**" // Do that enough, and you'll get lead poisoning. Follow the cliché, and arrive at the idea that someone who's too stoic (someone who regularly "bites the bullet") risks a good deal. Here's what the Mayo Clinic says about lead poisoning:

> Initially, lead poisoning can be hard to detect—even people who seem healthy can have high blood levels of lead. Signs and symptoms usually don't appear until dangerous amounts have accumulated.[4]

The figurative implications are fascinating.

> Lead poisoning symptoms in adults: High blood pressure, joint and muscle pain, difficulties with memory or concentration, headache, abdominal pain, mood disorders, reduced sperm count and abnormal sperm, miscarriage, stillbirth or premature birth in pregnant women.[5]

"…**kid in a candy store**" // Most kids in candy stores aren't giddy; they're frantic.

How did the kid end up there? Did he go alone? Did an adult take him? If the former, why is the kid unattended? If

---

4 "Lead Poisoning: Symptoms and Causes," Mayo Clinic, https://www.mayoclinic.org/diseases-conditions/lead-poisoning/symptoms-causes/syc-20354717.

5 Ibid.

the latter, what would ever possess a parent to take a child to a candy store? The kid becomes a monster when he wants candy; sugar doing what it does, he becomes a bigger monster after consuming it.

Candy is an archetypal food. When you're a kid, you're told never to take candy from strangers—"candy" being a synecdoche: a specific thing that serves as shorthand for an entire category of things.

What if it's the pederast who's taken the kid to the candy store?

"...**salt of the earth**" // The rich eat the poor, and the poor (if they're like salt) cause high blood pressure.

FIFTY-THREE

FEELING AND TECHNIQUE

G OOD POEMS make you feel something. Feeling is your point of entry into the poem. But your voyage can't end with feeling. Everything that a poem makes you feel is the result of certain technical decisions made by the poet. The serious study of poetry is largely about tracing the connections between your feelings and the poet's technical strategies.

In this sense, real poetry has much in common with serious music. In *A Singer's Notebook*, English tenor Ian Bostridge sketches a fascinating paradox:

> Music undoubtedly arouses emotion, but whether either the composer or the performer have to be in that emotional state to convey or incite it is doubtful. As a performer you can find yourself thinking about the oddest things, fleetingly, while delivering high emotion with a great deal of focus. That, I suppose, is what we mean by technique[.] [...] At the apogee of nineteenth-century Romanticism, tears became part of the performing and audience experience, but for singers they cannot but be problematic, tending as they do to interrupt breathing and phonation—in some senses a measure of how mannered a seemingly natural process must, in performance, be.[1]

In other words, to provoke emotion in his audience, the

---

1 Faber and Faber, 2011, pp. 81-82.

singer cannot permit himself to become emotional, since his emotion interferes with the mechanics by means of which he provokes emotion in his audience. If the singer becomes emotional, it isn't experienced by the audience as betokening profound sincerity; it's simply experienced as bad singing.

If you want simply to enjoy poetry or music, there's no need to spend much effort examining the mechanism behind the feelings they stimulate. There's no shame in this. Real art is made for real people, and our shortage of real art is nearly as tragic as our shortage of real people.

If you want to *create* poetry or music, however, you need to trace each feeling to the ruthlessly specific, often dryly technical decision the artist is making.

To illustrate, let's look at stanza 24 of John Keats's "The Eve of Saint Agnes." Porphyro, the young man in love with the beautiful Madeline, is hiding inside her bedroom closet. While this conduct would be more than enough to get Porphyro fired from his tenure-track teaching gig, we are led to assume that, in the universe of the poem, it amounts to little more than an intrepid lover's tenacity in service of Aphrodite.

The bedroom upon which he spies is described thusly:

> A casement high and triple-arched there was,
> All garlanded with carven imageries
> Of fruits, and flowers, and bunches of knotgrass,
> And diamonded with panes of quaint device,
> Innumerable of stains and splendid dyes,   5.
> As are the tiger-moth's deep-damasked wings;
> And in the midst, 'mong thousand heraldries,
> And twilight saints, and dim emblazonings,
> A shielded scutcheon blushed with blood of queens and
>   kings.

My students generally come away from these lines with a vague unease. The stanza seems somewhat, well…it seems somewhat *sexy*, even though Keats is describing interior design. Everything feels somehow eroticized.

Just as the singer can't be anguished and perform in such a way that communicates anguish, I can't imagine that Keats is sitting at his desk in a seizure of lustful suspense. Those experiencing seizures of lustful suspense are generally not at their most eloquent. No; Keats is *crafting* something.[2]

Let's explore Keats's stanza, and uncover some of the technical decisions producing his effect.

Line 2: "All garlanded with carven imageries"

garland] In addition to the expected definition ("A wreath made of flowers, leaves, etc., worn on the head like a crown, or hung about an object for decoration"), the *OED* offers:

1. "A wreath, chaplet, or coronet of some costly material, esp. of gold or silver work;"
2. "A wreath, crown, etc. worn as a mark of distinction;"
3. "The priest's fillet or band of wool worn in token of consecration to the service of a god;"
4. "The wreath or crown conferred upon the victor in the Greek and Roman games, or upon the hero of any great exploit;"
5. "[A floral wreath] as worn by a 'May Queen,' or by girls as the prize of some kind of competition."

"Garland," therefore, suggests opulence, distinction, triumph, female beauty, and devotion to God. This final definition is especially interesting, since, in stanza 25, Keats eroticizes prayer itself.

> Full on this casement shone the wintry moon,
> And threw warm gules[3] on Madeline's fair breast

---

2   There's no shortage of writers like Miss Scrawen in Hector Hugh Munro's "Tobermory," "…who wrote fiercely sensuous poetry and led a blameless life[.]" It's the use of "and" instead of "but" that tells you all you need to know. Indeed, it's likely that the two nineteenth-century writers we most associate with sexual license, Swinburne and Whitman, actually led rather chaste lives.

3   gules] The color red, as used in heraldry. See notes for stanza 24, line 7.

> As down she knelt for heaven's grace and boon.
> Rose-bloom fell on her hands, together pressed,
> And on her silver cross soft amethyst,   5.
> And on her hair a glory, like a saint.
> She seemed a splendid angel, newly dressed,
> Save wings, for heaven. Porphyro grew faint.
> She knelt, so pure a thing, so free from mortal taint.

The line between eroticism and religious fervor is a porous one.

Also, the stressed syllable in "garland" rhymes with its counterpart in "carven," which appears soon after. This is called "assonance" and contributes to the line's musical coherence.

carven imageries]   There's a provocative tension between a garland and "carven imageries:" the former suggests softness; the latter, hardness. This contrast recalls an idea from food science called "dynamic contrast," best summarized by Robert J. Hyde and Steven A. Witherly: "[T]he most highly palatable foods are likely to have higher levels of 'dynamic contrast' (moment-to-moment sensory contrast from the everchanging properties of foods manipulated in the mouth)."[4]

There's profound sensual appeal in anything exhibiting "dynamic contrast." The rhetoric of Petrarch's sonnets suggests these tensions. Here's Sir Thomas Wyatt's translation of No. 134:

> I find no peace, and all my war is done.
> I fear and hope. I burn, and freeze like ice.
> I fly above the wind, yet can I not arise.
> And naught I have, and all the world I seize on.
> That looseth nor locketh holdeth me in prison,   5.
> And holdeth me not (yet can I 'scape nowise),
> Nor letteth me live nor die at my device,
> And yet of death it giveth none occasion.

---

4 "Dynamic Contrast: A Sensory Contribution to Palatability." *Appetite*, Volume 21, Issue 1, 1993, pp. 1-16.

Withouten eyen, I see; and without tongue, I plain.[5]
I desire to perish, and yet I ask health.   10.
I love another, and thus I hate myself.
I feed me in sorrow, and laugh in all my pain.
Likewise displeaseth me both death and life,
And my delight is causer of this strife.

This is rhetorical "dynamic contrast:" the narrator has nei-
ther war nor peace; he hopes and fears, burns and freezes; he's
both airborne and earthbound, free and captive; even though
he has no tongue,[6] he complains; he wants to live and to die.

Much of eroticism's drama comes from "dynamic con-
trast"—hence, the frisson caused by the juxtaposition of "gar-
land" and "carven imageries."

Line 3: "Of fruits, and flowers, and bunches of knotgrass"

fruits] Fruit is sexy. In our literary tradition, going all the
way back to the Song of Songs, bodies (especially female bod-
ies) are compared to fruit. Different parts of the female anatomy
are described as "ripe," which means "ready to be harvested"
("ripe" and "reap" being related). It's been used in English as a
metaphor for sexual maturity since the 1300s.

Fruit is sweet, and, figuratively, so is sex. Indeed, "fruit"
comes from a Latin root for "to enjoy." Considering that we
use words like "fleshly" in connection with sex, it's telling that,
while we often hear of a fruit having flesh, not even meat (which
is *actual* flesh) is always described in those terms. And if sex is
brought to its conclusion, the result (a child) may be referred to
as "fruit"—as in "the fruit of the womb."

Among the consequences Adam and Eve suffer for eat-
ing the Forbidden Fruit is that they discover their own naked-
ness—a discovery inaugurating the phenomenon of "sexuality."
Indeed, in Christina Rossetti's *Goblin Market*, fruits symbolize
sexual indulgence so blatantly that they nearly stop symbolizing

5 plain] Complain.

6 tongue] A metonym for language or the human voice.

sexuality and rather *become* sexuality:

> She cried, "Laura," up the garden,
> "Did you miss me?
> Come and kiss me.
> Never mind my bruises.
> Hug me, kiss me, suck my juices   5.
> Squeezed from goblin fruits for you—
> Goblin pulp and goblin dew.
> Eat me, drink me, love me.
> Laura, make much of me.
> For your sake I have braved the glen   10.
> And had to do with goblin merchant men."[7]

flowers] The transition from bud to flower has long been used to describe female maturation. "Flower" once referred to virginity; to lose one's virginity was to be "deflowered." Between the 1400s and the 1700s, it was a metaphor for menstrual discharge. And Georgia O'Keeffe was neither the first nor the last to recognize that the vulva can look floral.

knotgrass] This plant appears in Shakespeare's *A Midsummer Night's Dream*:

> Get you gone, you dwarf,
> You minimus of hindering knotgrass,
> You bead, you acorn.[8]

Sidney Beisly's *The Plants and Flowers Named in Shakespeare's Works* offers a useful gloss:

> [It is a] very common plant, growing in uncultivated grounds, neglected fields, and by roadsides, having minute, pale flesh-colored flowers. A single plant often covers a considerable space of ground, and its presence indicates

---

7 464-474.

8 3.2.328-330.

bad husbandry.[9] The allusion [made in Shakespeare] is to the character of the plant as hindering the growth of useful plants, as it spreads in thick masses, and is very tough and deep-rooted. Evelyn calls it the very worst of garden weeds[.] […] Mr. Steevens, in a note on this passage, says, "it appears that knotgrass was anciently supposed to prevent the growth of any animal or child[.][10]

Knotgrass makes an appearance in *The Coxcomb*, by Beaumont and Fletcher (that playwriting power duo of the early 1600s), and in *The Night of the Burning Pestel* by Francis Beaumont alone.

A particularly rousing tribute to knotgrass appears in *The Juvenile Instructor and Companion*:

> What can be more common than the little humble knotgrass? And yet how little is it regarded by most people! […] The pinkish-white flowers are seated closely on the stem, and may be seen from May to September. They are redder and brighter, however, during the height of the summer season. The knotgrass is a useful little plant, for thousands of birds are nourished by its seeds and young shoots, and there is a caterpillar peculiarly attached to it which produces a very handsome moth. It is said that the plant forms a pasture which is very agreeable to the animals feeding on it. The knotgrass, however, has no affinity to the true grasses. There are nine British species of the family to which this flower belongs.[11]

And we'd be negligent if we didn't consult that august volume bearing the title *Culpeper's Complete Herbal, To Which Is Now Added Upwards Of One Hundred Additional Herbs, With A Display Of Their Medicinal And Occult Qualities, Physically Applied To The Cure Of All Disorders Incident To Mankind*. Since this is rather a mouthful, we'll refer to the volume by the concise abbreviation: *CCHTWINAUOOHAHWADOTMAOQPAT-*

---

9   husbandry] Cultivation.

10   Longman, 1864, pp. 52-23.

11   Vol. XX. – Vol. VIII., New Series, William Cooke, 1869, p. 292.

TCOADITM. We learn that knotgrass "grows in every county of this land by the highway sides, and by foot-paths in fields; as also by the sides of old walls." Furthermore:

> Saturn seems to me to own the herb, and yet some hold the Sun; out of doubt 'tis Saturn. The juice of the common kind of knotgrass is most effectual to stay bleeding of the mouth, being drank in steeled[12] or red wine; and the bleeding at the nose, to be applied to the forehead or temples, or to be squirted up into the nostrils. It is no less effectual to cool and temper the heat of the blood and stomach, and to stay any flux of the blood[13] and humors, as lasks,[14] bloody-flux,[15] women's courses,[16] and running of the reins.[17] It is singularly good to provoke urine, help the stranguary,[18] and allays the heat that comes thereby; and is powerful by urine to expel the gravel or stone in the kidneys and bladder, a dram of the powder of the herb being taken in wine for many days together. Being boiled in wine and drank, it is profitable to those that are stung or bitten by venomous creatures, and very effectual to stay all defluxions[19] of rheumatic humors upon the stomach and kills worms in the belly or stomach, quiets inward pains that arise from the heat, sharpness and corruption of blood and choler.[20] The distilled water hereof taken by itself or with the powder of the herb or seed, is very effectual to all the purposes aforesaid, and is accounted one of the most sovereign remedies to cool all manner of inflammations, breaking out through heat, hot swellings

---

12   steeled wine] Wine that, for vague medicinal reasons, has been mixed with steel filings.

13   flux of the blood] Hemorrhaging.

14   lasks] Diarrhea.

15   bloody-flux] I don't know how bloody-flux differs from "flux of the blood."

16   women's courses] Menstruation.

17   running of the reins] White genital discharge.

18   stranguary] A disease of the urinary organs.

19   defluxions] In the humoral theory of disease, the flow of elemental fluids from one body part to another.

20   choler] Bile.

and imposthumes,[21] gangrene and fistulous cankers,[22] or foul filthy ulcers, being applied or put into them; but especially for all sorts of ulcers and sores happening in the privy parts of men and women. It helps all fresh and green wounds, and speedily heals them. The juice dropped into the ears, cleanses them being foul, and having running matter in them.[23]

Back to line 3 as a whole ("Of fruits, and flowers, and bunches of knotgrass"), what nimbus of meaning radiates from this final noun? Even after all of these extended quotations, I'm not entirely sure. As a medicine, knotgrass was indicated for many ills involving the patient's nether-parts. Simply mentioning it might have been like mentioning a vaginal PH test in mixed company: it reminds the men in the room that the women have vaginas, and it reminds the women that the men are thinking about vaginas.

This interpretation seems implausible, since Keats is evoking a sense of purity, and there's nothing that negates any sense of purity quite like a vaginal discharge.

However, there's a teasing ambiguity about knotgrass which might have some indirect bearing on the erotic: although it's beautiful, it suggests neglect. Unwary wanderers get lost and detained in it. Knotgrass prevents things from developing and keeps them vulnerable.

Perhaps we ought not to focus on "knotgrass" but on the phrase "bunches of knotgrass." "Bunches" suggests decadence. To grab one M&M isn't decadent. Nor is it decadent to grab precisely 35 M&M'S. To grab a "bunch" of M&M'S, however, suggests not only amplitude, but the kind of hedonism we associate with Roman aristocrats. To grab a "bunch" of anything implies that record-keeping is beneath you; it implies power, and the exercise of power has always played an outsized role in seduction.

---

21 imposthumes] Abscesses.
22 fistulous cankers] Ulcerated sores.
23 Richard Evans, 1816, pp. 102-103.

There's also the "dynamic contrast" between (on the one hand) fruit and flowers, which are soft, sweet, and vulnerable, and (on the other hand) knotgrass, which tends to be rough. And "bunches of knotgrass" tend to be yet rougher still.

Line 4: "And diamonded with panes of quaint device"

diamonded]   Although Keats wasn't the first to use "diamond" as a verb, and although it isn't erotic per say, it is very beautiful.

panes]   "Pane" and "pain" are homonyms, the latter playing various roles in descriptions of romantic love.

quaint]   This word can be used as an adjective describing a bed and breakfast on Martha's Vineyard, or, as a noun, it can be used as a variant of "cunt." In its vulvular sense, "quaint" seems to have begun its life as a euphemistic understudy for "cunt," and then evolved into a direct reference to the external female genitalia. In a similar way, "retarded" began as a polite label for the feebleminded, and then evolved into an actual synonym for "feebleminded."

Although the naughty definition of "quaint" seems to have fallen away by the sixteenth century, the word remained steeped in the vapors of its old use.

Line 5: "Innumerable of stains and splendid dyes"

stains…dyes]   Whereas paint or lacquer are used to cover a surface, stains and dyes penetrate it, fuse with it, and make it into something new. This comes close to recalling the Biblical image of marital union: "and they shall become one flesh."

Line 6: "As are the tiger-moth's deep-damasked wings"

tiger-moth's]   According to the *Encyclopedia Britannica*, "tiger moth" isn't a taxonomically precise designation, since it applies to 11,000 different species of moth, encompassing a broad range of color palettes and design configurations. The evocative punch comes from "tiger," which is associated with feminine grace (the adjective "feline" is sometimes applied to the female body or temperament), exoticness, and mysterious menace.

deep-damasked] "Damask" is short for "Damascus;" as a verb, according to the *OED*, it means "to weave with richly-figured designs" and apparently derives from its use as a noun referring to luxury textiles from Damascus. Indeed, "damask" is used to modify a range of sensuous, exotic commodities: plums, blades, the patterns characteristic of such blades, violets, roses, rose-water, rose-scented toilet powder, and rose color as seen on a woman's face.

Line 7: "And twilight saints, and dim emblazonings"

saints] As we've already seen, Keats eroticizes religious devotion.

emblazoning] In past ages, if you were a nobleman, and wanted, say, a chair built that bore your coat of arms, you couldn't text the craftsman a JPG. But you needed your coat of arms to be rendered perfectly, since matters of heraldry were important. What evolved, therefore, was a highly codified, regularized formula for describing the elements comprising coats of arms. This system of description produces what is called a "blazon."

For instance, the official definition of "bend" is:

A diagonal piece from top right to bottom left. A bend which runs in the opposite diagonal direction is known in English Heraldry as a "bend sinister."[24]

---

24 Kandel, Edward M. "The Language of Blazon." *Coat of Arms*. No. 146. Summer 1989. Accessed on the Heraldry Society website.

And here's "embattled:"

> A line of partition crenellated as are the embrasures of a battlement. A piece in bend, bend sinister or horizontal usually has only its top edge embattled but if it is embattled also on its lower edge it is "embattled counter embattled."[25]

Elizabethan sonneteers adapted the idea of the blazon to their own rhetorical uses. Just as a heraldic blazon is a careful itemization of the components of a coat of arms, a poetic blazon is a careful itemization of a woman's features.

"Blazon," therefore, blends ideas of physical beauty, distinction, and antiquity.

Line 8: "A shielded scutcheon blushed with blood of queens and kings"

blushed] To "blush" is to have one's face redden out of modesty or shame, two qualities that play mysterious roles in the economy of the erotic. While modesty and shame would seem to be great enemies of the erotic, they can be among the most erotically provocative qualities. In recent years, we've attempted to demolish sexuality and to rebuild it on the rational basis of affirmative consent, transparency, and hygiene. Human nature, however, seems to have other ideas.[26]

In "That Our Desire is Increased by Difficulty," Michel de Montaigne writes:

> What is the use of that art of virginal shame, that sedate coldness, that severe countenance, that profession of ignorance of things that they know better than we who instruct them in them, but to increase in us the desire to conquer, to overwhelm and subdue to our appetite all this ceremony and these obstacles? For there is not only plea-

---

25 Ibid.

26 These issues are developed beautifully in Allan Bloom's *Love and Friendship,* Simon & Schuster, 1993.

sure but also glory in driving wild and seducing that soft sweetness and that childlike modesty, and in reducing a proud and commanding gravity to the mercy of our ardor. [...] Beauty, all-powerful as it is, has not the wherewithal to make itself relished without that interposition.[27]

Excellence in poetry is the result of a dialectical tension between the constraints of form (on the one hand) and our appetite for freedom (on the other). Likewise, eroticism might be the result of a dialectical tension between "ceremony" and "obstacles" (on the one hand) and the brutality of lust (on the other).

The brutality of lust is wittily (if bluntly) invoked by Kingsley Amis in *One Fat Englishman*:

A man's sexual aim [...] is to convert a creature who is cool, dry, calm, articulate, independent, purposeful into a creature that is the opposite of these; to demonstrate to an animal which is pretending not to be an animal that it is an animal.[28]

Feminism argues that rape isn't about sex, but rather about power. But, if literary sources can be trusted, it seems that, often, sex isn't even about sex. Here's an example from *Carmina Burana* of how erotically inviting innocence and vulnerability can be:

But the young girl,
Trembling like a trembling leaf,
Like a beginning pupil,
Who has not yet flinched at the cane,
Trembled at my flattering words.[29]   5.

---

27 Donald M. Frame, trans. *The Complete Works*. Everyman's Library, 2003. pp. 565-566.

28 Harcourt, Brace & World, Inc., 1963, p. 122.

29 David A. Traill, trans., Harvard University Press, 2018, p. 83.

In this connection, see Robert Burns's "My Love, She's But a Lassie Yet:"

> My love she's but a lassie yet,
> My love she's but a lassie yet.
> We'll let her stand a year or twa;
> She'll no be half sae saucy yet.[30]

Keats's poem directly eroticizes Madeline's innocence. The very "rules" for St. Agnes' Eve suggest a child's game of make-believe:

> They told her how, upon St. Agnes' Eve,
> Young virgins might have visions of delight,
> And soft adorings from their loves receive
> Upon the honeyed middle of the night,
> If ceremonies due they did aright;   5.
> As, supperless to bed they must retire,
> And couch supine their beauties, lily white;
> Nor look behind, nor sideways, but require
> Of Heaven with upward eyes for all that they
>   desire.[31]

When Madeline dances, she does so with "vague, regard-less eyes"[32]—in other words, eyes characterized by a childlike guilelessness and lack of self-consciousness. Porphyro relishes the possibility of seeing Madeline in a state of drowsy vulnerability:

> Which was, to lead him, in close secrecy,
> Even to Madeline's chamber, and there hide
> Him in a closet, of such privacy
> That he might see her beauty unespied,
> And win perhaps that night a peerless bride,   5.

---

30 Stanza 2.

31 46-54.

32 64.

While legion'd faeries paced the coverlet,
And pale enchantment held her sleepy-eyed.[33]

Not that I place much stock in the social sciences, but a 2012 University of Texas study might be useful here. As reported by *Slate*:

> A [...] group of 76 male participants was presented with [images of women] in a randomized sequence and asked what they thought of each woman's overall attractiveness, how easy it would be to "exploit" her using a variety of tactics (everything from seduction to physical force), and her appeal to them as either a short-term or a long-term partner. The results were mixed. Physical cues of vulnerability—the pictures of, say, short women and hefty ones—had no effect. These women were not necessarily seen as easy lays, nor were they judged as especially appealing partners for either a casual fling or a lifelong marriage. On the other hand, the more psychological and contextual cues—pictures of dimwitted- or immature-seeming women, for example, or of women who looked sleepy or intoxicated, did seem to have an effect: Not surprisingly, men rated them as being easy to bed. But more importantly, they were also perceived as being more physically attractive than female peers who seemed more lucid or quick-witted. This perceived attractiveness effect flipped completely when the participants were asked to judge these women as potential long-term partners. In other words, the woozy ladies were seen as sexy and desirable—but only for fleeting venereal meetings.[34]

The sexiest part of any Keats poem, however, is something it's nearly impossible to describe: the music of it. Some lines are like sips of good wine. We read aloud, and revel in the sensuous pleasure produced by the perfect pacing, the liquid modulations, the supple admixture of assonance and alliteration,

---

33   163-169.

34   Jesse Bering, "Do Men Find Dumb-Looking Women More Attractive?," *Slate*, May 23. 2012.

the luxuriant variousness of it all. Keats's music points to those promised lands beyond the frontiers of craft. Any competent poet can write a line of iambic pentameter. But only a master can manage something like this.

FIFTY-FOUR

DOGS, JEWS, AND FLAMES

I N *Decline and Fall of the Roman Empire*, Edward Gibbon sketches the final moments of Roman politician Cola de Rienzi:

> He fell senseless with the first stroke; the impotent revenge of his enemies inflicted a thousand wounds; and the senator's body was abandoned to the dogs, to the Jews, and to the flames.[1]

Notice the wording. "Enemies" are given agency: they "inflict." But then, the body is simply "abandoned" to forces apparently roiling on the periphery, each accorded a stately definite article. The pairing of "Jews" and "dogs" is cliché (Islamist literature, for instance, is never short on references to "Jewish dogs"), but to associate "Jews" and "flames" is poetically marvelous— though otherwise appalling, of course. Dogs are pathetic and opportunistic; flames, unapologetic and avenging. Also striking is the implication that the flames were waiting the whole while, getting themselves worked up for the anticipated barbeque.

Dogs and flames have a defining action in common: they both consume. It's "Jews" that doesn't belong. In the rhetoric of drama or humor, the surprise goes last: "The impotent revenge of his enemies inflicted a thousand wounds; and the senator's body was abandoned to the dogs, to the flames, and to the Jews."

---

1   Vol. XIII, Ch. LXX., John Murray, 1887, p. 248.

We're accustomed to the surprise appearing at the end, sometimes with variations. "The four most overrated things in the world," declared Christopher Hitchens, "are champagne, lobster, anal sex, and picnics."[2] Champagne and lobster are archetypal luxuries. People pursue luxuries, and, to the extent that most people are wrong, these luxuries are bound to be overrated. Hitchens's line would have been brilliant enough if he went with "champagne, lobster, and anal sex."

But "picnics" clinches it. And it does so for two reasons:

Firstly, it's a withering anticlimax, and an example of the literary device called "bathos," to be addressed comprehensively in Chapter Fifty-eight. We jump from "anal sex" which is shocking, and (still) slightly taboo, to the most innocent activity imaginable: "picnics."

Both "anal sex" and "picnics" are extremely evocative. That "anal sex" is evocative requires no explanation. "Picnics" conjures up the tasks, pleasures, and ambivalences associated with them:

1. The decision to have the picnic (usually made by the mother),
2. The preparation and packing of food,
3. The anxious checking of the weather,
4. The hassle of the entire thing, which gets blurred or effaced by our commitment to the purely abstract idea that picnics are "fun,"
5. The bees, the ants, the plug of chocolate ice cream that tumbles down the child's shirt, and the absence of any means to clean it up, and
6. The occasional moments of gaiety.

And secondly, there's the absurd, whimsical music of the word "picnic:" the trochaic quaintness of those two rhyming syllables. "Picnic" makes a terrific punchline. In *Pnin*, Vladimir Nabokov has his protagonist scanning the advertisements in a Russian émigré newspaper. He discovers "[a] somewhat Gogo-

---

2 Quoted by Ian Parker in "He Knew He Was Right: How a Former Socialist Became the Iraq War's Fiercest Defender." *The New Yorker*, October 8, 2006.

lian mortician" proud of his deluxe hearses, "which were also available for picnics."[3]

And, as if we didn't have enough reasons to praise Hitchens's line, here's another: the use of the Oxford comma after "sex." It heightens the drama, mandating a slight pause before the quasi-punchline. You're meant to teeter slightly on the edge of the canyon before being made to tumble into it.

It's thrilling to see a convention used well. It can be equally thrilling to see a convention violated intelligently. And this is what Gibbon does with "…to the dogs, to the Jews, and to the flames."

❧

Exercise Six

Pick a verb; "exhaust," for example. Find two nouns or noun-based phrases referring to phenomena that exhaust you: say, "marathons" and "unrequited love."

Now, go to www.randomwordgenerator.com, and look for good, juicy nouns referring to things that we don't typically think of as exhausting us: "error," "warnings," "childhood," "meaning," "science."

Experiment with each "surprising" noun, sandwiching it between the two "standard" nouns, in the following manner:

- "…as exhausting as marathons, error, or unrequited love."
- "…as exhausting as marathons, warnings, or unrequited love."
- "…as exhausting as marathons, childhood, or unrequited love."
- "…as exhausting as marathons, meaning, or unrequited love."
- "…as exhausting as marathons, science, or unrequited love."

---

3 Everyman's Library, 1957, p. 57.

FIFTY-FIVE

PARADOX

E ARLIER, I QUOTED Robert Herrick's "Delight in Disor-
der" in full. Here it is, again:

A sweet disorder in the dress
Kindles in clothes a wantonness:
A lawn[1] about the shoulders thrown
Into a fine distraction;
An erring lace, which here and there   5.
Enthralls the crimson stomacher;[2]
A cuff neglectful, and thereby
Ribands to flow confusedly;
A winning wave, deserving note,
In the tempestuous petticoat;   10.
A careless shoestring, in whose tie
I see a wild civility...
Do more bewitch me, than when Art
Is too precise in every part.

The *OED* offers five definitions of "paradox:"
1. "A statement or tenet contrary to received opinion or
belief, especially one that is difficult to believe."
2. "A figure of speech consisting of a conclusion or apodo-

---

1 lawn] Shawl.
2 stomacher] A garment bound over a woman's bodice.

sis[3] contrary to what the audience has been led to expect."
3. "An apparently absurd or self-contradictory statement or proposition, or a strongly counter-intuitive one, which investigation, analysis, or explanation may nevertheless prove to be well-founded or true."
4. "A proposition or statement that is (taken to be) actually self-contradictory, absurd, or intrinsically unreasonable."
5. "An argument, based on (apparently) acceptable premises and using (apparently) valid reasoning, which leads to a conclusion that is against sense, logically unacceptable, or self-contradictory; the conclusion of such an argument."

However, I shall propose a sixth sense of "paradox:"

6. A phrase which, for poetic effect, combines mutually exclusive words.

Line 12 of "Delight in Disorder" offers a good example: "wild civility." What could it possibly mean? Wildness isn't civil; civility isn't wild. There's no way that these words can be stretched into congruence.

However, "wild civility" makes a kind of sense. This sense cannot be paraphrased. It exists in the tension between the words themselves.

This type of paradox has long fascinated me. For years, I've been bewitched by a line from *The Renaissance* by Walter Pater, who was not only the patriarch of what would become the "Aesthetic movement" but one of the most interesting links between Gerard Manley Hopkins and Oscar Wilde, both of whom came beneath his influence during their Oxford years. The line comes from the chapter on Michelangelo's poetry:

> But his professed disciples did not share this temper; they are in love with his strength only, and seem not to feel his

---

3 apodosis] "The main clause of a conditional sentence" (*Merriam-Webster*).

grave and temperate sweetness.[4]

"[G]rave and temperate sweetness:" I've tried my best to trace this phrase's lineage. It seems to have been inspired by Edward Gibbon, who described his own "grave and temperate irony" (both in *Decline and Fall of the Roman Empire* and in his *Memoirs*) as a quality acquired by reading Pascal.

This, in turn, seems to reference the King James translation of Titus 2:2: "That the aged men be sober, grave, temperate, sound in faith, in charity, in patience."

While gravity and irony seem ill-pared, gravity and sweetness downright repel each other. When they're coerced into proximity, however, the words produce an elusive kind of sense—which is also nonsense.

It recalled other phrases I'd encountered over my reading life; phrases from Samuel Johnson ("greatness with ease, and gay severity"), from John Milton ("Truth, wisdom, sanctitude severe and pure"), from elsewhere in Edward Gibbon's *Decline and Fall of the Roman Empire* ("original and intrepid fanaticism"), from Michel de Montaigne, ("severe gentleness"), and from Pope Gregory, as quoted by the Venerable Bede, ("It is needful that you rejoice with fear and fear with joy.").

And it wasn't just in bygone eras when this linguistic tic appeared. Here's the final line of "The Geese" by the shamefully

---

4   Macmillan and Co., 1919, p. 91.

overlooked Hyam Plutzik:[5] "Value[6] the intermediate splendor of birds."[7]

The "intermediate splendor" is like "wild civility:" simultaneously vivid and illegible. "Splendor" cannot be "intermediate."

It soon became my good fortune, however, to discover James G. Williams's *Those Who Ponder Proverbs: Aphoristic Thinking and Biblical Literature*. In it, he writes:

> It is necessary at the outset to distinguish between literary paradox and the literary indication of paradox. By the former is meant the use of words and images in such a way that the conclusion or meaning comes as unexpected to those holding the prevailing opinions that the paradox presupposes. The literary indication of paradox is a reference to a paradox, in reality or in a fictional world. It may be artfully done, but the meaning of the language is not changed or negated.[8]

A "literary paradox" pushes against the very limits of lexical meaning, pointing to a mysterious, somehow remote, realm of truth. That's precisely what Herrick accomplishes with "wild

---

5 Even during Plutzik's brief professional life (he died in 1962, aged 51), he was subjected to preposterous nastiness. According to Tom Clark's *Charles Olson: The Allegory of a Poet's Life*:

> At the Wesleyan Spring Poetry Festival in the last week of April 1960 [Charles Olson] appeared on a two-man program with Hyam Plutzik, an academic poet published by Wesleyan University Press. Robert Duncan, also on the festival bill, and Norman O. Brown, Wesleyan's resident pop psychologist, led a demonstration of allegiance by a small but committed "pro-Olson claque"[.] […] As Plutzik's opening reading wore on, a subdued but audible rumble of impatience from the claque gradually turned into "sounds of muffled mockery" (North Atlantic Books, 2000, p. 289).

Duncan's behavior is disappointing; Olson's is despicable—but not surprising. He was apparently as graceless socially as he was poetically.

6 value] This is in the imperative mood.

7 *Apples From Shinar*. Wesleyan University Press, 1950, p. 15.

8 The Almond Press, 1981, p. 43.

civility."

↶

Exercise Seven

Divide a blank sheet of paper into three columns. Watch a movie or television show, and record those words that you find interesting. Adjectives go in the left-hand column; nouns, in the center; verbs, on the right.

These words were harvested from a 10-minute *Vice* documentary entitled "We Followed an Inmate to the Execution Chamber:"

Adjectives	Nouns	Verbs
addicted, black	angel, appetite	arrest, beat, begin
concerned, concrete	area, arm	botch, bother
eldest, fried, hard	banquet, belonging	change, come
incarcerated	bone, box, brother	commit, die
last, left, lethal	call, cell, crime	drink, drive
lifeless, material	chicken, city, clerk	eat, empty, faint
ordinary, other	coffee, confort	give, hurt, imagine
personal, real	company, cookie	include, inform
solid, sterile	conversation, court	kill, part, pray
strapped, strong	curtain, day	prepare, recycle
tearful, tired	document, empathy	relive, rely
early, unbelievable	energy, execution	remember, request
unloved, young	face, food, galaxy	return, rob
	girlfriend, gurney	sadden, say
	hand, home	schedule, set
	homocide, hotel	shoot, stage, start
	inmate, kingdom	suffer, table, take
	knife, life, love	tell, think
	mercy, money	transport
	mother, name, pain	
	patriarch, point	
	process, prophet	

	room, saint, shadow shoe, sibling, side snacks, son, street theater, T.V. unconsciousness universe, van, visitor week, window witness, word, year	

And now, throw the words into interesting combinations. Organize them into two columns: the lefthand column for Adjective-Noun phrases; the right, for Noun-Verb phrases.

Adjective-Noun	Noun-Verb
black banquet concrete document concrete mercy, hard sympathy incarcerated appetite lethal banquet, lethal mercy personal banquet, sterile money tearful banquet, tired banquet tired mercy unbelievable window young empathy	appetites botch bones stage courts eat documents imagine empathy remembers love includes patriarchs stage saints remember witnesses return

Some of these are particularly promising paradoxes:[9]
"Concrete mercy;" "Hard sympathy;" "Lethal mercy;" "Personal banquet;" "Unbelievable window."

---

9 The real winner, however, isn't a paradox at all, but "bones stage."

FIFTY-SIX

SPECIFICITY

"I mentioned that I was afraid I put into my journal too many little instances. JOHNSON: 'There is nothing, Sir, too little for so little a creature as man. It is by studying little things that we attain the great art of having as little misery and as much happiness as possible.'"
—James Boswell, *The Life of Samuel Johnson*

"Just to see [Plutarch] pick a trivial action in a man's life, or a word which seems unimportant: that is a treatise in itself."
—Michel de Montaigne [1]

"Goodbye to you also, dear friend, for the time being. Write me when the mood is on. Nothing is minutiæ to me which you write or think."
—Albert Jay Nock, "Study in Brussels"[2]

G ERARD MANLEY HOPKINS was a true original, synthesizing some severely disparate artistic and philosophical elements: proto-*fin de siècle* aestheticism, Catholicism of a particularly mirthless and self-lacerating type, devotion to the works of Franciscan Scholastic Duns Scotus, and just a

---

1   Donald Frame, trans. *The Complete Works*. A.A. Knopf, 2003, p. 140.
2   In *Snoring as a Fine Art, and Twelve Other Essays*. Richard R. Smith, 1958, p. 196.

touch of English nationalism. This fraught inner variousness recalls Walt Whitman's oft-quoted pronouncement:

> Do I contradict myself?
> Very well, then; I contradict myself.
> (I am large. I contain multitudes.)[3]

It's no surprise that Hopkins felt a kinship with Whitman. "I always knew in my heart Walt Whitman's mind to be more like my own than any other man's living," Hopkins admitted, before adding: "As he is a very great scoundrel this is not a pleasant confession."[4]

Sources indicate that Hopkins had a high-pitched, reedy voice. While I detest the phenomenon of "alternative facts" borne of wishful thinking, I hereby assert, on whatever authority I possess, that Hopkins' voice was impossibly deep, and sounded like the voice used by God to call the world into being.

You might agree after reading "God's Grandeur," an anthology mainstay. It begins:

> The world is charged with the grandeur of God.
> It will flame out, like shining from shook foil;
> It gathers to a greatness, like the ooze of oil
> Crushed. Why do men then now not reck[5] his rod?
> Generations have trod, have trod, have trod;   5.
> And all is seared with trade; bleared, smeared with toil;
> And wears man's smudge and shares man's smell: the soil
> Is bare now, nor can foot feel, being shod.

I'm confident that many of the best similes and metaphors in English poetry are written backwards. Hopkins compares the flaming of God's grandeur to "shining from shook foil," an image that's so awesomely specific that nobody could confect it as a means of illustrating an abstract idea.

---

3 "Song of Myself," 51.8-10.
4 In a letter to Robert Bridges, 1882.
5 reck] Heed.

Step outside on a summer afternoon. Place a square of foil in your palm. Notice its surface's angular dents. Notice its near-weightlessness. Notice how it shudders to a breeze that's almost too gentle to feel. Notice how reflected sunlight dances across it, occasionally contracting into an abrupt point so piercingly bright that you squint.

Hopkins had obviously experienced this and stored it away for future use.

Likewise, with "It gathers to a greatness, like the ooze of oil / Crushed." We all know how a droplet of olive oil looks on a countertop: how it glows, how it refracts the pattern of whatever's underneath it, how its edges remain curiously clean. The droplet never tapers off at the margins, but stays somehow self-consolidated, so that the perimeter seems to push the oil upward into a three-dimensional shape.

Now, imagine the olive being crushed, let's say, by a thin stone cylinder of only slightly greater diameter than the olive itself. You cannot see the force being applied to the olive, but only the slowly, silently expanding circle of oil. It swells like a greedy prism, gathering centimeters of tabletop into the scope of its refraction.

Hopkins was erudite enough to know that the verb traditionally used for the extraction of oil from an olive is "express." While today we speak of "self-expression" as a joyful form of liberation, Hopkins is more likely to have regarded it as a masochistically tense, painful enterprise.[6]

> It will flame out, like shining from shook foil;
> It gathers to a greatness, like the ooze of oil
> Crushed.

It's all so beautifully, excruciatingly precise.

The rhetorical technique Hopkins is using is called "ba-

---

6 As an example of this older use of "express," check out John Webster's *The White Devil*, when Antonelli says: "Perfumes, the more they are chafed, the more they render / Their pleasing scents; and so affliction / Expresseth virtue fully" (1.1.45-47).

thos," which is when the poet compares or juxtaposes something dramatic with something commonplace. Bathos is often used for comedic effect, as when Woody Allen says: "I don't want to achieve immortality through my work; I want to achieve immortality through not dying."[7]

Bathos of a very different kind shows up when the poet has no idea what he's doing. In the introduction to their anthology, *Very Bad Poetry*, Kathryn and Ross Petras write:

> So what is a very bad poem? Usually it is testimony to a poet's well-honed sense of the anticlimactic. A poet must be immeasurably moved by some grandiose emotion or event—say, a horrific catastrophe—commit it to paper, then veer from the sublime to the pedestrian at precisely the right—which is to say, the wrong—moment. One minute the poet is describing the sinking of a ferry, the next mentioning how much the fare was.[8]

Bathos can also be an effective way to discuss tragedy when "real life" feels rather like a bad joke. Hamlet's father's ghost is flabbergasted that Gertrude could have gone from him (a substantial man) to petty, pointless, hard-hearted Claudius. "Ay, that incestuous, that adulterate beast," he rages,

> With witchcraft of his wits, with traitorous gifts—
> O wicked wit and gifts, that have the power
> So to seduce!—won to his shameful lust
> The will of my most seeming-virtuous queen.   5.
> O Hamlet, what a falling off there was!
> From me, whose love was of that dignity
> That went hand in hand even with the vow
> I made to her in marriage, and to decline
> Upon a wretch whose natural gifts were poor   10.
> To those of mine.[9]

---

7   Source uncertain.
8   Vintage Books, 1997, p. xvi.
9   1.5. 49-59.

Hamlet echoes this in his confrontation with Gertrude. He hands her two portraits: one of her former, and one of her present husband. "Look here upon this picture and on this," he says,

> The counterfeit presentiment of two brothers.
> See what grace was seated on his brow,
> Hyperion's[10] curls, the front of Jove[11] himself,
> An eye like Mars'[12] to threaten and command,   5.
> A station like the herald Mercury[13]
> New-lighted on a heaven-kissing hill,
> A combination and a form indeed
> Where every god did seem to set his seal
> To give the world assurance of a man.   10.
> This was your husband. Look you now what follows.

He replaces it with a portrait of her present husband, and says:

> Here is your husband, like a mildewed ear
> Blasting his wholesome brother. Have you eyes?[14]

Bathos has long been put to diverse uses. To the best of my knowledge, however, what Hopkins generates is new; we'll call it the Bathetic Sublime. The grand must be astonishingly grand; the specific, astonishingly specific. Hopkins' religious and philosophical priorities were well-calibrated for minute observation, for he believed in something called "inscape." *The Norton Anthology of English Literature* says:

> [Hopkins] felt that everything in the universe was characterized by what he called inscape, the distinctive design that constitutes individual identity. This identity is not

---

10 Hyperion] Greek god of light.

11 Jove] AKA Jupiter, King of the Gods; Roman equivalent of Zeus.

12 Mars] Roman god of war.

13 Mercury] Roman god of merchants and mountebanks.

14 3.4. 63-75.

static but dynamic. Each being in the universe "selves,"
that is, enacts its identity.[15]

In other words, there's a sacred thing-ness which makes
every single thing the thing that it is. To think in these terms re-
quires that you go through the world asking questions of every-
thing, even (or especially) of those things that don't possess an
obvious personality or distinctness. This is conducive to a par-
ticularizing sense of the world. It's conducive, indeed, to poetry.

Concision is among the defining features of poetry; the
poet forces a few words to say a great deal. Figurative language is
a common mechanism for this. When Robert Burns announces
"My love is like a red, red rose," he's asking us to recall the rose's
defining features, to pinpoint those that might be compared
with feminine beauty, and then to make the connections. We
supply the relevant information; the simile tells us what, exactly,
to supply.

But roses are generic. When you hear "rose," you don't
imagine a rose, but rather, the *idea* of a rose. A rose is to flowers
what the *Mona Lisa* is to art. Poets avoid vagueness when they
keep their figurative language hyper-specific. John Milton does
this (often annoyingly) with "epic similes." In this scene from
Paradise Lost, the fallen, rebellious angels are assembled at their
new headquarters, Pandemonium,[16] debating how to retaliate
against God:

> Others with vast Typhoean rage more fell
> Rend up both rocks and hills, and ride the air
> In whirlwind. Hell scarce holds the wild uproar,
> As when—

When Milton writes "as when," beware: a labyrinthine simile is

---

15 Stephen Greenblatt et al., ed. "Gerard Manley Hopkins." *The Norton
Anthology of English Literature*. 8th ed. Vol. 2. W. W. Norton & Company,
2006, p. 2159.

16 Pandemonium] Literally, "All Demons." Milton coined this word.

coming.

> As when Alcides from Oechalia crowned
> With conquest, felt th' envenomed robe, and tore   5.
> Through pain up by the roots Thessalian pines,
> And Lichas from the top of Oeta threw
> Into th' Euboic Sea.[17]

Regardless of any other accusations one might level against Milton, a lack of specificity cannot be among them. All that's required of the reader is that he can identify Alcides,[18] Oechalia,[19] Thessalian pines,[20] Lichas,[21] Oeta,[22] and the Euboic Sea.[23] Even though I adore Milton, I admit that this sort of thing is preposterous.

A valiant Miltonist might fly to the Great Man's defense, pointing out that in the 1660s, classical learning was more current than it is today, and that Milton isn't being particularly showy. Fair enough. Today's readers (myself included) are pathetically ignorant in many areas.

You'll observe, however, that *King Lear* doesn't require footnotes for an average audience to get it. In 3.2, we find Lear on the heath, screaming at the weather:

> Blow, winds, and crack your cheeks! Rage! Blow!
> You cataracts and hurricanoes, spout
> Till you have drenched our steeples, drowned the cocks!
> You sulphurous and thought-executing fires,
> Vaunt-couriers to oak-cleaving thunderbolts,   5.
> Singe my white head! And thou, all-shaking thunder,
> Strike flat the thick rotundity of the world!

---

17 2.539–546.

18 Alcides] Another name for Hercules.

19 Oechalia] Town in ancient Greece.

20 Thessalian pines] The Pineios River in Thessaly.

21 Lichas] Hercules' servant.

22 Oeta] A mountain.

23 Euboic Sea] Appendage of the Aegean.

Crack nature's molds, all germens spill at once
That make ingrateful man!

Most people who know the context will have little difficulty figuring out what's going on, even if they're unsure as to the meaning of "crack your cheeks," "cataracts," "vaunt-couriers," and "germens."

An analogous claim cannot be made for that bit of Milton I've quoted.

There must, then, be another mode of specificity: somewhere equidistant between red, red roses and Classical quasi-arcana.

Let's travel East. Here's a verse by Bullhe Shāh, collected in *Sufi Lyrics*:

[T]he mind is a bundle of fiber. Sit in a corner somewhere and beat it.[24]

It's a reference to the craft of rope making, which evidently involved hammering a bunch of disparate fibers so that they coalesce into a rope.

Your mind is likely well-stocked with flower-related information; as for rope making, however, you're forced to *think*, and to follow the metaphor. And as you mentally unpack the circumstances of rope making, you discover a ballooning number of ways that the metaphor is apt. The metaphor gets more impressive the more you think about it.

T.S. Eliot was among the very few poets with enough chutzpah to disparage the greatest play in English. In "Hamlet and His Problems," Eliot argues the sort of point you can only argue if you happen to be T.S. Eliot. "So far from being Shakespeare's masterpiece," he opines, "the play is most certainly an artistic failure." But things soon take a serious turn. (This is something that one knows better than to expect from Eliot's

---

24 Harvard University Press, 2015, verse 17.

comrade Ezra Pound, who tends to follow up an absurd opinion with yet another absurd opinion.) Eliot declares:

> The only way of expressing emotion in the form of art is by finding an "objective correlative"; in other words, a set of objects, a situation, a chain of events which shall be the formula of that particular emotion; such that when the external facts, which must terminate in sensory experience, are given, the emotion is immediately evoked.[25]

Eliot's dislike of *Hamlet* lies in its protagonist's endless bellyaching about his plight—bellyaching that remains abstract due to its lack of an Objective Correlative.

An example might be useful. Since I'm blessed to spend nearly all of my reading time on masterpieces, it's tough for me to find illustrative garbage. Fair warning: we're going to have to go *low*.

According to the current *Billboard* Top Ten, a song called "Stay" (Justin Bieber, et al.) is doing brisk business. Here's a representative stanza:

> I do the same thing I told you that I never would.
> I told you I changed, even when I knew I never could.
> I know that I can't find nobody [*sic*] else as good as you.
> I need you to stay, need you to stay. Hey.
> I do the same thing I told you that I never would.   5.
> I told you I changed, even when I knew I never could.
> I know that I can't find nobody [*sic*] else as good as you.
> I need you to stay, need you to stay. Yeah.[26]

Regarding *Moby-Dick*, Clive James wrote that "[T]here is surely a case for saying that the story of Captain Ahab's contest with the great white whale is one of those books you can't get

---

25   Quoted in James Edwin Miller's *T.S. Eliot: The Making of an American Poet, 1888-1922*. Penn State University Press, 2005, p. 348.
26   Transcribed from YouTube.

started with even after you have finished reading them."[27] "Stay" is the opposite: it's a town you've already passed through before you've even reached it.

What to say of it? The repetition of "I" at the beginning of each line is a rhetorical device, which (as I'm sure Mr. Bieber knows) is called anaphora (Greek for "carrying back"). And "would" does indeed rhyme with "could." God be praised. And speaking of God, the stanza may be understood as a vernacular paraphrase of Romans 7:19: "For the good that I would, I do not; but the evil which I would not, that I do."

Oy.

All joking aside, however, there's nothing in this stanza that isn't an abstraction—and a boring abstraction, at that. There isn't a single image. There isn't "a set of objects, a situation, [or] a chain of events" that might constitute "the formula of [Mr. Bieber's] particular emotion;" there aren't any "external facts" by means of which "the emotion is immediately evoked."

It's just a guy, kvetching.

Now, we need something of comparable stature to demonstrate the Objective Correlative in action. It embarrasses me enough to confess that my musical tastes in high school were so debased, but actually to quote Sixpence None the Richer's 1998 hit single "Kiss Me" forces this writer to confront some ugly parts of himself. However, the educator must sometimes forgo his own comfort in the interest of his vocation, and "Kiss Me" supplies accessible and illuminating examples of how the Objective Correlative is accomplished.

Let's take a look at stanzas 1 and 3:

Kiss me out in the bearded barley,
Nightly beside the green, green grass.
Swing, swing; swing the spinning step.
You wear those shoes and I will wear that dress.

[…]

---

27 *Cultural Amnesia: Notes in the Margin of My Time.* Picador, 2007, p. 65.

Kiss me down by the broken tree house.
Swing me upon its hanging tire.
Bring, bring—bring your flowered hat;
We'll take the trail marked on your father's map.[28]

Yes, the rhyming is crappy. "Step" does not rhyme with "dress;" "hat" does not rhyme with "map." And (yes), while I see the appeal of heavy-petting *upon* the green, green grass, whatever is *beside* said grass must be lush indeed to make it preferable.

However, this song translates abstract feelings into concrete images: "bearded barley;" "the spinning step." Shoes (for the boy) and a dress (for the girl) are concrete enough, but we get "*those* shoes;" "*that* dress."

These items have significance to the characters. We don't know exactly what significance, but we know what general kind of significance, and this is more than adequate. "Kiss me down by the broken tree house. / Swing me upon its hanging tire." The landscape is charged with a significance that only comes of familiarity. "*The* broken treehouse;" it's as if someone asked "… which treehouse?" and was answered "*the* broken treehouse," as if nobody could possibly doubt which treehouse was being referred to. A lesser songwriter would give us an abstraction, like "We were innocent, and life was simple;" this lyric gives us "We'll take the trail marked on your father's map." Lovely.

---

28 Transcribed from YouTube.

FIFTY-SEVEN

(SPECIFICITY, CONTINUED) "FOR ON HIS VISAGE WAS IN LITTLE DRAWN"

IN "A Lover's Complaint," Shakespeare writes:

For on his visage was in little drawn
What largeness thinks in Paradise was sawn.[1] [2]

This is the relationship between the specific and the general.

---

1 sawn] Seen.
2 90-91.

(SPECIFICITY, CONTINUED)
TECHNIQUE OFFERS ITS OWN SPECIFICITY

A POEM BESET BY abstractions can still be great if the rhyme and prosody are handled with astonishing mastery. Swinburne's "Dolores" is one such work, comprising 440 lines of the most shocking, beautiful poetry ever written in English. Although that's the sort of length we normally associate with narrative poetry, "Dolores" is a lyric. Swinburne is nothing if not a rule-breaker, and he figures out how to render the length a positive asset, creating a driving, feverish incantation in praise of "Dolores"—a mythical entity who's one part Virgin Mary and one part patron saint of sadomasochism. It begins:

> Cold eyelids that hide like a jewel
> Hard eyes that grow soft for an hour;
> The heavy white limbs, and the cruel
> Red mouth like a venomous flower;
> When these are gone by with their glories,　　　　5.
> What shall rest of thee then, what remain,
> O mystic and sombre Dolores,
> Our Lady of Pain?

Its rhyme and prosody graph as follows:

1. a.　Cold eyelids that hide like a jewel　u / u u / u u / u
2. b.　Hard eyes that grow soft for an hour;　u / u u / u u / u

3. a. The heavy white limbs, and the cruel u / u u / u u / u
4. b. Red mouth like a venomous flower; u / u u / u u / u
5. c. When these are gone by with their glories, u / u u / u u / u
6. d. What shall rest of thee then, what remain, u u / u u / u u /
7. c. O mystic and somber Dolores, u / u u / u u / u
8. d. Our Lady of Pain? u / u u /

If we understand poetry as comprising two components, "sound" and "sense," we find that, even in this opening stanza, there's a good deal of abstraction and imprecision.

> Lines 1 – 2:
> Cold eyelids that hide like a jewel
> Hard eyes that grow soft for an hour;

Do "cold eyelids" and a "jewel" have volition? Is the first line saying that "cold eyelids" hide in the same manner as a "jewel" hides? Or are "hard eyes" being hidden? And if so, what's doing the hiding: "cold eyelids" or a "jewel?" Furthermore, are all "hard eyes" being hidden, or just those "that grow soft for an hour?"

"Jewel" and "hard eyes" are abstractions; so is "an hour," since it's being used to mean "a certain span of time," and not a concrete unit of 60 minutes.

> Lines 3 – 8:
> The heavy white limbs, and the cruel
> Red mouth like a venomous flower;
> When these are gone by with their glories,
> What shall rest of thee then, what remain,
> O mystic and somber Dolores,
> Our Lady of Pain?

Abstractions: "heavy;" "white;" "cruel;" "red mouth;" "venomous;" "flower;" "gone by;" "glories;" "remain;" "mystic."

The poem manages to render excusable not only prolixity and abstraction, but even over-stretched (sometimes nearly preposterous) rhymes. Over the 440 lines, "Dolores" is rhymed with: "glories;" "stories;" "floor is;" "adore is;" "core is;" "pour is;" "door is;" "implore is;" "more is." He gives up trying after stanza 33, with around 40% of the poem left to go. It's as if even Swinburne begins to doubt just how far these rhymes may be pushed while remaining just this side of absurdity.

The poem vindicates itself through music. In his three-volume *A History of English Prosody: From the Twelfth Century to the Present Day,*[1] George Saintsbury describes Swinburne as "the one living master of English prosody" and "a prosodist magician." Regarding "Dolores" specifically, he comments that the poem's music is "almost ideally suitable for the great series of pictures and situations that the poem contains."[2] Even quasi-pornographic content and the occasional lapse into abstraction can be made great through music.

Swinburne can get away with it. I can't, and I doubt that you can, either. Better stick with specificity.

---

1 W.H. Auden boasted of having used every form of prosody discussed in this massive work.

2 For Saintsbury's complete take on Swinburne, refer to Vol. III, Macmillan and Co, 1910, pp. 334-352.

III

CONCLUSION

FIFTY-NINE

IT IS AGAINST THIS WHICH WE ARE FIGHTING

I N A RECENT issue of *The Journal*,[1] the distinguished literary magazine of The Ohio State University, there appears something that claims to be a poem. It bears the title "Yelp Page for My Cunt," and begins thusly:

Recommended Reviews
TIGHT
oh my god you're tight[3]
The tightest I've ever (… *more*)
so fucking tight[4] holy s(… *more*)   5.
can't last too long here
You wouldn't believe how ti(… *more*)
[*View more reviews*]

The apparent proprietress of the cunt at issue is a young woman named Shakthi Shrima, whose parents must be very proud. The poem has two parts: the first is formatted like a Yelp review. Superscripted numbers conduct the curious reader to further text, formatted like footnotes; this is the second part. The beginning of footnote #4 reads:

I remember this guy too, his eager fingers splaying
past my parted mouth in the moment before their thrust

---

1 Issue 43.2, Spring 2019.

into my cunt. […]

I don't find this scandalous, exactly. Men are seldom ambivalent about the female form. A text conducting so minute a survey of the landscape is unlikely to meet with strenuous disapproval. That a young woman would actually volunteer this information is an interesting development; that she'd volunteer it with such obvious self-importance is adorable.

Keep at it, my dear. Just as all art aspires to the condition of music, all vulgarity aspires to the condition of a medical file. And medical files are boring.

While you are toiling away, however, my readers and I will be writing poems.

SIXTY

I'LL MEET YOU THERE

I N "An Anatomy of the World: The First Anniversary,"
John Donne writes:

Verse hath a middle nature: Heaven keeps souls;
The Grave keeps bodies; Verse, the fame enrolls.[1]

He's proposing that "verse" is a sort of "place" equidistant
between Heaven and Earth, and that this is the home of fame,
which gives the earthly eternal life, and gives the eternal a pres-
ence in our actual lives.

I'll meet you there.

---

1 473-474.

SIXTY-ONE

"UPON A REVEALED PARADISE"

I N "Further Notes on Edgar Poe," Charles Baudelaire writes:

It is this admirable and immortal instinct for Beauty that makes us consider the Earth and its shows as a glimpse, a correspondence, of Heaven. The unquenchable thirst for all that lies beyond, and which life reveals, is the liveliest proof of our immortality. It is at once by means of and through poetry, by means of and through music, that the soul gets an inkling of the glories that lie beyond the grave; and when an exquisite poem melts us into tears, those tears are not the proof of an excess of pleasure, but rather, evidence of a certain petulant, impatient sorrow— of a nervous postulation—of a nature exiled amid the imperfect, and eager to seize immediately, on this very earth, upon a revealed paradise.[1]

Amen.

---

1 In *The Painter of Modern Life and Other Essays*. Phaidon Press Limited, 2010.

SIXTY-TWO

THERE'S NOTHING STRANGE ABOUT AN AFTERLIFE

O N MAY 11, 2022, *The New York Times* published "The Strange Afterlife of George Carlin." "Nearly 14 years after his death," observes Dave Itzkoff, "his provocative humor has been embraced by people across the political spectrum. What happens when comedy outlasts the era it was made for?"

Great art is made for all eras, and there's nothing strange about an afterlife.

SIXTY-THREE

NOISE OF TEARING

"When Kemble was living at Lausanne, he used to feel rather jealous of Mont Blanc; he disliked to hear people always asking, 'How does Mont Blanc look this morning?'"
—Samuel Rogers, *Table-Talk and Recollections*

"I suspect that sentience only evolved on Earth once carnivores did[.]"
—Colin McGinn, *Prehension: The Hand and the Emergence of Humanity*[1]

"No strange move can I make
Without noise of tearing."
—Stephen Crane, XL.

W E ONCE BELIEVED in Ultimate Harmony; we believed in a cosmic order, and that if the individual oriented himself correctly, he could harmonize his existence with Creation itself, and be at peace. As Boethius writes in *The Consolation of Philosophy*:

How happy is mankind
If the love that orders the stars above

---

1 The MIT Press, 2015, p. 93.

Rules, too, in your hearts.[2]

Modernity's loathsome trinity (Charles Darwin, Sigmund Freud, and Karl Marx) proved that Reality's bottom line isn't peace but frenzied conflict. Marx maintained that History was the chronicle of class hatred. Freud demonstrated that what you recognize as You is a patchwork of defense mechanisms, that your personality is "born in sin" (as it were), and that a "normal" self is little more than a truce always on the verge of dissolution. And Darwin observed that when you "lean and loafe at your ease, observing a spear of summer grass" (to quote Whitman), listening to the birds, you aren't listening to the sounds of Edenic order, but rather, to the sounds of war.

My own experience tends to vindicate the Existentialist view. I'm not proud of this; I'd welcome the suggestions of anyone who's discovered the trick of making the world feel like something other than a phantasmagoria.

Jacobo Timerman's *Prisoner Without a Name, Cell Without a Number* is a memoir of his imprisonment and torture during Argentina's "Dirty War." "Perhaps I'm experiencing the same problem as Argentina," he writes, "an unwillingness to be aware of one's own drama."[3]

You cannot think of your life as worthwhile unless you believe it has drama; you cannot have drama without believing that your life has transcendent meaning. We're molested by the message that we're nothing more than better-evolved ferrets; that "spirituality" can never hope to be more than an inward-looking enterprise, because there's nothing outside of yourself; that the best we can do is to validate ourselves through yoga, meditation, or some other form of self-affirmation.

It's the absolute worst of both worlds. You're expected to believe that you "own" yourself, and, therefore, make your own destiny; at the same time, you're discouraged from believing that any of this is transcendently significant. You're expected

---

2 David R. Slavitt, trans., Harvard University Press, 2008, II.VIII. p. 58.

3 Alfred A. Knopf, 1981, p. 36.

to suffer like an operatic protagonist, but without the cosmic satisfaction of being an operatic protagonist.

Let's unapologetically reject this. Human life is sacred. God is personally invested in our struggle-riven lives. Our decisions ripple outward through everything.

Only Religion and Art can assure us that we're *real*.

This past semester, I taught William Blake's *The Marriage of Heaven and Hell*, which I'd read many times, but had never taught. It includes a brace of deviant "proverbs;" they're like the biblical proverbs—if King Solomon were a pagan lunatic.

When I was a teenager, some of those proverbs, oddly enough, helped me to consolidate an approach to life which I've found useful, namely: "Dip him in the river who loves water," and, "If the fool would persist in his folly, he would become wise."

I take these to mean that moderation isn't absolutely good. Certain things should be lavishly immoderate. The love that you develop for your life's work, for instance, should be immoderate.

Don't misunderstand: Stoicism often makes sense. But the greatest human achievements are incompatible with stoicism, because greatness itself is inherently immoderate: Thelonious Monk's musicianship, Bernini's sculptures, Bach's *Mass in B Minor*, Shakespeare's *Hamlet*, William Holman Hunt's *The Finding of the Savior in the Temple*, and so many others.

Contemporary American culture would seem to celebrate "redemptive immoderation." We're told to "reach for the stars;" it's the stuff of every inspirational cliché.

In practice, however, "redemptive immoderation" is seldom encouraged. Bourgeois tranquility is frustrated by immoderation. Sacred excess is either resisted or unnoticed. If a suburban audience were to see *Othello* (and really get it), those "pillars of the community" would be sobbing like children. The appropriate response to Paganini is stupefaction. To those that have eyes and ears, great art is strange.

It's a lucky man who can avoid using his mind. But if you're condemned to use it, use it ferociously. A dynamic mind should give a faint whiff and a fainter snarl of grinding gears.

TEMPLATES

ONE

BALLAD

CERTAIN POETIC FORMS carry particular associations. The ballad is associated with vernacular storytelling. It's a democratic, egalitarian form. That doesn't mean, however, that it must be used in this way. A poem can produce added layers of meaning when it presents a dissonance between the subject matter and the form's associations. For instance, the sonnet is associated with courtly love. John Donne, however, gets dramatic mileage by using the sonnet as an artifact of spiritual torment. Likewise, feel free to wield the ballad subversively.

The ballad is one of those poetic forms where the meter is essential. It can be mapped as follows:

Line Number	Rhyme	Number of Iambs	
1.	a.	4.	
2.	b.	3.	
3.	a.	4.	
4.	b.	3.	
5.	c.	4.	
6.	d.	3.	
7.	c.	4.	
8.	d.	3.	
9.	e.	4.	
10.	f.	3.	
11.	e.	4.	
12.	f.	3.	

To make things easier on yourself, the odd-numbered lines can remain unrhymed. This is among the few situations where ease may be compatible with aesthetic refinement, since, when only the even-numbered lines rhyme, there's produced a pleasing tension at the end of each odd-numbered line.

The Ballad of the White Horse by G.K. Chesterton is among the most underrated book-length poems of the twentieth century and is competitive with the best poems of any century. Although he shifts between different forms of ballad stanza, if one were to "take the average," it would look like this:

Line Number	Rhyme	Number of Iambs	
1.	x.	4.	
2.	a.	3.	
3.	b.	4.	
4.	b.	4.	
5.	b.	4.	
6.	a.	3.	

In *The Ballad of Reading Gaol*, Oscar Wilde organizes his stanzas thusly:

Line Number	Rhyme	Number of Iambs	
1.	x.	4.	
2.	a.	3.	
3.	x.	4.	
4.	a.	3.	
5.	x.	4.	
6.	a.	3.	

TWO

EPIGRAM

I N 1885, Peter Carl Fabergé began producing jeweled eggs for Russian royalty to give as Easter gifts. They are commonly known as "Fabergé eggs," and they're difficult to characterize. "Jewelry" is used to adorn the face or body, which gives it, in a roundabout sort of way, a utilitarian dimension. But Fabergé eggs aren't worn.

Theoretically, they should teeter on the brink of kitsch. Take the "1887 Third Imperial Egg," for instance. When it appeared at auction in 1964, the catalogue described it thusly:

> Fourteen-karat gold watch in reeded egg-shaped case with seventy-five-point old-mine diamond clasp by Vacheron & Constantin; on eighteen-karat three-tone gold stand exquisitely wrought with an annulus, bordered with wave scrollings and pairs of corbel-like legs cirelé with a capping of roses, pendants of tiny leaves depending to animalistic feet with ring stretcher; the annulus bears three medallions of cabochon sapphires surmounted by tiny bowknotted ribbons set with minute diamonds, which support very finely ciselé three-tone gold swags of roses and leaves which continue downward and over the pairs of legs.[1]

It seems like the jewelry analogue to the drag queen. But nothing that's a mere 3¼ inches high can quite qualify as kitsch. Although it's tiny, it can't qualify as a "trinket," which implies cheapness of materials and laxity of craftsmanship. And the House of Fabergé was sublimely devoted to quality; Peter Carl Fabergé was famous for making his pieces seem as though they'd descended from heaven, New-Jerusalem-like, fully formed,

---

1 Parke-Bernet Catalogue (Lot No. 259), 6 – 7 March 1964.

perfectly expressed, and flawless. The sheer dramatic force of the craftsmanship is such that it moderates the punch produced by the astonishing worth of its raw materials: the two varieties of gold, the diamond clasps, the dusting of "minute" diamonds, and the cabochon sapphires.

The Fabergé egg, then, is a paradox. It's ostentatious, but private. Its raw materials (which, in any other context, would be the show-stealer) are humbled by something more precious than Preciousness itself. It's unique, but "common" enough to be given away.

At its best, the epigram is like a Fabergé egg. Unlike, say, the sonnet, the epigram doesn't have a specified line count, a rhyme or metrical scheme, or a structure. The epigram can best be understood as a mode of address or a rhetorical mood. Epigrams are intended to have a lapidary permanence. But they often address specific occasions (major or minor), contribute to a specific debate or conversation, pay tribute to someone deserving of honor, or deflate some bombastic schmuck.

Alexander Pope was a master of the epigram. Here are two about wit, which then referred not exclusively to humor (as it does now), but to general intellectual nimbleness:

> Wit is like Faith by such warm fools professed,
> Who, to be saved by one, must damn the rest.

And:

> Now wits gain praise by copying other wits
> As one hog lives on what another shits.

John Donne was no slouch in the epigram department. Here's "Antiquary:"

> If in his study he hath so much care
> To hang all old strange things, let his wife beware.

And here's "An Obscure Writer:"

Philo with twelve years' study hath been grieved
To be understood. When will he be believed?

Ben Jonson has two epigrams addressed to his own body parts. Here's "On Groin:"

Groin, come of age, his state[2] sold out of hand
For his whore: Groin doth still occupy his land.

And here's "On Gut:"

Gut eats all day, and lechers all the night,
So all his meat he tasteth over, twice;
And striving so to double his delight,
He makes himself a thoroughfare of vice.
Thus in his belly can he change a sin: 5.
Lust, it comes out, that gluttony went in.[3]

And here's the always-provocative John Wilmot, 2nd Earl of Rochester, ensuring that one Ms. Cary Frazier attains her modest (or, indeed, immodest) sliver of immortality:

Her father gave her dildoes six;
Her mother made 'em up a score.
But she loves naught but living pricks,
And swears by God she'll frig[4] no more.

---

2 state] Estate, i.e., property or possessions.

3 In *The Anatomy of Melancholy*, Robert Burton quotes Saint Ambrose: "As hunger […] is a friend of virginity, so is it an enemy to lasciviousness, but fullness overthrows chastity, and fostereth all manner of provocations." Gluttony and sexual license were seen as kindred vices, which is odd, because they seem fundamentally different. Gluttony requires only food, and food is not expected to give its consent. Sexual license, however, tends to require another human being, and, no matter how vigorously we slander previous generations of men as being a pack of patriarchal rapists, the woman's willing participation was always rather the point.

4 frig] Masturbate.

And as for the flattering epigram, we should return it to the role it once enjoyed in social networking and job-hunting. What, for instance, can a prospective employer really know about you from your job application, which is, perforce, a skeletal professional history fleshed out with tendentious comment and boring half-lies? A job application can never be stylish. If we insist on artifice from our applicants, why not provide the possibility of skillful artifice? Imagine how humane and amiable it would be if we had the custom of writing an epigram to someone we'd like to work for. The process would enable the applicant to retain his dignity.

And as for the boss, he'd actually be able to learn something about the applicant, since an epigram is revealing:

1. Is the applicant meticulous? Was care taken to ensure that rhyme and meter aren't just technically correct, but also fluent?

2. Does the applicant have a sense of irony? If so, what kind of irony, exactly? If his sense of ironic detachment is too developed, he will likely neglect his professional duties. If it's too narrow, however, he's sure to be a mirthless putz.

3. It isn't just the irony's strength that matters, but also its peculiar character. Is the applicant's humor gentle or tough; elevated or vulgar; self-effacing or superior; relaxed or posed?

4. Is he able to command his wit so that it demonstrates the ideal balance of boldness and propriety?

5. To what extent is the applicant showing off? To what extent is he attempting to make effort appear effortless?

In our current system, the applicant prepares one basic resume, and then tailors it here and there in order most effectively to speak to the job's demands. An epigram-based system, however, would require a fresh epigram for each application. Each application would constitute a unique test, just as the job, if you're lucky enough to get it, will confront you with a parade of unique challenges, each requiring skill, judgment, and just a bit of improvisational panache.

THREE

GHAZAL

T HIS FORM IS so difficult to abstract into a diagram that I begin by providing one of my own ghazals by way of example:

> Pour your gentle wine on them.
> Rinse away the brine on them.
>
> May they be at ease with Time,
> Knowing its design on them.
>
> Their bewildered questions are   5.
> Fixed on you, and mine on them.
>
> Poet, formless are their woes.
> Make your song a spine for them.[5]

What we have, then, is a series of queerly rhymed couplets. There's a "refrain phrase" ("on them," in this case) concluding each couplet's second line, the word before which is rhymed with corresponding words in the other couplets. The opening couplet employs this pattern in both of its lines.

It might be graphed accordingly:

---

5 Published as Ghazal No. 3 in *Still Telling What is Told*. Argus Huber, 2020.

	Line Number		Rhyme	
Stanza One	1.		a.	Refrain Phrase
	2.		a.	Refrain Phrase
Stanza Two	3.			
	4.		a.	Refrain Phrase
Stanza Three	5.			
	6.		a.	Refrain Phrase
Stanza Four	7.			
	8.		a.	Refrain Phrase

It's best to go about it without any preconceived ideas regarding what you might want to "say;" this form is more purely musical and atmospheric than any other. I suggest that you begin by selecting a refrain phrase and rhyme (even if it's rather arbitrary), use a rhyming dictionary to copy every possibility, and then begin piecing it together like a puzzle. There's an element of randomness in this exercise that sometimes produces exceptional beauty, and sometimes produces drivel. Spin the wheel and take your chance.

FOUR

SESTINA

FOR AN INTRODUCTION to the sestina, refer to Chapter Thirty-Four ("Elaboration").

	Line Number	End-Word Number	
Stanza One	i.	1.	
	ii.	2.	
	iii.	3.	
	iv.	4.	
	v.	5.	
	vi.	6.	
Stanza Two	i.	6.	
	ii.	1.	
	iii.	5.	
	iv.	2.	
	v.	4.	
	vi.	3.	
Stanza Three	i.	3.	
	ii.	6.	
	iii.	4.	
	iv.	1.	
	v.	2.	
	vi.	5.	
Stanza Four	i.	5.	
	ii.	3.	
	iii.	2.	
	iv.	6.	
	v.	1.	
	vi.	4.	

Stanza Five	i.	4.	
	ii.	5.	
	iii.	1.	
	iv.	3.	
	v.	6.	
	vi.	2.	
Stanza Six	i.	2.	
	ii.	4.	
	iii.	6.	
	iv.	5.	
	v.	3.	
	vi.	1.	

FIVE

SONNET (PETRARCHAN / ITALIAN)

Line Number		Rhyme	
1.	Octave	a.	
2.		b.	
3.		b.	
4.		a.	
5.		a.	
6.		b.	
7.		b.	
8.		a.	
9.	Sestet	[Flexible]	
10.			
11.			
12.			
13.			
14.			

My favorite rhyme scheme for the sestet is:

9.	c.	
10.	d.	
11.	e.	
12.	c.	
13.	d.	
14.	e.	

With this rhyme scheme, you can write three complete lines without having to worry about rhyming anything. Then, you can decide if you're going to use them as lines 9 – 11:

9.	c.		
10.	d.		3-Line Unit
11.	e.		
12.	c.		
13.	d.		
14.	e.		

—lines 12 – 14:

9.	c.		
10.	d.		
11.	e.		
12.	c.		3-Line Unit
13.	d.		
14.	e.		

—lines 10 – 12:

9.	c.		
10.	d.		
11.	e.		3-Line Unit
12.	c.		
13.	d.		
14.	e.		

—or lines 11 – 13:

9.	c.		
10.	d.		
11.	e.		
12.	c.		3-Line Unit
13.	d.		
14.	e.		

SIX

SONNET (SHAKESPEAREAN / ENGLISH)

Line Number	Rhyme		
1.	a.	Quatrain One	
2.	b.		
3.	a.		
4.	b.		
5.	c.	Quatrain Two	
6.	d.		
7.	c.		
8.	d.		
9.	e.	Quatrain Three	
10.	f.		
11.	e.		
12.	f.		
13.	g.	Cou-plet	
14.	g.		

Tradition suggests that each quatrain maintain its independence. The quatrain is imagined as a type of paragraph—a discrete component of a machine. However, if you melt them into each other, you have opportunities to write blocks of lines before having to worry about rhyming anything. If you approach it like this, for instance, you can begin with one unit of four unrhymed lines, and one of three unrhymed lines:

1.	a.	Quatrain One		4-Line Unit
2.	b.			
3.	a.			
4.	b.			
5.	c.	Quatrain Two		
6.	d.			
7.	c.			
8.	d.			
9.	e.	Quatrain Three		3-Line Unit
10.	f.			
11.	e.			
12.	f.			
13.	g.	Couplet		
14.	g.			

Exercise Eight

Here's a scaffold for an English sonnet. Lines 3 – 6 and 11 – 13 have been filled with excerpts from Hamlet's famous soliloquy in 3.1. Improvise around the quotes to complete the sonnet.

Line Number	Rhyme	
1.	a.	
2.	b.	
3.	a.	For in that sleep of death, what dreams may come,
4.	b.	When we have shuffled off this mortal coil,
5.	c.	Must give us pause. There's the respect
6.	d.	That makes Calamity of so long life.
7.	c.	
8.	d.	
9.	e.	
10.	f.	
11.	e.	Thus conscience does make cowards of us all,
12.	f.	And thus the native hue of Resolution
13.	g.	Is sicklied o'er, with the pale cast of Thought.
14.	g.	

To produce the most dramatic effect, rhyming words should either be of the same syllable count, or be arranged in such a way that the shorter word appears first. Therefore:

- Lines 1, 2, and 9 should end in words of 1 syllable.
- Line 7 should end in a word of at least 3 syllables.
- Line 10 should end in any word of between 1 and 3 syllables.
- Lines 8 and 14 are up for grabs.

SEVEN

TERZA RIMA

THIS FORM WAS invented by the medieval Italian poet Dante Alighieri for the *Divine Comedy*—a three-book narrative poem about the afterlife. Terza Rima is easier in Italian than in English, as the former is much richer in rhyme. For that very reason, it's satisfying if you can get it right.

Line Number	Rhyme	
1.	a.	
2.	b.	
3.	a.	
4.	b.	
5.	c.	
6.	b.	
7.	c.	
8.	d.	
9.	c.	
10.	d.	
11.	e.	
12.	d.	
13.	e.	
14.	f.	
15.	e.	

EIGHT

TRIOLET

Line Number	Rhyme		
1.	a.		
2.	b.		
3.	a.		
4.	a.	Repeat Line 1	
5.	a.		
6.	b.		
7.	a.	Repeat Line 1	
8.	b.	Repeat Line 2	

By way of example, here's an untitled triolet by Robert Bridges:

> When first we met, we did not guess
> That Love would prove so hard a master;
> Of more than common friendliness
> When first we met, we did not guess
> Who could foretell this sore distress,   5.
> This irretrievable disaster
> When first we met?—We did not guess
> That Love would prove so hard a master.

And here's "The Minaret at Jaffa," which I wrote back in 2002:

> The minaret at Jaffa served
> A sniper till the city fell.
> Emaciated boys observed
> The minaret that Jaffa served,
> And prayed: "This city be preserved   5.
> From the Foreign Infidel!"
> The minaret at Jaffa served
> A sniper till the city fell.[1]

While the triolet is a fairly unforgiving form, there are a few easier points of entry. You can use a triolet as a means of elaborating an unrhymed couplet, which can be slotted into lines 1 – 2 / 7 – 8:

1.	a.		Unrhymed Couplet
2.	b.		
3.	a.		
4.	a.		
5.	a.		
6.	b.		
7.	a.		Unrhymed Couplet
8.	b.		

---

1 First published in *Understandings* (Argus Huber, 2021).

—lines 5 – 6:

1.	a.		
2.	b.		
3.	a.		
4.	a.		
5.	a.		Unrhymed Couplet
6.	b.		
7.	a.		
8.	b.		

—or lines 6 – 7:

1.	a.		
2.	b.		
3.	a.		
4.	a.		
5.	a.		
6.	b.		Unrhymed Couplet
7.	a.		
8.	b.		

NINE

VILLANELLE

T HE VILLANELLE is the triple axel jump of poetic forms.

	Line Number	Rhyme		
Stanza One	1.	a.	Refrain i.	
	2.	b.		
	3.	a.	Refrain ii.	
Stanza Two	4.	a.		
	5.	b.		
	6.	a.	Refrain i.	
Stanza Three	7.	a.		
	8.	b.		
	9.	a.	Refrain ii.	
Stanza Four	10.	a.		
	11.	b.		
	12.	a.	Refrain i.	
Stanza Five	13.	a.		
	14.	b.		
	15.	a.	Refrain ii.	
Stanza Six	16.	a.		
	17.	b.		
	18.	a.	Refrain i.	
	19.	a.	Refrain ii.	

The perfect villanelle is Dylan Thomas's "Do Not Go Gentle Into That Good Night"—which I won't reproduce here, since it remains under copyright. I'll direct you, therefore, to the website of the Poetry Foundation, where this text is accessible.

ANTHOLOGY

In compiling this miniature anthology, I've restricted myself to poems that are in the public domain. I wouldn't want the absence of recent works to be misconstrued as indicating a curmudgeonly bias against anything published after 1920.

"The Seafarer"
ANONYMOUS
Translated from the Anglo-Saxon by EZRA POUND

Ezra Pound was bad for poetry—not as bad as Allen Ginsberg, but close. Ginsberg valorized semi-literacy; Pound valorized the opposite: bookish-seeming obscurity. I say "seeming" because there wasn't much behind his brash erudition. Pound was to poetry what Jacques Lacan was to academic prose: a vindication of those nasty impulses to which clever young people are already vulnerable.

Vladimir Nabokov concurs. In a letter to Philip Rahav dated May 21, 1949, he volunteers: "I am sorry you did not ask me what I think of the disgusting and entirely second-rate Mr. Pound[.]"[1] Nabokov elaborates on these feelings in a letter to William F. Buckley, dated March 26, 1973:

> Did the copy of *Transparent Things* I sent you through my publisher reach you? I did get the sumptuous *Pound Era* [by Hugh Kenner], which you were so kind to send me. Though I detest Pound and the costume jewelry of his verse, I must say Kenner's approach is very interesting particularly when he discusses other writers of that era[.][2]

Ambrose Bierce has this to say:

---

1 *Selected Letters: 1940 – 1977.* Harcourt Brace Jovanovich, 1989, p. 93.

2 Ibid. p. 514.

> I've not seen Ezra Pound's books, but the "Goodly Fere" was submitted to me in manuscript and highly commended by me. Some that were previously submitted e s c a p e d my approval by a wide margin.[3]

Pound's translation of "The Seafarer," however, stands out like an oil lamp in an otherwise destroyed city—destroyed, perhaps, by the fascists who Pound supported with a fidelity that suggests True Love. Anglo-Saxon (Old English) verse isn't held together by the kind of rhyme and meter that we may be used to; these techniques wouldn't be introduced into England until after the Norman Invasion of 1066. Rather, each line is characterized by an alliterative scheme—a particular consonant that predominates. And Pound deftly reproduces this.

"The Seafarer" simply must be read aloud—or, not so much read as *roared*. Do it in your garage or cellar, where you can get a good echo. Savor the rhythm. It's as savage as the landscape it describes.[4]

May I for my own self song's truth reckon,
Journey's jargon, how I in harsh days
Hardship endured oft.
Bitter breast-cares[5] have I abided,
Known on my keel many a care's hold,   5.
And dire sea-surge, and there I oft spent
Narrow nightwatch nigh the ship's head
While she tossed close to cliffs. Coldly afflicted,

---

3 *The Poems of Ambrose Bierce*. University of Nebraska Press, 1995, p. 188.

4 Those who are interested in learning more about this piece (its history, and the philosophy of translation animating it) should consult Timothy Billings's critical edition of Pound's *Cathay* (Fordham University Press, 2018).

5 breast-cares] Anxiety. This is an example of a kenning, a common Anglo-Saxon poetic device. A kenning is a compounded literary euphemism. Other examples in this text are "mood-lofty" (happy) [40], "flood-ways" (sea) [53], "whale's acre" (sea) [61], "sword-hate" (violence) [71], and "flesh-cover" (body) [96].

My feet were by frost benumbed.
Chill its chains are; chafing sighs   10.
Hew my heart round and hunger begot
Mere-weary mood. Lest man know not
That he on dry land loveliest liveth,
List how I, care-wretched, on ice-cold sea,
Weathered the winter, wretched outcast   15.
Deprived of my kinsmen;
Hung with hard ice-flakes, where hail-scur flew,
There I heard naught save the harsh sea
And ice-cold wave, at whiles the swan cries,
Did for my games the gannet's clamor,   20.
Sea-fowls' loudness was for me laughter,
The mews' singing all my mead-drink.
Storms, on the stone-cliffs beaten, fell on the stern
In icy feathers; full oft the eagle screamed
With spray on his pinion.   25.
                Not any protector
May make merry man faring needy.
This he little believes, who aye in winsome life
Abides 'mid burghers some heavy business,
Wealthy and wine-flushed, how I weary oft   30.
Must bide above brine.
Neareth nightshade, snoweth from north,
Frost froze the land, hail fell on earth then
Corn of the coldest. Nathless there knocketh now
The heart's thought that I on high streams   35.
The salt-wavy tumult traverse alone.
Moaneth alway my mind's lust
That I fare forth, that I afar hence
Seek out a foreign fastness.
For this there's no mood-lofty man over earth's midst,   40.
Not though he be given his good, but will have in his youth
    greed;
Nor his deed to the daring, nor his king to the faithful
But shall have his sorrow for sea-fare
Whatever his lord will.

He hath not heart for harping, nor in ring-having[6]   45.
Nor winsomeness to wife, nor world's delight
Nor any whit else save the wave's slash,
Yet longing comes upon him to fare forth on the water.
Bosque taketh blossom, cometh beauty of berries,
Fields to fairness, land fares brisker,   50.
All this admonisheth man eager of mood,
The heart turns to travel so that he then thinks
On flood-ways to be far departing.
Cuckoo[7] calleth with gloomy crying,

------

6   ring-having] A kenning for "wealth." In Anglo-Saxon literature, a king is often called a "ring-giver;" he distributes golden rings to his bravest and most loyal subjects. "Ring-having," therefore, would suggest not only wealth, but wealth bestowed by a king in exchange for demonstrations of the manly virtues.

7   cuckoo] The symbolism of the cuckoo is ancient and complex. In *Works and Days*, Hesiod discusses the circumstances under which a "late plougher" might make up for lost time:

> If you do plough late, this will be a remedy for you: when the cuckoo in the leaves of the oak tree first calls and gives pleasure to mortals on the boundless earth, if at that time Zeus rains on the third day without ceasing, neither exceeding the hoof-print of an ox nor falling short of it—in this way the late plougher will vie with the early plougher (Glenn W. Most, trans., Harvard University Press, 2018, p. 127).

The inauguration of the cuckoo's song is a milestone in the agricultural calendar, and therefore a matter connected with individual destiny. In *The Folklore of Birds*, Edward A. Armstrong elaborates on Hesiod's instructions: "From being associated with changes in the weather, the cuckoo acquired a reputation as forecaster of the weather and other events" (Collins, 1958).

In that beguiling work of pseudo-scholarship, *The White Goddess: a Historical Grammar of Poetic Myth*, Robert Graves writes:

> "Where?" is the question that should always weigh most heavily with poets who are burdened with the single poetic theme of life and death. As Professor Ifor Williams has pointed out, it is because the cuckoo utters its "Where?" so constantly that it is represented in early Welsh poetry as a kill-joy: "for 'cw-cw', pronounced 'ku-ku' means 'where? where?' It cries: 'Where is my love gone? Where are my lost companions?'" (Octagon Books, 1976, p. 251.)

And finally, the cuckoo is said to steal other birds' nests, thereby associating it with dispossession.

He singeth summerward, bodeth sorrow,   55.
The bitter heart's blood. Burgher knows not —
He the prosperous man — what some perform
Where wandering them widest draweth.
So that but now my heart burst from my breast-lock,
My mood 'mid the mere-flood,   60.
Over the whale's acre, would wander wide.
On earth's shelter cometh oft to me,
Eager and ready, the crying lone-flyer,
Whets for the whale-path the heart irresistibly,
O'er tracks of ocean; seeing that anyhow   65.
My lord deems to me this dead life
On loan and on land, I believe not
That any earth-weal eternal standeth
Save there be somewhat calamitous
That, ere a man's tide go, turn it to twain.   70.
Disease or oldness or sword-hate
Beats out the breath from doom-gripped body.
And for this, every earl whatever, for those speaking after—
Laud of the living, boasteth some last word,
That he will work ere he pass onward,   75.
Frame on the fair earth 'gainst foes his malice,
Daring ado, ...
So that all men shall honour him after
And his laud beyond them remain 'mid the English,
Aye, forever, a lasting life's-blast,   80.
Delight mid the doughty.
                          Days little durable,
And all arrogance of earthen riches,
There come now no kings nor Cæsars
Nor gold-giving lords like those gone.   85.
Howe'er in mirth most magnified,
Whoe'er lived in life most lordliest,
Drear all this excellence, delights undurable!
Waneth the watch, but the world holdeth.
Tomb hideth trouble. The blade is layed low.   90.
Earthly glory ageth and seareth.

No man at all going the earth's gait,
But age fares against him, his face paleth,
Grey-haired he groaneth, knows gone companions,
Lordly men are to earth o'ergiven,   95.
Nor may he then the flesh-cover, whose life ceaseth,
Nor eat the sweet nor feel the sorry,
Nor stir hand nor think in mid heart,
And though he strew the grave with gold,
His born brothers, their buried bodies   100.
Be an unlikely treasure hoard.

☙

"Love Among the Ruins"
ROBERT BROWNING

Robert Browning's heftiest contribution to English litera-
ture is a poetic form, the dramatic monologue, which is rather
like a Shakespearean soliloquy, but without the play on either
side of it. A good dramatic monologue implies the foregoing ac-
tion in the monologue itself, so that a complex plot and precise,
nuanced characterization are compressed into something that
can be read in one sitting.

Although this selection isn't a dramatic monologue, it
showcases Browning's formal mastery and dramatic control.

W here the quiet-colored end of evening smiles
        Miles and miles
On the solitary pastures where our sheep,
        Half-asleep,
Tinkle homeward through the twilight, stray or stop   5.
        As they crop,—
Was the site once of a city great and gay,
        (So they say)
Of our country's very capital, its prince

  Ages since   10.
Held his court in, gathered councils, wielding far
   Peace or war.

Now, the country does not even boast a tree,
   As you see,
To distinguish slopes of verdure,[8] certain rills   15.
   From the hills
Intersect and give a name to, (else they run
   Into one)
Where the domed and daring palace shot its spires
   Up like fires   20.
O'er the hundred-gated circuit of a wall
   Bounding all,
Made of marble, men might march on nor be pressed,
   Twelve abreast.

And such plenty and perfection, see, of grass   25.
   Never was!
Such a carpet as, this summertime, o'erspreads
   And embeds
Every vestige of the city, guessed alone,
   Stock or stone—   30.
Where a multitude of men breathed joy and woe
   Long ago;
Lust of glory pricked their hearts up, dread of shame
   Struck them tame;
And that glory and that shame alike, the gold   35.
   Bought and sold.

Now, the single little turret that remains
   On the plains,
By the caper[9] overrooted, by the gourd
   Overscored,   40.

---

8 verdure] Greenery.
9 caper] A shrub, *Capparis spinosa*.

While the patching houseleek's[10] head of blossom winks
 Through the chinks[11]—
Marks the basement whence a tower in ancient time
 Sprang sublime,
And a burning ring all round, the chariots traced   45.
 As they raced,
And the monarch and his minions and his dames
 Viewed the games.

And I know, while thus the quiet-colored eve
 Smiles to leave   50.
To their folding, all our many-tinkling fleece
 In such peace,
And the slopes and rills in undistinguished grey
 Melt away—
That a girl with eager eyes and yellow hair   55.
 Waits me there
In the turret, whence the charioteers caught soul
 For the goal,
When the king looked, where she looks now, breathless, dumb,
 Till I come.   60.

But he looked upon the city, every side,
 Far and wide,
All the mountains topped with temples, all the glades'
 Colonnades,

---

10 houseleek] "Any of various perennial plants constituting the genus *Sempervivum* (family *Crassulaceae*), comprising succulents native to southern Eurasia and North Africa, with a basal rosette of leaves and red, pink, or yellow flowers; esp. [...] *S. tectorum*, with pink flowers and a thick stem and leaves, formerly planted on the roofs of houses as protection against lightning" (*OED*).

11 chink] Fissure. The word dates to the late 1300s, and might have initially been an onomatopoetic imitating the sound that a hard material makes when it's fractured. The word first appears as an ethnic slur for the Chinese in the late 1800s. The *OED* suggests (but cannot establish definitively) that "chink" refers to the narrow eyes of East Asians, which resemble fissures.

All the causeys,[12] bridges, aqueducts,—and then,   65.
    All the men!
When I do come, she will speak not, she will stand,
    Either hand
On my shoulder, give her eyes the first embrace
    Of my face,   70.
Ere we rush, ere we extinguish sight and speech
    Each on each.

In one year they sent a million fighters forth
    South and north,
And they built their gods a brazen[13] pillar high   75.
    As the sky,
Yet reserved a thousand chariots in full force,—
    Gold, of course.
O heart! O blood that freezes, blood that burns!
    Earth's returns   80.
For whole centuries of folly, noise and sin!
    Shut them in,
With their triumphs and their glories and the rest!
    Love is best.

ᖇᖇ

"Were My Heart as Some Men's Are"
THOMAS CAMPION

Thomas Campion was the Leonard Cohen of the late sixteenth and early seventeenth centuries: an artist combining consummate musicianship with meticulous lyrical craft. His dexterity on the lute gave him a profound understanding of the music of language.

---

12 causeys] "A raised [roadway] formed on a mound, across a hollow, esp. low wet ground, a bog, marsh, lake, arm of the sea, etc.; a raised footway by the side of a carriage road liable to be submerged in wet weather" (*OED*).

13 brazen] Made of brass.

His *Observations in the Art of English Poesie* is a must-read for any aspiring songwriter.

W̲ere my heart as some men's are, thy errors would not
   move me,
But thy faults I curious find, and speak because I love thee:
Patience is a thing divine, and far, I grant, above me.

Foes sometimes befriend us more, our blacker deeds objecting,
Than th' obsequious bosom-guest with false respect affecting:
Friendship is the Glass[14] of Truth, our hidden stains detecting.

While I use of eyes enjoy, and inward light of reason,
Thy observer will I be and censor, but in season:[15]
Hidden mischief to conceal in State[16] and Love is treason.

∽

from *The Ballad of the White Horse*
G.K. CHESTERTON

G.K. Chesterton was one of those maddening creatures who managed to do everything, and to do it well. I'd call him the Swiss Army knife of the written word—but a Swiss Army knife does *nothing* well. He wrote fiction, literary criticism, philosophy, journalism, Christian apologetics, theology, polemics, and (of course) poetry.

The selection below comes from Book I of *The Ballad of the White Horse*, an epic poem about King Alfred the Great. The poem's most conspicuous strength is how comfortably it assumes the ancient epic register—this, in an age that witnessed the birth of air mail and the Chevrolet. The epic mode must be

---

14 Glass] Mirror.

15 but in season] At the appropriate time.

16 State] Affairs of state.

comfortably inhabited; otherwise, it becomes either an academic exercise or a silly affectation.

Before the gods that made the gods
Had seen their sunrise pass,
The White Horse[17] of the White Horse Vale
Was cut out of the grass.

Before the gods that made the gods   5.
Had drunk at dawn their fill,
The White Horse of the White Horse Vale
Was hoary on the hill.

Age beyond age on British land,   10.
Aeons on aeons gone,
Was peace and war in western hills,
And the White Horse looked on.

For the White Horse knew England
When there was none to know;   15.
He saw the first oar break or bend,
He saw heaven fall and the world end,
O God, how long ago.

For the end of the world was long ago—
And all we dwell today   20.
As children of some second birth,
Like a strange people left on earth
After a judgment day.

For the end of the world was long ago,
When the ends of the world waxed free,   25.

---

17   The White Horse]   An immense, stylized horse-shape gouged into a hilltop in Uffington, England, and accentuated with powdered white chalk packed into the gashes. It dates from the Iron Age.

When Rome was sunk in a waste of slaves,
And the sun drowned in the sea.

When Caesar's sun fell out of the sky[18]
And whoso hearkened right
Could only hear the plunging   30.
Of the nations in the night.

When the ends of the earth came marching in
To torch and cresset gleam,
And the roads of the world that lead to Rome
Were filled with faces that moved like foam,   35.
Like faces in a dream.

And men rode out of the eastern lands,
Broad river and burning plain;
Trees that are Titan flowers[19] to see,
And tiger skies, striped horribly,   40.
With tints of tropic rain.

Where Ind's[20] enameled peaks arise
Around that inmost one,
Where ancient eagles on its brink,
Vast as archangels, gather and drink   45.
The sacrament of the sun.

And men brake out of the northern lands,
Enormous lands alone,
Where a spell is laid upon life and lust
And the rain is changed to a silver dust   50.
And the sea to a great green stone.

And a Shape that moveth murkily

---

18 Caesar's sun…the sky] A major comet, circa 44 BC.
19 Titan flowers] A reference to the tremendous flower of the *Amorphophal-lus titanum*, which can reach ten feet in height.
20 Ind's] India's.

In mirrors of ice and night,
Hath blanched with fear all beasts and birds,
As death and a shock of evil words   55.
Blast a man's hair with white.

And the cry of the palms and the purple moons,
Or the cry of the frost and foam,
Swept ever around an inmost place,
And the din of distant race on race   60.
Cried and replied round Rome.

And there was death on the Emperor
And night upon the Pope;
And Alfred, hiding in deep grass,
Hardened his heart with hope.   65.

A sea-folk blinder than the sea
Broke all about his land,
But Alfred up against them bare
And gripped the ground and grasped the air,
Staggered, and strove to stand.   70.

He bent them back with spear and spade,
With desperate dyke and wall,
With foemen leaning on his shield
And roaring on him when he reeled;
And no help came at all.   75.

He broke them with a broken sword
A little towards the sea,
And for one hour of panting peace,
Ringed with a roar that would not cease,
With golden crown and girded fleece   80.
Made laws under a tree.

* * *21

---

21 This divider belongs to the full, original text.

The Northmen came about our land
A Christless chivalry:
Who knew not of the arch or pen,
Great, beautiful half-witted men   85.
From the sunrise and the sea.

Misshapen ships stood on the deep
Full of strange gold and fire,
And hairy men, as huge as sin
With hornéd heads, came wading in   90.
Through the long, low sea-mire.

Our towns were shaken of tall kings
With scarlet beards like blood;
The world turned empty where they trod,
They took the kindly Cross of God   95.
And cut it up for wood.

Their souls were drifting as the sea,
And all good towns and lands
They only saw with heavy eyes,
And broke with heavy hands.   100.

Their gods were sadder than the sea,
Gods of a wandering will,
Who cried for blood like beasts at night,
Sadly, from hill to hill.

They seemed as trees walking the earth,   105.
As witless and as tall,
Yet they took hold upon the heavens
And no help came at all.

They bred like birds in English woods,
They rooted like the rose,   110.
When Alfred came to Athelney[22]

_____

22 Athelney] A village in Somerset, England.

To hide him from their bows.

There was not English armor left,
Nor any English thing,
When Alfred came to Athelney   115.
To be an English king.

For earthquake swallowing earthquake
Uprent the Wessex tree;
The whirlpool of the pagan sway
Had swirled his sires as sticks away   120.
When a flood smites the sea.

And the great kings of Wessex
Wearied and sank in gore,
And even their ghosts in that great stress
Grew greyer and greyer, less and less,   125.
With the lords that died in Lyonesse[23]
And the king that comes no more.

And the God of the Golden Dragon
Was dumb upon his throne,
And the lord of the Golden Dragon   130.
Ran in the woods alone.

And if ever he climbed the crest of luck
And set the flag before,
Returning as a wheel returns,
Came ruin and the rain that burns,   135.
And all began once more.

And naught was left King Alfred
But shameful tears of rage,
In the island in the river
In the end of all his age.   140.

---

23 Lyonesse] A lost mythic kingdom in ancient British lore.

&cs;

"My Mary"
WILLIAM COWPER

Most clichés are true; that's how they become cliché in the first place. Absence really does make the heart grow fonder, politicians really are dishonest, and war really is hell. Exceptions are rare; one of them is that great poets are insane. The three heavy hitters of English verse, Chaucer, Shakespeare, and Milton, all had decent table manners, and they bathed, if not every day (the past is a smelly place), then certainly no less frequently than their peers.

The most conspicuous exception was William Blake, who really was out of his mind. Another is William Cowper. In "My Mary," he writes of his beloved:

> For could I view nor them nor thee,
> What sight worth seeing could I see?
> The sun would rise in vain for me,
> My Mary![24]

It's one of the ancient arrows in the amatory poet's rhetorical quiver that the girl is brighter than the sun. The luminescence of feminine beauty is so vital to the Western poetic imagination that entire forests have been felled to announce it. Female beauty risks undermining reforestation efforts worldwide.

However, "[t]he sun would rise in vain for me" suggests an actual despair that transcends the complications of the poet's love life. One senses that this is a familiar feeling for our narrator. The poet's despair breathes life into the cliché.

---

24 29-32.

The twentieth year is wellnigh past
Since first our sky was overcast;
Ah, would that this might be the last,
                My Mary!

Thy spirits have a fainter flow;   5.
I see thee daily weaker grow—
'Twas my distress that brought thee low,
                My Mary!

Thy needles, once a shining store,
For my sake restless heretofore,   10.
Now rust disused, and shine no more,
                My Mary!

For though thou gladly wouldst fulfil
The same kind office[25] for me still,
Thy sight now seconds[26] not thy will,   15.
                My Mary!

But well thou play'dst the housewife's part,
And all thy threads with magic art
Have wound themselves about this heart,
                My Mary!   20.

Thy indistinct expressions seem
Like language uttered in a dream;
Yet me they charm, whate'er the theme,
                My Mary!

Thy silver locks, once auburn bright,   25.
Are still more lovely in my sight

---

25 office] Responsibility.
26   second] To be the second person to agree to some proposal, thereby
endowing it with greater validity than it had when it could be dismissed as
the will of one man.

Than golden beams of orient[27] light,
      My Mary!

For could I view nor them nor thee,
What sight worth seeing could I see?   30.
The sun would rise in vain for me,
      My Mary!

Partakers of thy sad decline,
Thy hands their little force resign;
Yet, gently pressed, press gently mine,   35.
      My Mary!

Such feebleness of limbs thou prov'st
That now at every step thou mov'st,
Upheld by two; yet still thou lov'st,
      My Mary!   40.

And still to love, though pressed with ill,
In wintry age to feel no chill,
With me is to be lovely still,
      My Mary!

But ah! by constant heed I know   45.
How oft the sadness that I show
Transforms thy smiles to looks of woe,
      My Mary!

And should my future lot be cast
With much resemblance of the past,   50.
Thy worn-out heart will break at last,
      My Mary!

---

27 orient] Eastern, referring to Asia, and, by extension, things originating there. "Orient" implies mystery, opulence, exoticness, and vague menace.

∾

Three Poems
COUNTEE CULLEN

Countee Cullen deserved the reputation that ultimately went to Langston Hughes: "poet laureate" of the Harlem Renaissance, and therefore, by extension, most significant black poet in the United States. Hughes was a different sort of creature. In inventing a new style, which, he felt, was an organic outgrowth of the African American experience, Hughes removed himself from the sphere of recognized poetic standards, and thereby made an easier grading rubric for himself. Countee Cullen, however, attempted to climb the same mountain that poets have always attempted to climb. He went up against the best, and proved himself the equal of any lyric poet in English. His mastery was a blow against the racism that glibly assumed that blacks lacked aesthetic or intellectual nuance. Needless to say, Countee Cullen's poems never stopped a single lynching, but (in all fairness) nor did Langston Hughes's.

"Gods"
COUNTEE CULLEN

I fast and pray and go to church,
And put my penny in,
But God's not fooled by such slight tricks,
And I'm not saved from sin.

I cannot hide from Him the gods   5.
That revel in my heart,
Nor can I find an easy word
To tell them to depart:

God's alabaster turrets gleam

Too high for me to win,   10.
Unless He turns His face and lets
Me bring my own gods in.

"Uncle Jim"
COUNTEE CULLEN

"White folks is white," says uncle Jim;
"A platitude," I sneer;
And then I tell him so is milk,
And the froth upon his beer.

His heart walled up with bitterness,   5.
He smokes his pungent pipe,
And nods at me as if to say,
"Young fool, you'll soon be ripe!"

I have a friend who eats his heart
Always with grief of mine,   10.
Who drinks my joy as tipplers drain
Deep goblets filled with wine.

I wonder why here at his side,
Face-in-the-grass with him,
My mind should stray the Grecian urn[28]   15.

---

28 Grecian urn] A reference to Keats's "Ode on a Grecian Urn," in which
the narrator circumambulates the urn, describing the scenes carved into the
sides. He concludes:

> Thou, silent form, dost tease us out of thought
> As doth eternity: Cold Pastoral!
> When old age shall this generation waste,
> Thou shalt remain, in midst of other woe
> Than ours, a friend to man, to whom thou say'st,
> "Beauty is truth, truth beauty,—that is all
> Ye know on earth, and all ye need to know."

The urn represents an escape from pain, for it represents an escape from the

To muse on uncle Jim.

"Only the Polished Skeleton"
COUNTEE CULLEN

The heart has need of some deceit
To make its pistons rise and fall;
For less than this it would not beat.
Nor flush the sluggish vein at all.

With subterfuge and fraud the mind   5.
Must fend and parry thrust for thrust,
With logic brutal and unkind
Beat off the onslaughts of the dust.

Only the polished skeleton,
Of flesh relieved and pauperized,   10.
Can rest at ease and think upon
The worth of all it so despised.

☙

Three Poems
WALTER DE LA MARE

Walter de la Mare began writing in the late Victorian peri-
od, continued through the Edwardian interlude, witnessed the

---

present. This liberation points toward a reality in which Beauty and Truth
are unified. Uncle Jim must be somehow "untrue" because he speaks in plat-
itudes, which aren't beautiful. Beauty (and therefore, Truth) is to be found in
the louche bohemia which the narrator has chosen, sprawled upon the grass
with his same-sex lover. But the narrator's self-transplanting seems not fully
to have "taken;" he's assumed the burden of a lie (of a milieu that isn't properly
his) so that he might access Truth. And the narrator half-acknowledges that
his real birthright, his real inheritance, comes not from Keats, but from his
half-literate uncle.

First World War, witnessed the Second World War, and died during the year that Elvis Presley released "Heartbreak Hotel." Such a long life, spread across such an eventful 83 years, isn't without thorns. De la Mare was considered an out-of-touch dotard by the time he was in his forties, at which point he still had another four decades to go.

For the Modernists (T.S. Eliot and friends), Walter de la Mare represented everything allegedly dull and sclerotic that must be transcended. De la Mare was "respectable" in the most damning way. To report that you'd been raised in a home where Walter de la Mare was beloved was to imply that you'd been forced to overcome high-grade bourgeois stultification. Vladimir Nabokov defended him, but Nabokov was nearly alone among top-tier men of letters.

To the extent that I have my finger on the pulse of anything, it does appear that Walter de la Mare's poetic *œuvre* is just beginning to stimulate something resembling appreciation. In other words, he was always one hell of a poet, and folks are now beginning to see it.

"Rose"
WALTER DE LA MARE

T hree centuries now are gone
Since Thomas Campion
Left men his airs,[29] his verse, his heedful prose.
Few other memories
Have we of him, or his,   5.
And, of his sister, none, but that her name was Rose.

Woodruff,[30] far moschatel[31]
May the more fragrant smell

---

29 airs] Tunes.
30 Woodruff] *Galium odoratum.*
31 moschatel] *Adoxa moschatellina.*

When into brittle dust their blossoming goes.
His, too, a garden sweet,   10.
Where rarest beauties meet,
And, as a child, he shared them with this Rose.

Faded, past changing, now,
Cheek, mouth, and childish brow.
Where, too, her phantom wanders no man knows.   15.
Yet, when in undertone
That eager lute pines on,
Pleading of things he loves, it sings of Rose.

"To E.T.: 1917"[32]
WALTER DE LA MARE

You sleep too well—too far away,
For sorrowing word to soothe or wound;
Your very quiet seems to say
How longed-for a peace you have found.

Else, had not death so lured you on,   5.
You would have grieved—'twixt joy and fear—
To know how my small loving son
Had wept for you, my dear.

"For All the Grief"
WALTER DE LA MARE

For all the grief I have given with words

---

32   1917] Shorthand for the Great War. To write a funerary poem and mention 1917 in the title is to do more than imply that the poem's subject was killed in battle.

May now a few clear flowers blow,[33]
In the dust, and the heat, and the silence of birds,
Where the friendless go.

For the thing unsaid that heart asked of me   5.
Be a dark, cool water calling—calling
To the footsore, benighted, solitary,
When the shadows are falling.

O, be beauty for all my blindness,
A moon in the air where the weary wend,   10.
And dews burdened with loving-kindness
In the dark of the end.

ᖇ

"To His Mistress Going to Bed"
JOHN DONNE

John Donne was a playboy who developed into an An-
glican priest. In this latter incarnation, he eroticized the divine
as, in his earlier incarnation, he'd intellectualized the erotic. He
belonged to the "metaphysical" movement in poetry, which was
characterized (among other things) by complex similes and
metaphors, called "conceits." Donne understood Creation itself
as a conceit—a mechanism in which everything is connected
to everything else: order and disorder, love and hate, certain-
ty and doubt, faith and fear, the divine and the secular, mercy
and justice, the sublime and the quotidian, the aethereal and the
physical, the timeless and the time-bound, the religious-ecstatic
and the sexual-ecstatic.

I've been teaching Donne for years. Although my female
students have found some of his amatory poems appealing,
their response to the piece reproduced here is almost always
negative. I suspect that the zeitgeist is to blame. We elevate fe-
male sexual desire to the status of the sacred. Ours is a world

---

33 blow] Bloom.

that encourages the composition of poems like "A Yelp Review of my Cunt."[34] However, the male sexual appetite, which is expressed nowhere better than in "To His Mistress Going to Bed," remains a great taboo.

Come, madam, come; all rest my powers defy.
Until I labor, I in labor lie.
The foe, oft-times having the foe in sight,
Is tired with standing though he never fight.
Off with that girdle, like heaven's zone[35] glistering,   5.
But a far fairer world encompassing.
Unpin that spangled breastplate which you wear,
That th'eyes of busy[36] fools may be stopped there.
Unlace yourself, for that harmonious chime,
Tells me from you, that now it is bed time.   10.
Off with that happy busk, which I envy,
That still can be, and still can stand so nigh.
Your gown going off, such beauteous state[37] reveals,
As when from flowery meads[38] th'hill's shadow steals.
Off with that wiry coronet and show   15.
The hairy diadem which on you doth grow.
Now off with those shoes, and then safely tread

---

34 See Chapter 59.

35   zone] Among the *OED*'s definitions: [1] "Any region extending around the earth and comprised between definite limits, e.g. between two parallels of latitude. Also [in astronomy] applied to a similar region in the heavens or on the surface of a planet or the sun;" "A girdle or belt, as a part of dress. (Chiefly poetic.) Hence, any encircling band;" [3] "The girdle of Orion."

36   busy] Among the *OED*'s definitions: [1] "[A]ctive in what does not concern one; prying, inquisitive, gossiping; meddlesome, officious, interfering;" [2] "Constantly or habitually occupied;" [3] "Solicitous, concerned; anxious, uneasy, troubled; careful, attentive. Of desires, prayers, etc.: earnest, eager, persistent; (of suffering) severe, continual."

37   state] Condition, but also a polity; in line 27, Donne will compare his beloved to a piece of real estate.

38   meads] Meadows.

In this love's hallowed temple: this soft bed.
In such white robes heaven's angels used to be
Received by men. Thou angel bringst with thee   20.
A heaven like Mahomet's paradise.[39] And though
Ill spirits walk in white, we easily know,
By this these angels from an evil sprite:
Those set our hairs, but these, our flesh, upright.
    License my roving hands, and let them go   25.
Before, behind, between, above, below.
O my America! my new-found-land,
My kingdom, safeliest when with one man manned.
My mine of precious stones, my empirie;[40]
How blest am I in this discovering thee!   30.
To enter in these bonds is to be free.
Then where my hand is set, my seal shall be.
    Full nakedness! All joys are due to thee;
As souls unbodied, bodies unclothed must be
To taste whole joys. Gems which you women use   35.
Are like Atalanta's balls,[41] cast in men's views,

---

39 Mahomet's paradise] This is an allusion to the Muslim imagination of heaven, which purportedly involves fleshly delights.

40 empirie] A derivative of "empire." Donne catalogues the ways in which he will master his beloved: he will penetrate her as a miner penetrates the earth (29); he will conquer her as a warrior conquers a kingdom (28); he will discover and exploit her as Europeans discover and exploit the New World (27). According to the *OED*, however, "empirie" is also associated with "empiricism;" the etymology is anchored in a Greek word referring to a "practice founded upon experiment and observation, especially in medicine[.]" Donne will subject his beloved to his gaze, thereby rendering her as vulnerable as anything that has come beneath scientific scrutiny. European engagement with the New World had started only recently, and what we might recognize as science was still in its infancy. Donne is therefore surveying "current events" for fresh paradigms to help him conceptualize and delineate the nature of his lust.

41 Atalanta's balls] I can't do better than Smithsonian Education, which sketches the story thusly:

> Atalanta was the fastest person in Greece, but she was in no hurry to get married. [...] She loved racing and games and the outdoors. [...] One day, [...] Hippomenes asked for her hand in marriage. Atalanta liked him, but she told him that she would marry him only if he could beat her in a race. She knew that

That when a fool's eye lighteth on a gem,
His earthly soul may covet theirs, not them.
Like pictures, or like books' gay coverings made
For laymen, are all women thus arrayed.   40.
Themselves are mystic books which only we
(Whom their imputed grace will dignify)
Must see revealed. Then since that I may know
As liberally as to a Midwife, show
Thyself. Cast all, yea, this white linen hence.   45.
There is no penance due to innocence.
To teach thee, I am naked first; why then
What needst thou have more covering than a man.[42]

ᘒ

"Full Moon"
ROBERT GRAVES

Robert Graves was one of the "World War One poets"—
that cohort of English soldier-lyricists who so vividly chroni-
cled the Great War, capturing both the perverse novelty of
mechanized slaughter and war's eternal tragedy. Graves was un-
like many of his comrades, such as Isaac Rosenberg or Wilfred
Owen. Not only did he survive the war (despite, at one point,
having been declared dead, and thrown onto a heap of corps-
es), but he had a long, distinguished literary career, lasting un-

---

could never happen. Hippomenes looked for help from [...]
Aphrodite. The goddess gave him three beautiful golden apples
from her garden. [...] [During the race, Hippomenes] took one
of the apples from the pocket of his tunic and threw it ahead
of [Atalanta]. She saw it rolling and stopped to pick it up. Hip-
pomenes threw another apple. She stopped and picked it up. He
threw the third apple. She stopped, she picked it up, he passed
her, and he won.

42 What needst...than a man] This rhetorical question can be read in two
(equally saucy) ways, which may be paraphrased thusly: [1] "You can 'wear'
me—a naked man—as if I were a garment; this is the only garment you
require." [2] "You don't need any more clothes than I'm wearing—and I'm
naked."

til his death in 1985. In addition to poetry, Graves wrote war memoirs, historical novels, works of classical scholarship, and a bewitching, faintly deranged study of comparative folklore entitled *The White Goddess: An Historical Grammar of Poetic Myth.*

When compared with his contemporaries (including the Modernist trinity: T.S. Eliot, Ezra Pound, and James Joyce), Robert Graves can seem awfully old fashioned. He uses rhyme and meter, and tends to make sense. Reactionary stuff, that.

But an honest, generous-spirited critic must admit that Graves's poetry is free of the inflated rhetoric, prolixity, and general bloatedness that Modernism found so objectionable. His work is generally clean and purposeful.

Unjust prejudices often withstand common sense, however. My teacher Robert Creeley served as a private tutor to Graves's children in the 1950s, when they were all living in Deià, Majorca. In a 1953 letter to Irving Layton, Creeley confessed:

> I find his poems very damn dull, and slight, finally. Likewise […], there is a hell of a pretension in the address. I am by no means a sober man, […] but do get bugged by a cute flippancy when I can't see the call for such.[43]

Irving Layton replied:

> I found your remarks about Graves interesting. Reluctantly, I'm forced to agree with you about the quality of his poetry. Little spontaneity in it, smells too much of the midnight oil, has too conscious an air about it.[44]

I love Creeley and Layton. But I also love "the midnight oil;" I love the dignity of poems that eschew spontaneity in favor of lucidity and competence. And I imagine that the midnight oil was burning brightly when Graves wrote "Full Moon."

---

43 Ekbert Faas and Sabrina Reed, ed. *Irving Layton and Robert Creeley: The Complete Correspondence, 1953 – 1978*. McGill-Queen's University Press, 1990, p. 10.

44 Ibid., p. 14.

As I walked out that sultry night,
I heard the stroke of One.
The moon attained to her full height,
Stood beaming like the Sun:
She exorcised the ghostly wheat   5.
To mute assent in Love's defeat,
Whose tryst had now begun.

The fields lay sick beneath my tread,
A tedious owlet cried;
The nightingale above my head   10.
With this or that replied—
Like man and wife who nightly keep
Inconsequent debate in sleep
As they dream side by side.

Your phantom wore the moon's cold mask,   15.
My phantom wore the same;
Forgetful of the feverish task
In hope of which they came,
Each image held the other's eyes
And watched a grey distraction rise   20.
To cloud the eager flame—

To cloud the eager flame of love,
To fog the shining gate:
They held the tyrannous queen above
Sole mover of their fate,   25.
They glared as marble statues glare
Across the tessellated stair
Or down the halls of state.

And now warm earth was Arctic sea,
Each breath came dagger-keen;   30.
Two bergs of glinting ice were we,
The broad moon sailed between;

There swam the mermaids, tailed and finned,
And Love went by upon the wind
As though it had not been.   35.

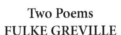

Two Poems
FULKE GREVILLE

Cælica IV.
FULKE GREVILLE

Y ou little stars that live in skies
And glory in Apollo's glory,
In whose aspècts conjoinèd lies
The heaven's will and nature's story,
Joy to be likened to those eyes,   5.
Which eyes make all eyes glad or sorry;
For when you force thoughts from above,
These overrule your force by love.

And thou, O Love, which in these eyes
Hast married Reason with Affection,   10.
And made them saints of Beauty's skies,
Where joys are shadows of perfection,
Lend me thy wings that I may rise
Up, not by worth, but thy election;
For I have vowed in strangest fashion   15.
To love and never seek compassion.

Cælica XXIX.
FULKE GREVILLE

Faction, that ever dwells
In courts[45] where wit[46] excels,
Hath set defiance.
Fortune[47] and Love have sworn
That they were never born   5.
Of one alliance.

Cupid, that doth aspire
To be god of desire,
Swears he gives laws:
That where his arrows hit   10.
Some joy, some sorrow it—
Fortune, no cause.

Fortune swears weakest hearts,
The books of Cupid's arts,
Turn with her wheel.[48]   15.
Senses themselves shall prove
Venture hath place in love.
Ask them that feel.

This discord it begot,
Atheists, that honor not   20.
Nature, thought good.
Fortune should ever dwell
In courts, where wits excel.[49]

---

45 courts] Royal courts.
46 wit] Not merely a sense of humor, but an intelligent and sociable sensibility.
47 fortune] Luck.
48 her wheel] In the iconography of the time, Fortune was pictured as a wheel, spinning randomly, dispensing destinies to people without any correspondence to their own decisions.
49 In courts, where wits excel] The placement of the comma suggests that courts are the places "where wits excel." Line two, however, lacks the comma:

Love keep the wood.[50]

Thus to the wood went I   25.
With love to live and die;[51]
Fortune's forlorn.
Experience of my youth
Thus makes me think the truth
In desert born.   30.

My saint is dear to me.
Myra herself is she,
She fair and true—
Myra that knows to move
Passions of love with love.   35.
Fortune, Adieu.

∿

Three Poems
THOMAS HARDY

Thomas Hardy's engagingly grim vision of the world, articulated in thousands of pages of fiction and poetry, did to Victorian sentimentalism what an elephant gun would do to a tufted titmouse. Philip Larkin, the twentieth century's curmudgeon laureate, claimed Hardy as a crucial influence.

"In courts where wit excels" suggesting that the narrator is referring to a particular court where wit excels, in contrast to the others, where it apparently doesn't.

50 wood] The forest.

51 Thus to the wood went I / With love to live and die] Unclear. Is he saying that he went lovingly into the forest to live and die, or is he describing a personification of love—a companion with whom he's retreating into the forest?

"The Levelled Churchyard"
THOMAS HARDY

"O passenger,[52] pray list[53] and catch
Our sighs and piteous groans,
Half stifled in this jumbled patch
Of wrenched memorial stones!

"We, late-lamented, resting here,   5.
Are mixed to human jam,
And each to each exclaims in fear:
'I know not which I am!'

"The wicked people have annexed[54]
The verses on the good;   10.
A roaring drunkard sports the text
Teetotal Tommy should!

"Where we are huddled none can trace,
And if our names remain,
They pave some path or porch or place   15.
Where we have never lain!

"There's not a modest maiden elf
But dreads the final trumpet,
Lest half of her should rise herself,
And half some sturdy strumpet!   20.

"From restorations of Thy fane,[55]
From smoothings of Thy sward,[56]

---

52 passenger] Passerby.
53 list] Listen.
54 annexed] To be pronounced as an iamb: "an-NEXED."
55 fane] Temple.
56 sward] Lawn.

From zealous Churchmen's pick and plane[57]
Deliver us O Lord! Amen!"

"After Schiller"[58]
THOMAS HARDY

Knight, a true sister-love
This heart retains;
Ask me no other love,
That way lie pains!

Calm must I view thee come,   5.
Calm see thee go;
Tale-telling tears of thine
I must not know!

"Neutral Tones"
THOMAS HARDY

We stood by a pond that winter day,
And the sun was white, as though chidden of God,
And a few leaves lay on the starving sod;
– They had fallen from an ash, and were gray.

Your eyes on me were as eyes that rove   5.
Over tedious riddles of years ago;
And some words played between us to and fro
On which lost the more by our love.

The smile on your mouth was the deadest thing

---

57 pick and plane] As in the tools.
58 Schiller] Friedrich Schiller, German poet.

Alive enough to have strength to die;   10.
And a grin of bitterness swept thereby
Like an ominous bird a-wing….

Since then, keen lessons that love deceives,
And wrings with wrong, have shaped to me
Your face, and the God-curst sun, and a tree,   15.
And a pond edged with grayish leaves.

Seven Poems
ROBERT HERRICK

In "So Long," Walt Whitman writes: "[T]his is no book[;] / Who touches this touches a man[.]" Whitman is telling us that his book is neither a bundle of discrete poems nor a chronical of a life; rather, it *is* a life—a living thing invested with the variety, passion, contradiction, and ambiguity found in any person.

Robert Herrick's body of work is similar. Flip through *The Poems of Robert Herrick*,[59] and you'll discover piety and iconoclasm, passion and frivolity, spiritualized love and downright lust.

However, Herrick differs from Whitman in one crucial respect. Whitman's poems assume an unbounded shape and vernacular tone reflecting his ideas about human nature and democracy. Herrick goes in the opposite direction, with formally tight epigrams. This combination of formal tightness and human openness is what ostensibly endeared Herrick to Robert Creeley, whose sense of the self was open and exploratory, but who remained, temperamentally, a sort of formal minimalist.

---

59 Oxford University Press, 1965.

"The Departure of the Good Dæmon"[60]
ROBERT HERRICK

What can I do in poetry
Now the good spirit's gone from me?
Why, nothing now, but lonely sit,
And over-read what I have writ.

"To Sylvia"
ROBERT HERRICK

I am holy while I stand
Circum-crossed by thy pure hand.
But, when that is gone again,
I, as others, am profane.

"To Julia"
ROBERT HERRICK

Julia, when thy Herrick dies,
Close thou up thy poet's eyes;
And his last breath, let it be
Taken in by none but thee.

---

60 Dæmon] A god, not to be confused with "demon."

"To Music, to Becalm a Sweet-Sick Youth"
ROBERT HERRICK

Charms that call down the moon from out her sphere:
On this sick youth work your enchantments here.
Bind up his senses with your numbers[61] so
As to entrance his pain or cure his woe.
Fall gently, gently, and awhile him keep,   5.
Lost in the civil wilderness of sleep.
That done, then let him, dispossessed of pain,
Like to a slumbering bride, awake again.

"The Eyes"
ROBERT HERRICK

'Tis a known principal in war:
The eyes be first that conquered are.[62]

"The Difference Betwixt Kings and Subjects"
ROBERT HERRICK

Twixt kings and subjects there's this mighty odds:
Subjects are taught by men; kings, by the gods.

---

61 numbers] Poetry or song.

62 This seems to be taken from Tacitus' *Germania*, which was quoted in Edward Gibbon's *Decline and Fall of the Roman Empire*, Ch. 12:

> As for the Harii, they are superior in strength to the other peoples I have just mentioned, and they pander to their savage instincts by choice of trickery and time. They black their shields and dye their bodies black and choose pitch dark nights for their battles. The terrifying shadow of such a fiendish army inspires a mortal panic, for no enemy can stand so strange and devilish a sight. Defeat in battle always begins with the eyes.

"Another Upon Her Weeping"
ROBERT HERRICK

She by the river sate, and sitting there,
She wept, and made it deeper by a tear.

❧

"The Wreck of the Deutschland"
*To the happy memory of five Franciscan Nuns,
exiles by the Falck Laws, drowned between
midnight & morning of December 7, 1875*
GERARD MANLEY HOPKINS

Gerard Manley Hopkins is an extreme rarity: a superb poet without any contemporary audience. A Jesuit priest, Hopkins made no significant effort to publish his work. Indeed, it was only a handful of intimate friends who knew that he wrote at all—and they were never particularly encouraging. After his death at 44, the consensus among his friends was that he'd wasted his life—that he'd never been cut out for the priesthood, and that his poems were an idiosyncratic mess. Despite this isolation, Hopkins's poems never became pathological. This is because he was always looking outward, not only toward God, but toward God's signature in the commonplace.

In "The Wreck of the Deutschland," Hopkins attempts to coerce the English language into doing the impossible. There's a weird dialectic at work: the poem represents the volatile, ever-pulsing, self-renewing confrontation between the poet's aggressive will to say the unsayable and the protest mounted by Language herself.

The structure is curious. An introductory prayer occupies nearly 30% of the poem; it isn't until the passage of 80 lines that we are introduced to the poem's subject. As with so much of Hopkins, it's bizarre and marvelous.

I object to the poem only in one respect. In *The Claude Glass: Use and Meaning of the Black Mirror in Western Art*, Arnaud Maillet writes:

> A specialist in physiological optics, [Hermann von] Helmholtz worked to define the notion of brightness. In fact, the reality the painter would represent presents extreme differences in brightness, that is, in luminosities; put another way, there are infinite tones for a single color on a scale from dark to light. But the colors available on an artist's palette cannot offer such a wide variety of tones: the visual impression, the brightness of a sheet of paper, even in full sunlight, cannot equal the luminosity of the sun itself. On the other hand, the human eye is sensitive to the relations between different levels of brightness; these are therefore experienced not absolutely but relatively. The artist must then seek to produce on the eye of the spectator of average sensitivity the dazzling light of the sun as well as the repose of moonlight. It is a question no longer of copying reality but of giving a "translation of his impression into another scale of sensitiveness, which belongs to a different degree of impressibility of the observing eye."[63]

In Hopkins, the consistent, nearly hysterical vigor of "tone" is well suited to shorter works, which rely upon concentration. In something as long as "The Wreck of the Deutschland," however, the dazzling brightness might be lost. Since everything is so dazzlingly bright, few things are permitted to stand out by means of contrast.

But it seems unsportsmanlike to complain about too much genius in a poem.

Note: I have decided not to define obscure words, since to define them would suggest that they are the only potential barriers to understanding. You can know the etymology of every single word in the poem, and still stand dumbstruck in its presence. It's so overwhelmingly mysterious, so mysteriously over-

---

63 Zone Books, 2009, pp. 117-118.

whelming, that I suggest you simply read aloud, and immerse yourself in the thing. I've been thinking about this poem for over twenty years, and I think I'll need another twenty before I finally "get it."

Part the First

T hou mastering me
God! giver of breath and bread;
World's strand, sway of the sea;
Lord of living & dead;
Thou hast bound bones & veins in me, fastened me flesh,   5.
And after it álmost únmade, what with dread,
Thy doing: & dost thou touch me afresh?
Over again I feel thy finger & find theé.

I did say yes
O at lightning & lashed rod;   10.
Thou heardst me truer than tongue confess
Thy terror, O Christ, O God;
Thou knowest the walls, altar & hour & night:
The swoon of a heart that the sweep & the hurl of thee trod
Hard down with a horror of height: 15.
And the midriff astrain with leaning of, laced with fire of
    stress.

The frown of his face
Before me, the hurtle of hell
Behind, where, where was a, where was a place?
I whirled out wings that spell   20.
And fled with a fling of the heart to the heart of the Host.
My heart, but you were dovewinged, I can tell,
Carrier-witted, I am bold to boast,
To flash from the flame to the flame then, tower from the grace
    to the grace.

I am soft sift   25.
In an hourglass—at the wall
Fast, but mined with a motion, a drift,
And it crowds & it combs to the fall;
I steady as a water in a well, to a poise, to a pane,
But roped with, always, all the way down from the tall   30.
Fells or flanks of the voel, a vein
Of the gospel proffer, a pressure, a principle, Christ's gift.

I kiss my hand
To the stars, lovely-asunder
Starlight, wafting him out of it; and   35.
Glow, glory in thunder;
Kiss my hand to the dappled-with-damson west:
Since, tho' he is under the world's splendor & wonder,
His mystery must be instressed, stressed;
For I greet him the days I meet him, & bless when I
       understand.   40.

Not out of his bliss
Springs the stress felt
Nor first from heaven (and few know this)
Swings the stroke dealt—
Stroke & a stress that stars & storms deliver,   45.
That guilt is hushed by, hearts are flushed by & melt—
But it rides time like riding a river
(And here the faithful waver, the faithless fable & miss).

It dates from day
Of his going in Galilee;   50.
Warm-laid grave of a womb-life grey;
Manger, maiden's knee;
The dense and the driven Passion, & frightful sweat:
Thence the discharge of it, there its swelling to be,
Tho' felt before, though in high flood yet—   55.
What none would have known of it, only the heart, being hard
       at bay,

Is out with it! Oh,
We lash with the best or worst
Word last! How a lush-kept plush-capped sloe
Will, mouthed to flesh-burst,   60.
Gush!—flush the man, the being with it, sour or sweet,
Brim, in a flash, full!—Hither then, last or first,
To hero of Calvary, Christ's feet—
Never ask if meaning it, wanting it, warned of it—men go.

Be adored among men,   65.
God, three-numberéd form;
Wring thy rebel, dogged in den,
Man's malice, with wrecking & storm.
Beyond saying sweet, past telling of tongue,
Thou art lightning & love, I found it, a winter & warm;   70.
Father & fondler of heart thou hast wrung:
Hast thy dark descending & most art merciful then.

With an anvil-ding
And with fire in him forge thy will
Or rather, rather then, stealing as Spring   75.
Through him, melt him but master him still:
Whether át ónce, as once at a crash Paul,
Or as Austin, a lingering-out sweet skill,
Make mercy in all of us, out of us all
Mastery, but be adored, but be adored king.   80.

Part the Second

"Some find me a sword; some
The flange & the rail; flame,
Fang, or flood" goes Death on drum,
And storms bugle his fame.
But wé dréam we are rooted in earth—Dust!   85.
Flesh falls within sight of us, we, though our flower the same,

Wave with the meadow, forget that there must
The sour scythe cringe, & the blear share come.

On Saturday sailed from Bremen,
American-outward-bound,   90.
Take settler & seamen, tell men with women,
Two hundred souls in the round—
O Father, not under thy feathers nor ever as guessing
The goal was a shoal, of a fourth the doom to be drowned;
Yet díd the dark side of the bay of thy blessing   95.
Not vault them, the million of rounds of thy mercy not reeve
    even them in?[64]

Into the snows she sweeps,
Hurling the haven behind,
The Deutschland, on Sunday; & so the sky keeps,
For the infinite air is unkind,   100.
And the sea flint-flake, black-backed in the regular blow,
Sitting Eastnortheast, in cursed quarter, the wind;
Wiry & white-fiery & whírlwind-swivellèd snow
Spins to the widow-making unchilding unfathering deeps.

She drove in the dark to leeward,   105.
She struck—not a reef or a rock
But the combs of a smother of sand: night drew her
Dead to the Kentish Knock;
And she beat the bank down with her bows & the ride of her
    keel:
The breakers rolled on her beam with ruinous shock;   110.
And canvass & compass, the whorl & the wheel
Idle forever to waft her or wind her with, these she endured.

Hope had grown grey hairs,
Hope had mourning on,
Trenched with tears, carved with cares,   115.
Hope was twelve hours gone;

---

64 This was the poem's first stanza that Hopkins wrote.

And frightful a nightfall folded rueful a day
Nor rescue, only rocket & light ship, shone,
And lives at last were washing away:
To the shrouds they took,—they shook in the hurling &
    horrible airs.   120.

One stirred from the rigging to save
The wild woman-kind below,
With a rope's end round the man, handy & brave—
He was pitched to his death at a blow,
For all his dreadnought breast & braids of thew: 125.
They could tell him for hours, dandled the to & fro
Through the cobbled foam-fleece. What could he do
With the burl of the fountains of air, buck & the flood of the
    wave?

They fought with God's cold—
And they could not & fell to the deck   130.
(Crushed them) or water (and drowned them) or rolled
With the sea-romp over the wreck.
Night roared, with the heart-break hearing a heart-broke
    rabble,
The woman's wailing, the crying of child without check—
Till a lioness arose breasting the babble,   135.
A prophetess towered in the tumult, a virginal tongue told.

Ah, touched in your bower of bone
Are you! turned for an exquisite smart,
Have you! make words break from me here all alone,
Do you!—mother of being in me, heart.   140.
O unteachably after evil, but uttering truth,
Why, tears! is it? tears; such a melting, a madrigal start!
Never-eldering revel & river of youth,
What can it be, this glee? the good you have there of your
    own?

Sister, a sister calling   145.

A master, her master & mine!—
And the inboard seas run swirling & hawling;
The rash smart sloggering brine
Blinds her; but shé that weather sees óne thing, one;
Has óne fetch ín her: she rears herself to divine   150.
Ears, & the call of the tall nun
To the men in the tops & the tackle rode over the storm's
    brawling.

She was first of a five & came
Of a coifèd sisterhood.
(O Deutschland, double a desperate name!   155.
O world wide of its good!
But Gertrude, lily, & Luther, are two of a town,
Christ's lily & beast of the waste wood:
From life's dawn it is drawn down,
Abel is Cain's brother and breasts they have sucked the same.)
    160.

Loathed for a love men knew in them,
Banned by the land of their birth,
Rhine refused them, Thames would ruin them;
Surf, snow, river & earth
Gnashed: but thou art above, thou Orion of light;   165.
Thy unchancelling poising palms were weighing the worth,
Thou martyr-master: in thy sight
Storm flakes were scroll-leaved flowers, lily showers—sweet
    heaven was astrew in them.

Five! the finding & sake   170.
And cipher of suffering Christ.
Mark, the mark is of man's make
And the word of it Sacrificed.
But he scores it in scarlet himself on his own bespoken,
Before-time-taken, dearest prizèd & priced—   175.
Stigma, signal, cinquefoil token
For lettering of the lamb's fleece, ruddying of the rose-flake.

Joy fall to thee, father Francis,
Drawn to the life that died;
With the gnarls of the nails in thee, niche of the lance, his   180.
Lovescape crucified
And seal of his seraph-arrival! & these thy daughters
And five-livèd & leavèd favor & pride,
Are sisterly sealed in wild waters,
To bathe in his fall-gold mercies, to breathe in his all-fire
glances.   185.

Away in the loveable west,
On a pastoral forehead of Wales,
I was under a roof here, I was at rest,
And they the prey of the gales;
She to the black-about air, to the breaker, the thickly   190.
Falling flakes, to the throng that catches and quails
Was calling "O Christ, Christ, come quickly":
The cross to her she calls Christ to her, christens her wildworst
    Best.

The majesty! what did she mean?
Breathe, arch & original Breath.   195.
Is it lóve in her of the béing as her lóver had béen?
Breathe, body of lovely Death.
They were else-minded then, altogether, the men
Wóke thee with a we are périshing in the wéather of
    Gennésaréth.
Or ís it that she cried for the crown then,   200.
The keener to come at the comfort for feeling the combating
    keen?

For how to the heart's cheering
The down-dugged ground-hugged grey
Hovers off, the jay-blue heavens appearing
Of pied & peeled May!   205.
Blue-beating & hoary-glow height; or night, still higher,
With belled fire & the moth-soft Milky way,

What by your measure is the heaven of desire,
The treasure never eyesight got, nor was ever guessed what for
    the hearing?

Nó, but it was nót these.   210.
The jading & jar of the cart,
Time's tásking, it is fathers that asking for ease
Of the sodden-with-its-sorrowing heart,
Not danger, electrical horror; then further it finds
The appealing of the Passion is tenderer in prayer apart: 215.
Other, I gather, in measure her mind's
Burden, in wind's burly & beat of endragonèd seas.

But how shall I...make me room there:
Reach me a...Fancy, come faster—
Strike you the sight of it? look at it loom there,   220.
Thing that she...there then! the Master,
Ipse, the only one, Christ, King, Head:
He was to cure the extremity where he had cast her;
Do, deal, lord it with living and dead;
Let him ride, her pride, in his triumph, dispatch and have done
    with his doom there.   225.

Ah! there was a heart right!
There was single eye!
Read the unshapeable shock night
And knew the who & the why;
Wording it how but by him that present & past,   230.
Heaven & earth are word of, worded by?—
The Simon Peter of a soul! to the blast
Tárpéían-fast, but a blown beacon of light.

Jesu, heart's light,
Jesu, maid's son,   235.
What was the feast followed the night
Thou hadst glory of this nun?—
Féast of the óne wóman withóut stáin.

For so conceivèd, so to conceive thee is done;
But here was heart-throe, birth of a brain,   240.
Word, that heard & kept thee & uttered thee óutríght.

Well, shé has thée for the pain, for the
Patience; but pity of the rest of them!
Heart, go & bleed at a bitterer vein for the
Comfortless unconfessed of them—   245.
No not uncomforted: lovely-felicitous Providence
Fínger of a ténder of, O of a féathery délicacy, the bréast of the
Maiden could obey so, be a bell to, ring óf it, and
Startle the poor sheep back! is the shipwrack then a harvest,
        does tempest carry the grain for thee?

I admire thee, master of the tides,   250.
Of the Yore-flood, of the year's fall;
The recurb & the recovery of the gulf's sides,
The girth of it & the wharf of it & the wall;
Staunching, quenching ocean of a motionable mind;
Ground of being, & granite of it: pást áll   255.
Grásp Gód, thróned behínd
Death with a sovereignty that heeds but hides, bodes but
        abides;

With a mercy that outrides
The all of water, an ark
For the listener; for the lingerer with a love glides   260.
Lower than death & the dark;
A vein for the visiting of the past-prayer, pent in prison,
The-last-breath penitent spirits—the uttermost mark
Our passion-plungèd giant risen,
The Christ of the Father compassionate, fetched in the storm
        of his stridès.   265.

Now burn, new born to the world,
Doubled-naturèd name,
The heaven-flung, heart-fleshed, maiden-furled

Miracle-in-Mary-of-flame,
Mid-numberèd he in three of the thunder-throne!   270.
Not a dooms-day dazzle in his coming nor dark as he came;
Kind, but royally reclaiming his own;
A released shówer, let flásh to the shíre, not a líghtning of fíre
    hard-húrled.

Dame, at our door
Drówned, & among óur shóals,   275.
Remember us in the roads, the heaven-haven of the reward:
Our Kíng back, Oh, upon Énglish sóuls!
Let him easter in us, be a dayspring to the dimness of us, be a
    crimson-cresseted east,
More brightening her, rare-dear Britain, as his reign rolls,
Pride, rose, prince, hero of us, high-priest,   280.
Our héarts' charity's héarth's fíre, our thóughts' chivalry's
    thróng's Lórd.

∽

**from *A Shropshire Lad*
A.E. HOUSMAN**

To write simple poetry well requires a complex mind. A.E. Housman had just such a mind. Although his style is direct and pure, each line is underwritten, or "sponsored," by the intellectual capital he'd collected as one of the twentieth century's leading philologists. His poems are minor-key pastorals addressing the various calamities of Existence. Even when setting a poem in an urban landscape, he executes his purpose with the straightforwardness and faux-naïve candor we recognize from folk ballads.

The protagonist of Vladimir Nabokov's *Pale Fire* says:

> *A Shropshire Lad* vies with *In Memoriam* of Alfred Tennyson [...] in representing, perhaps (no, delete this craven "perhaps"), the highest achievement of English poetry in

a hundred years[.][65]

Nabokov's identification with Housman makes sense, for Nabokov was himself a complex genius who wrote simple poems.[66] In his introduction to the *Collected Poems*, Thomas Karshan writes:

> [Nabokov's] key words of praise are "clear" or "intelligible" [...], "pure" [...], "harmonious" or "well structured" [...], "correct" [...]—and, perhaps most often, "simple" [...]. In the opening of his first-ever review, published in *Rul'* on 17 November 1922, Nabokov passionately expresses the sentiment that informs all his criticism: "In our black days, when countless hooligan 'poetasters' torture the Russian muse, it is sweet to open a booklet of simple and intelligible verses." It is no objection to the poet in question that in him Nabokov finds "the shadow of a somehow pleasing old-fashionedness." In a review written nearly five years later, on 31 August 1927, Nabokov praises another minor figure whose "quiet modest poetry is, as it were, written not in emigration, but in a thicket of alder trees, in a miraculously unchanged leafy Russia, where there is no place for communist blockheads."[67]

It's always better to have a pregnant simplicity than a barren complexity.

A Shropshire Lad, LI.
A.E. HOUSMAN

Loitering with a vacant eye
Along the Grecian gallery,

---

65 Knopf Doubleday, 1992, p. 205.

66 Those who are familiar only with Nabokov's fiction will be shocked at how simple his poems are.

67 Penguin Classics, 2012, p. xix.

And brooding on my heavy ill,
I met a statue standing still.
Still in marble stone stood he,   5.
And steadfastly he looked at me.
"Well met," I thought the look would say,
"We both were fashioned far away;
We neither knew, when we were young,
These Londoners we live among."   10.

Still he stood and eyed me hard,
An earnest and a grave regard:
"What, lad, drooping with your lot?
I too would be where I am not.
I too survey that endless line   15.
Of men whose thoughts are not as mine.
Years, ere you stood up from rest,
On my neck the collar pressed;
Years, when you lay down your ill,
I shall stand and bear it still.   20.
Courage, lad, 'tis not for long:
Stand, quit you[68] like stone, be strong."
So I thought his look would say;
And light on me my trouble lay,
And I stepped out in flesh and bone   25.
Manful like the man of stone.

A Shropshire Lad, LVI. / "The Day of Battle"
A.E. HOUSMAN

"Far I hear the bugle blow
To call me where I would not go,
And the guns begin the song,
'Soldier, fly or stay for long.'

---

68 Quit you] Conduct yourself.

"Comrade, if to turn and fly   5.
Made a soldier never die,
Fly I would, for who would not?
'Tis sure no pleasure to be shot.

"But since the man that runs away
Lives to die another day,   10.
And cowards' funerals, when they come,
Are not wept so well at home,

"Therefore, though the best is bad,
Stand and do the best, my lad;
Stand and fight and see your slain,   15.
And take the bullet in your brain."

⌘

Two Poems
HENRY KING

Henry King, Bishop of Chichester, is best remembered as the author of "An Exequy to his Matchless, Never-to-be-Forgotten Friend" (the title is sometimes abbreviated to "Exequy on His Wife"). An exequy is a funeral rite, and Bishop King's elegy is among the best of its kind. It's enough to demolish the ridiculous modern assumption that "back then," when death was so much more constant a presence, people didn't mourn as we do now—that death wasn't such a "big deal."

Although his *œuvre* was by no means extensive, the two poems reprinted below demonstrate that he was more than a "one-hit wonder."

"A Contemplation Upon Flowers"[69]
HENRY KING

Brave flowers, that I could gallant[70] it like you,
And be as little vain.
You come abroad,[71] and make a harmless show,
And to your beds of earth again.
You are not proud. You know your birth,   5.
For your embroidered garments are from earth.

You do obey your months and times, but I
Would have it ever spring.
My fate would know no winter, never die,
Nor think of such a thing.   10.
O that I could my bed of earth but view
And smile, and look as cheerfully as you.

O teach me to see Death, and not to fear,
But rather, to take truce.
How often have I seen you at a bier,[72]
And there look fresh and spruce.[73]
You fragrant flowers, then teach me that my breath,
Like yours, may sweeten and perfume my death.

---

69 Poets have been comparing people to flowers for so long that it's solidly
cliché. Pay close attention to how King redeems this trope from cliché, and, in
so doing, discovers real meaning and drama.

70 gallant] From the *OED*: [1] "To play the gallant or dandy, to 'cut a dash';"
[2] "To play the gallant, flirt, dally with."

71 abroad] Outside.

72 bier] The platform upon which a coffin is placed.

73 spruce] "Of a person or his or her behavior or demeanor: lively, brisk,
spry" (*OED*).

"The Legacy"[74]
HENRY KING

My dearest love, when thou and I must part,
And the icy hand of death shall seize that heart
Which is all thine, within some spacious will
I'll leave no blanks for legacies to fill.
Tis my ambition to die one of those   5.
Who but himself hath nothing to dispose.[75]

And since that is already thine, what need
I to re-give it by some newer deed?[76]
Yet take it once again. Free circumstance
Does oft the value of mean[77] things advance.   10.
Who thus repeats what he bequeathed before
Proclaims his bounty richer than his store.

But let me not upon my love bestow
What is not worth the giving. I do owe
Somewhat to dust. My body's pampered care   15.
Hungry corruption[78] and the worm will share.
That moldering relic which in earth must lie
Would prove a gift of horror to thine eye.

With this cast rag of my mortality
Let all my faults and errors buried be.   20.

---

74 legacy] "A sum of money, or a specified article, given to another by will" (*OED*).

75 dispose] "To bestow, make over, hand over; to deal out, dispense, distribute" (*OED*).

76 deed] "An instrument in writing (which for this purpose includes printing or other legible representation of words on parchment or paper), purporting to effect some legal disposition, and sealed and delivered by the disposing party or parties" (*OED*).

77 mean] Lowly.

78 corruption] Decay.

And as my sear-cloth[79] rots, so may kind fate
Those worst acts of my life incinerate.
He shall in story fill a glorious room
Whose ashes and whose sins sleep in one tomb.

If now to my cold hearse thou deign to bring   25.
Some melting sighs as thy last offering,
My peaceful exequys are crowned. Nor shall
I ask more honor at my funeral.
Thou wilt more richly balm[80] me with thy tears
Than all the nard[81] fragrant Arabia bears.   30.

And as the Paphian queen[82] by her griefs shower
Brought up her dead love's spirit in a flower,
So by those precious drops rained from thine eyes,
Out of my dust, O may some virtue rise!

---

79 sear-cloth] Burial shroud. For "sear," the *OED* offers: [1] "To dry up, to
wither away;" [2] "To cause to wither, to blight;" [3] "To burn or char (animal
tissues) by the application of a hot iron; to cauterize (a wound, the stump of an
amputated limb, etc.) in order to destroy virus or prevent the flow of blood;"
[4] "Figurative. Chiefly after 1 Timothy 4:2, to render (the conscience) incapa-
ble of feeling." Also, recall the opening lines of Milton's "Lycidas:"

> Yet once more, O ye laurels, and once more
> Ye myrtles brown, with ivy never sere,
> I come to pluck your berries harsh and crude,
> And with forced fingers rude
> Shatter your leaves before the mellowing year.

80 balm] As a noun, "balm" refers both to a soothing medicament and to
the preservatives pumped into a corpse (as in "embalm"). Both senses are
relevant here.

81 nard] "A fragrant ointment or perfume prepared from the rhizome of the
plant of the same name [...] and much prized in antiquity. [...] Now chiefly
literary and in references to Mark 14:3, John 12:3" (*OED*). I must say that I've
never heard an accent that can pronounce "nard" in such a way that makes it
seem other than preposterous, and vaguely lewd.

82 Paphian queen] According to *The Oxford Dictionary of Phrase and Fable*:

> Of or relating to Paphos, a Cypriot city held to be the birthplace of
> Aphrodite or Venus and formerly sacred to her; Paphian in literary use
> can thus mean relating to love and sexual desire, and the goddess may
> be referred to as the Paphian Goddess or Paphian Queen (526).

And like thy better genius[83] thee attend,   35.
Till thou in my dark period shalt end.

Lastly, my constant truth let me commend
To him thou choosest next to be thy friend.
For (witness all things good) I would not have
Thy youth and beauty married to my grave.   40.
'Twould show thou didst repent the style[84] of wife
Should'st thou relapse into a single life.

They with preposterous grief the world delude
Who mourn for their lost mates in solitude,
Since widowhood more strongly doth enforce   45.
The much-lamented lot of their divorce.
Themselves then of their losses guilty are
Who may, yet will not, suffer[85] a repair.

Those were barbarian wives that did invent
Weeping to death at the husband's monument,   50.
But in more civil rites she doth approve
Her first, who ventures on a second love;
For else it may be thought, if she refrain,
She sped so ill she durst not try again.

Up then my love! and choose some worthier one   55.
Who may supply my room when I am gone.
So will the stock of our affection thrive
No less in death, than were I still alive.
And in my urn I shall rejoice, that I

---

83   genius] "With reference to classical pagan belief: the tutelary god or at-
tendant spirit allotted to every person at birth to govern his or her fortunes
and determine personal character, and finally to conduct him or her out of
the world. Also: a guardian spirit similarly associated with a place, institution,
thing, etc." (*OED*).

84   style] Title.

85   suffer] Tolerate.

Am both testator[86] thus and legacy.   60.

☙

"The Unfortunate Lover"
ANDREW MARVELL

The Latin phrase "*Carpe diem!*" ("Seize the day!") is the stuff of motivational speakers and the more revolting kind of high school guidance counselor. The imperative to seize the day seems Yankee-Puritan to the core. Wake up, boys! There's money to be made! Competition to be trounced! Marketable skills to be acquired! *Carpe diem!*

In traditional poetry, however, "*carpe diem*" has rather different associations; it refers to a rhetorical strategy whereby a lustful man attempts to cajole a (quite understandably) resistant woman into sex. "Time flies," pleads the lad. "Before you know it, we'll both be old and decrepit; for the moment, however, our limbs are supple, the air is balmy, and I have my dad's credit card. Therefore, let's find us a cheap motel room, pronto! To do otherwise would be to dishonor Life itself. *Carpe diem!*"

The most famous poem in this genre is Andrew Marvell's "To His Coy Mistress," which contains one of the most grotesque images in canonical English poetry:

> Thy beauty shall no more be found,
> Nor, in thy marble vault, shall sound
> My echoing song. Then worms shall try
> That long-preserved virginity[.][87]

You read that correctly. "You should let me schtup you," the argument runs, "because, even if you refuse, you're eventually going to die, after which you'll be schtupped by worms, and, even though I'm ugly, tactless, and not very bright, I can't possibly be worse than a worm." That Marvell is apparently trying to

---

86 Testator] One who makes a will.

87 25-28.

be playful makes it all the worse.

You'll be grateful that I'm steering us clear of annelid-shepherdess sex in favor of one of Marvell's poems that should get at least some of the attention currently hogged by "To His Coy Mistress." Enjoy.

Alas, how pleasant are their days
With whom the infant Love yet plays!
Sorted by pairs, they still are seen
By fountains cool and shadows green.
But soon these flames do lose their light   5.
Like meteors of a summer's night,
Nor can they to that region climb
To make impression upon Time.

'Twas in a shipwreck, when the seas
Ruled, and the winds did what they please,   10.
That my poor lover floating lay,
And, ere brought forth, was cast away:
Till at the last the master-wave
Upon the rock his mother drave;
And there she split against the stone   15.
In a Caesarean séctíon.[88]

The sea him lent those bitter tears
Which at his eyes he always bears;
And from the winds the sighs he bore
Which through his surging breast do roar.   20.
No day he saw but that which breaks
Through frighted clouds in forkèd streaks,
While round the rattling thunder hurled,
As at the funeral of the world.

---

88   séctíon] We're meant to stretch two syllables into three.

While Nature to his birth presents   25.
This masque[89] of quarrelling elements,
A numerous fleet of cormorants black
That sailed insulting o'er the wrack
Received into their cruel care
Th' unfortunate and abject heir: 30.
Guardians most fit to entertain
The orphan of the hurricane.

They fed him up with hopes and air,
Which soon digested to despair,
And as one cormorant fed him, still   35.
Another on his heart did bill.
Thus while they famish him, and feast,
He both consumèd, and increased:
And languishèd with doubtful breath,
The amphibíum[90] of Life and Death.   40.

And now, when angry heaven would
Behold a spectacle of blood,
Fortune and he are called to play
At sharp before it all the day:
And tyrant Love his breast does ply   45.
With all his winged artillery,
Whilst he, betwixt the flames and waves,
Like Ajax,[91] the mad tempest braves.

See how he naked and fierce does stand,
Cuffing the thunder with one hand,   50.
While with the other he does lock
And grapple with the stubborn rock
From which he with each wave rebounds,
Torn into flames and ragg'd with wounds,

---

89 masque] A courtly drama.
90 amphibíum] An archaic spelling of "amphibian," which combines the Greek word for "of both kinds" with the word for "life."
91 Ajax] A warrior in Greek mythology.

And all he 'says,[92] a lover dressed   55.
In his own blood does relish best.

This is the only banneret[93]
That ever Love created yet:
Who though, by the malignant stars,
Forcèd to live in storms and wars,   60.
Yet dying, leaves a perfume here
And music within every ear;
And he in story only rules,
In a field sable a lover gules.[94]

♋

"To His Mistress"
ALEXANDER MONTGOMERIE

I'd never heard of this poem until stumbling upon it in *101 Sonnets*, edited by Don Paterson.[95] I've done something naughty: this poem is written in the Scottish dialect, and I've "updated" the spelling of those words that could withstand it sans loss of meaning. When I read Chaucer, I understand 85% of it, at best—and I can't imagine that I'm alone. And whatever makes sense only does so because I "translate" it in my own mind. So why not give the reader (who might be less comfortable than I with weird spelling) a little hand? "To His Mistress" is such an excellent poem that it would be a shame if it were to be sequestered from its potential audience by anything avoidable.

---

92 'says] An abbreviation of "assays."

93 banneret] A small banner.

94 gules] Heraldic red. "Field sable" refers to a dark brown background on a coat of arms.

95 Faber and Faber, 1999.

So sweet a kiss yistrene[96] from thee I reft,[97]
In bowing down thy body on the bed,
That even my life within thy lips I left,
Since from thee my spirits would never shed.
To follow thee, it from my body fled,   5.
And left my corpse as cold as any key.
But when the danger of my death I dread,
To seek my sprit, I sent my heart to thee.
But it was so enamored with thine eye,
With thee it minded likewise to remain;   10.
So thou has kept captive all the three,
More glad to bide then to return again.
Except thy breath their places had supplied,
Even in thine arms, there doubtless had I died.

❧

Four Poems
E.A. ROBINSON

Many who've never heard of E.A. Robinson know his work: his poem "Richard Cory" was adapted by Simon & Garfunkel into a song on the *Sounds of Silence* record. It's about a young, debonaire aristocrat who, despite having everything required for the "perfect" life, kills himself for no apparent reason.

This was E.A. Robinson's specialty: portraits of people attempting to accommodate the painful riddle that is an individual human life. Robinson suffered what we'd now reductively label "depression;" a lesser poet would have used poetry as a means of catharsis. Robinson, however, chooses a different approach; he uses poetry to distance himself from his own feelings, to examine them, and then to dramatize them with shocking objectivity and precision. Although Robinson often writes about desperation, his tone is never overheated. It reminds me

---

96 yistrene] Last night.
97 reft] Plundered.

of paintings like Caravaggio's *Crucifixion of Saint Peter*, where the most frenzied bewilderment is depicted with the coolest, most meticulous craft.

"Veteran Sirens"
E.A. ROBINSON

The ghost of Ninon[98] would be sorry now
To laugh at them, were she to see them here,
So brave and so alert for learning how
To fence with reason for another year.

Age offers a far comelier diadem   5.
Than theirs; but anguish has no eye for grace,
When time's malicious mercy cautions them
To think a while of number and of space.

The burning hope, the worn expectancy,
The martyred humor, and the maimed allure,   10.
Cry out for time to end his levity,
And age to soften its investiture;

But they, though others fade and are still fair,
Defy their fairness and are unsubdued;
Although they suffer, they may not forswear   15.
The patient ardor of the unpursued.

Poor flesh, to fight the calendar so long;
Poor vanity, so quaint and yet so brave;
Poor folly, so deceived and yet so strong,
So far from Ninon and so near the grave.   20.

---

98 Ninon] Ninon de l'Enclos, a French courtesan.

"Erasmus"[99]
E.A. ROBINSON

When he protested, not too solemnly,
That for a world's achieving maintenance
The crust of overdone divinity
Lacked aliment, they called it recreance;[100]
And when he chose through his own glass[101] to scan   5.
Sick Europe, and reduced, unyieldingly,
The monk within the cassock to the man
Within the monk, they called it heresy.
And when he made so perilously bold
As to be scattered forth in black and white,   10.
Good fathers looked askance at him and rolled
Their inward eyes in anguish and affright;
There were some of them did shake at what was told,
And they shook best who knew that he was right.

"The Pity of the Leaves"
E.A. ROBINSON

Vengeful across the cold November moors,
Loud with ancestral shame there came the bleak,
Sad wind that shrieked, and answered with a shriek,
Reverberant through lonely corridors.

---

99   Erasmus] Desiderius Erasmus Roterodamus, a Reformation-era Catholic priest and scholar. His erudition, intellectual independence, feeling for nuance, and sense of irony have made him an informal patron saint of free inquiry.

100   recreance] Cowardice, unfaithfulness.

101   glass] Although Robinson is referring to the lens of a scientific instrument, "glass" once referred to a mirror. We examine ourselves in a mirror; we examine something outside of ourselves via a lens. This paradox hovers over Robinson's use of the word.

The old man heard it; and he heard, perforce,   5.
Words out of lips that were no more to speak—
Words of the past that shook the old man's cheek
Like dead, remembered footsteps on old floors.

And then there were the leaves that plagued him so!
The brown, thin leaves that on the stones outside   10.
Skipped with a freezing whisper. Now and then
They stopped, and stayed there—just to let him know
How dead they were; but if the old man cried,
They fluttered off like withered souls of men.

"Reunion"
E.A. ROBINSON

By some derision of wild circumstance
Not then our pleasure somehow to perceive,
Last night we fell together to achieve
A light eclipse of years. But the pale chance
Of youth resumed was lost. Time gave a glance   5.
At each of us, and there was no reprieve;
And when there was at last a way to leave,
Farewell was a foreseen extravagance.

Tonight the west has yet a failing red,
While silence whispers of all things not here;   10.
And round there where the fire was that is dead,
Dusk-hidden tenants that are chairs appear.
The same old stars will soon be overhead,
But not so friendly and not quite so near.

∾

Astrophel and Stella, **Sixth Song**
SIR PHILIP SIDNEY

O you that hear this voice,
O you that see this face,
Say whether of the choice
Deserves the former place:
Fear not to judge this bate,[102]   5.
For it is void of hate.

This side doth Beauty take.
For that doth Music speak;
Fit orators to make
The strongest judgements weak: 10.
The bar[103] to plead their right
Is only true delight.

Thus doth the Voice and Face,
These gentle lawyers, wage,
Like loving brothers' case   15.
For father's heritage,[104]
That each, while each contends,
Itself to other lends.

For Beauty beautifies
With heavenly hue and grace   20.
The heavenly harmonies;
And in this faultless face
The perfect beauties be
A perfect harmony.

_____

102 bate] Contention.
103 bar] Courtroom.
104 heritage] Inheritance.

Music more lofty swells   25.
In speeches nobly placed;
Beauty as far excels
In action aptly graced;
A friend each party draws
To countenance[105] his cause.   30.

Love more affected seems
To Beauty's lovely light,
And wonder more esteems
Of Music's wondrous might;
But both to both so bent,   35.
As both in both are spent.

Music doth witness call
The Ear, his truth to try;
Beauty brings to the hall
The judgement of the Eye: 40.
Both in their objects such
As no exceptions touch.

The common sense, which might
Be arbiter of this,
To be, forsooth, upright,   45.
To both sides partial is:
He lays on this chief praise,
Chief praise on that he lays.

Then Reason, princess high,
Whose throne is in the mind,   50.
Which music can in sky
And hidden beauties find:
Say whether thou wilt crown
With limitless renown.

---

105   countenance] Support.

❧

from "**Dolores**"
(*Notre-Dame des Sept Douleurs*)
ALGERNON CHARLES SWINBURNE

Swinburne was the poet laureate of sadomasochism. That he could get away with publishing something like "Dolores" in the 1860s forces us to rethink our idea of the Victorian era as one of merciless repression. It might have been the era which destroyed Oscar Wilde, but it also permitted Swinburne to become an important man of letters on the basis of poems like this.

A certain kind of Christian obsession with crucifixes, torture, redemptive pain, sin-absolving blood, and martyrdom often teeters on the edge of something slightly disreputable. This is what Christopher Hitchens saw in Mel Gibson's *The Passion of the Christ*, writing: "Gibson's film is fascinated with [pain], to an almost lingering and lascivious degree[.]"[106]

In "Dolores," Swinburne makes Mel Gibson seem positively squeamish, reimagining the Virgin Mary as a patron saint of S&M. The result is sometimes magisterial, sometimes grotesque, and sometimes both simultaneously.

It's an easy poem from which to select an extract; over the course of its 440 lines, nothing much happens, so there's no "plot" that an editor must be considerate not to obscure. "Dolores" is like a hymn, repeating the same sentiment in every possible variation. It's both dynamic and static. It's like a dervish, whirling in place.

"Dolores" is the perfect example of how meter and prosody can excuse (and even elevate) subject matter that might otherwise be sickening. It certainly gives John Keats's dictum ("Beauty is Truth; Truth, Beauty") a run for its money.

---

106 "The Gospel According to Mel." *Vanity Fair*, March 2004.

Cold eyelids that hide like a jewel
Hard eyes that grow soft for an hour;
The heavy white limbs, and the cruel
Red mouth like a venomous flower;
When these are gone by with their glories,   5.
What shall rest of thee then, what remain,
O mystic and sombre Dolores,
Our Lady of Pain?

Seven sorrows the priests give their Virgin;
But thy sins, which are seventy times seven,   10.
Seven ages would fail thee to purge in,
And then they would haunt thee in heaven:
Fierce midnights and famishing morrows,
And the loves that complete and control
All the joys of the flesh, all the sorrows   15.
That wear out the soul.

O garment not golden but gilded,
O garden where all men may dwell,
O tower not of ivory, but builded
By hands that reach heaven from hell;   20.
O mystical rose of the mire,
O house not of gold but of gain,
O house of unquenchable fire,
Our Lady of Pain!

O lips full of lust and of laughter,   25.
Curled snakes that are fed from my breast,
Bite hard, lest remembrance come after
And press with new lips where you pressed.
For my heart too springs up at the pressure,
Mine eyelids too moisten and burn;   30.
Ah, feed me and fill me with pleasure,
Ere pain come in turn.

In yesterday's reach and tomorrow's,
Out of sight though they lie of today,
There have been and there yet shall be sorrows   35.
That smite not and bite not in play.
The life and the love thou despisest,
These hurt us indeed, and in vain,
O wise among women, and wisest,
Our Lady of Pain.   40.

Who gave thee thy wisdom? what stories
That stung thee, what visions that smote?
Wert thou pure and a maiden, Dolores,
When desire took thee first by the throat?
What bud was the shell of a blossom   45.
That all men may smell to and pluck?
What milk fed thee first at what bosom?
What sins gave thee suck?

We shift and bedeck and bedrape us,
Thou art noble and nude and antique;   50.
Libitina[107] thy mother, Priapus[108]
Thy father, a Tuscan and Greek.
We play with light loves in the portal,
And wince and relent and refrain.
Loves die, and we know thee immortal,   55.
Our Lady of Pain.

Fruits fail and love dies and time ranges;
Thou art fed with perpetual breath,
And alive after infinite changes,
And fresh from the kisses of death;   60.
Of languors rekindled and rallied,
Of barren delights and unclean,
Things monstrous and fruitless, a pallid
And poisonous queen.

---

107 Libitina] The Roman goddess of death.
108 Priapus] A Greek god associated with male potency.

Could you hurt me, sweet lips, though I hurt you?　　　65.
Men touch them, and change in a trice
The lilies and languors of virtue
For the raptures and roses of vice;
Those lie where thy foot on the floor is,
These crown and caress thee and chain,　　　70.
O splendid and sterile Dolores,
Our Lady of Pain.

There are sins it may be to discover,
There are deeds it may be to delight.
What new work wilt thou find for thy lover,　　　75.
What new passions for daytime or night?
What spells that they know not a word of
Whose lives are as leaves overblown?
What tortures undreamt of, unheard of,
Unwritten, unknown?　　　80.

Ah beautiful passionate body
That never has ached with a heart!
On thy mouth though the kisses are bloody,
Though they sting till it shudder and smart,
More kind than the love we adore is,　　　85.
They hurt not the heart or the brain,
O bitter and tender Dolores,
Our Lady of Pain.

As our kisses relax and redouble,
From the lips and the foam and the fangs　　　90.
Shall no new sin be born for men's trouble,
No dream of impossible pangs?
With the sweet of the sins of old ages
Wilt thou satiate thy soul as of yore?
Too sweet is the rind, say the sages,　　　95.
Too bitter the core.

Hast thou told all thy secrets the last time,

And bared all thy beauties to one?
Ah, where shall we go then for pastime,
If the worst that can be has been done?   100.
But sweet as the rind was the core is;
We are fain of thee still, we are fain,
O sanguine and subtle Dolores,
Our Lady of Pain.

By the hunger of change and emotion,   105.
By the thirst of unbearable things,
By despair, the twin-born of devotion,
By the pleasure that winces and stings,
The delight that consumes the desire,
The desire that outruns the delight,   110.
By the cruelty deaf as a fire
And blind as the night,

By the ravenous teeth that have smitten
Through the kisses that blossom and bud,
By the lips intertwisted and bitten   115.
Till the foam has a savour of blood,
By the pulse as it rises and falters,
By the hands as they slacken and strain,
I adjure thee, respond from thine altars,
Our Lady of Pain.   120.

Wilt thou smile as a woman disdaining
The light fire in the veins of a boy?
But he comes to thee sad, without feigning,
Who has wearied of sorrow and joy;
Less careful of labor and glory   125.
Than the elders whose hair has uncurled:
And young, but with fancies as hoary[109]
And grey as the world.

---

109 hoary] Grey, old. Given the context, one might be excused for assuming that it means "of or relating to a whore."

I have passed from the outermost portal
To the shrine where a sin is a prayer;   130.
What care though the service be mortal?
O our Lady of Torture, what care?
All thine the last wine that I pour is,
The last in the chalice we drain,
O fierce and luxurious Dolores,   135.
Our Lady of Pain.

All thine the new wine of desire,
The fruit of four lips as they clung
Till the hair and the eyelids took fire,
The foam of a serpentine tongue,   140.
The froth of the serpents of pleasure,
More salt than the foam of the sea,
Now felt as a flame, now at leisure
As wine shed for me.

Ah thy people, thy children, thy chosen,   145.
Marked cross from the womb and perverse!
They have found out the secret to cozen[110]
The gods that constrain us and curse;
They alone, they are wise, and none other;
Give me place, even me, in their train,   150.
O my sister, my spouse, and my mother,
Our Lady of Pain.

For the crown of our life as it closes
Is darkness, the fruit thereof dust;
No thorns go as deep as a rose's,   155.
And love is more cruel than lust.
Time turns the old days to derision,
Our loves into corpses or wives;
And marriage and death and division
Make barren our lives.   160.

---

110 cozen] Deceive.

And pale from the past we draw nigh thee,
And satiate with comfortless hours;
And we know thee, how all men belie thee,
And we gather the fruit of thy flowers;
The passion that slays and recovers,   165.
The pangs and the kisses that rain
On the lips and the limbs of thy lovers,
Our Lady of Pain.

The desire of thy furious embraces
Is more than the wisdom of years,   170.
On the blossom though blood lie in traces,
Though the foliage be sodden with tears.
For the lords in whose keeping the door is
That opens on all who draw breath
Gave the cypress to love, my Dolores,   175.
The myrtle to death.

And they laughed, changing hands in the measure,
And they mixed and made peace after strife;
Pain melted in tears, and was pleasure;
Death tingled with blood, and was life.   180.
Like lovers they melted and tingled,
In the dusk of thine innermost fane;[111]
In the darkness they murmured and mingled,
Our Lady of Pain.

In a twilight where virtues are vices,   185.
In thy chapels, unknown of the sun,
To a tune that enthralls and entices,
They were wed, and the twain were as one.
For the tune from thine altar hath sounded
Since God bade the world's work begin,   190.
And the fume of thine incense abounded,
To sweeten the sin.

---

111   fane] Temple.

Love listens, and paler than ashes,
Through his curls as the crown on them slips,
Lifts languid wet eyelids and lashes,   195.
And laughs with insatiable lips.
Thou shalt hush him with heavy caresses,
With music that scares the profane;
Thou shalt darken his eyes with thy tresses,
Our Lady of Pain.   200.

⌒⌣

from *The Ballad of Reading Gaol*[112]
OSCAR WILDE

We have important examples in our literary tradition of poets whose careers are bisected by some crisis, establishing an unambiguous Before and After. With T.S. Eliot, we have (on one side of the "wall") the obliterating nihilism of *The Waste Land*, and (on the other) the calm certainty and Christian hope of *Four Quartets*. With John Donne, we have (on one side of the "wall") the cavalier sensuality of *Songs and Sonnets*, and (on the other) the godly terror of the *Holy Sonnets*. In middle age, Walt Whitman transforms from a hack journalist to the psalmist of American democracy.

Oscar Wilde's biography is so devastating because, although he would have had an After, he died before that After had an opportunity to take shape. Before his imprisonment for homosexuality, he was the leading exponent of Aestheticism—a philosophy that privileged radical superficiality over substance, and Hellenistic hedonism over Victorian moralizing.

As evidenced by *De Profundis*, his book-length letter addressed from prison to Lord Alfred Douglas, his erstwhile lover, Wilde experienced a Christian conversion under the strain of captivity. This was the man who'd only recently quipped that

---

112   *The Ballad of Reading Gaol* was originally published not under Wilde's name (which was too much sullied by scandal), but under his prison number: C.3.3.

"[i]t is only shallow people who do not judge by appearances."
That was Before. He anticipates the nature and disposition of his
After when he writes:

> [S]orrow is the ultimate type[113] both in life and art. Be-
> hind Joy and Laughter there may be a temperament,
> coarse, hard, and callous. But behind Sorrow there is al-
> ways Sorrow. Pain, unlike Pleasure, wears no mask. [...]
> For this reason there is no truth comparable to Sorrow.
> There are times when Sorrow seems to me to be the only
> truth. Other things may be illusions of the eye or the ap-
> petite, made to blind the one and cloy the other, but out
> of Sorrow have the worlds been built, and at the birth of a
> child or a star there is pain. More than this, there is about
> Sorrow an intense, an extraordinary reality. I have said of
> myself that I was one who stood in symbolic relations to
> the art and culture of my age. There is not a single wretch-
> ed man in this wretched place along with me who does
> not stand in symbolic relations to the very secret of life.
> For the secret of life is suffering. It is what is hidden be-
> hind everything.[114]

Oscar Wilde died three years after his release, which was
enough time for him to write but one substantial literary work:
The Ballad of Reading Gaol, which only hints at what his After
might have looked like.

I.

He did not wear his scarlet coat,
For blood and wine are red,
And blood and wine were on his hands
When they found him with the dead,

---

113 type] Original template, model.
114 Nicholas Frankel, ed. *The Annotated Prison Writings of Oscar Wilde*.
Harvard University Press, 2018, p. 187.

The poor dead woman whom he loved,   5.
And murdered in her bed.

He walked amongst the Trial Men
In a suit of shabby gray;
A cricket cap was on his head,
And his step seemed light and gay;   10.
But I never saw a man who looked
So wistfully at the day.

I never saw a man who looked
With such a wistful eye
Upon that little tent of blue   15.
Which prisoners call the sky,
And at every drifting cloud that went
With sails of silver by.

I walked, with other souls in pain,
Within another ring,   20.
And was wondering if the man had done
A great or little thing,
When a voice behind me whispered low,
"That fellow's got to swing."

Dear Christ! the very prison walls   25.
Suddenly seemed to reel,
And the sky above my head became
Like a casque of scorching steel;
And, though I was a soul in pain,
My pain I could not feel.   30.

I only knew what hunted thought
Quickened his step, and why
He looked upon the garish day
With such a wistful eye;
The man had killed the thing he loved,   35.
And so he had to die.

Yet each man kills the thing he loves,
By each let this be heard;
Some do it with a bitter look:
Some with a flattering word.   40.
The coward does it with a kiss,
The brave man with a sword!

Some kill their love when they are young,
And some when they are old;
Some strangle with the hands of Lust,   45.
Some with the hands of Gold:
The kindest use a knife, because
The dead so soon grow cold.

Some love too little, some too long,
Some sell, and others buy;   50.
Some do the deed with many tears,
And some without a sigh:
For each man kills the thing he loves,
Yet each man does not die.

He does not die a death of shame   55.
On a day of dark disgrace,
Nor have a noose about his neck,
Nor a cloth upon his face,
Nor drop feet foremost through the floor
Into an empty space.   60.

He does not sit with silent men
Who watch him night and day;
Who watch him when he tries to weep,
And when he tries to pray;
Who watch him lest himself should rob   65.
The prison of its prey.

He does not wake at dawn to see
Dread figures throng his room:

The shivering Chaplain robed in white,
The Sheriff stern with gloom, 70.
And the Governor all in shiny black,
With the yellow face of Doom.

He does not rise in piteous haste
To put on convict-clothes,
While some coarse-mouthed Doctor gloats, and notes 75.
Each new and nerve-twitched pose,
Fingering a watch whose little ticks
Are like horrible hammer-blows.

He does not know that sickening thirst
That sands one's throat, before 80.
The hangman with his gardener's gloves
Slips through the padded door,
And binds one with three leathern thongs,[115]
That the throat may thirst no more.

He does not bend his head to hear 85.
The Burial Office[116] read,
Nor, while the terror of his soul
Tells him he is not dead,
Cross his own coffin, as he moves
Into the hideous shed. 90.

He does not stare upon the air
Through a little roof of glass:
He does not pray with lips of clay
For his agony to pass;
Nor feel upon his shuddering cheek 95.
The kiss of Caiaphas.[117]

---

115 thongs] Cords or straps.
116 Office] A ceremonial duty.
117 Caiaphas] The Jewish High Priest who orchestrated Christ's execution.

II.

Six weeks our guardsman walked the yard
In the suit of shabby gray:
His cricket cap was on his head,
And his step seemed light and gay,   100.
But I never saw a man who looked
So wistfully at the day.

I never saw a man who looked
With such a wistful eye
Upon that little tent of blue   105.
Which prisoners call the sky,
And at every wandering cloud that trailed
Its ravelled fleeces by.

He did not wring his hands, as do
Those witless men who dare   110.
To try to rear[118] the changeling[119] Hope
In the cave of black Despair:
He only looked upon the sun,
And drank the morning air.

He did not wring his hands nor weep,   115.
Nor did he peek or pine,
But he drank the air as though it held
Some healthful anodyne;[120]
With open mouth he drank the sun
As though it had been wine!   120.

And I and all the souls in pain,

---

118   rear] To raise a child.

119   changeling] In European folklore, a humanoid creature left in the place from which an actual human baby has been abducted, usually by malevolent spirits.

120   anodyne] A soothing or painkilling medicament.

Who tramped the other ring,
Forgot if we ourselves had done
A great or little thing,
And watched with gaze of dull amaze   125.
The man who had to swing.

For strange it was to see him pass
With a step so light and gay,
And strange it was to see him look
So wistfully at the day,   130.
And strange it was to think that he
Had such a debt to pay.

For oak and elm have pleasant leaves
That in the springtime shoot:
But grim to see is the gallows-tree,   135.
With its adder-bitten root,
And, green or dry, a man must die
Before it bears its fruit!

The loftiest place is that seat of grace
For which all worldlings[121] try: 140.
But who would stand in hempen band
Upon a scaffold high,
And through a murderer's collar take
His last look at the sky?

It is sweet to dance to violins   145.
When Love and Life are fair:
To dance to flutes, to dance to lutes
Is delicate and rare:
But it is not sweet with nimble feet
To dance upon the air!   150.

So with curious eyes and sick surmise
We watched him day by day,

---

121 worldlings] A person of mundane concerns.

And wondered if each one of us
Would end the self-same way,
For none can tell to what red Hell   155.
His sightless soul may stray.

At last the dead man walked no more
Amongst the Trial Men,
And I knew that he was standing up
In the black dock's[122] dreadful pen,   160.
And that never would I see his face
In God's sweet world again.

Like two doomed ships that pass in storm
We had crossed each other's way:
But we made no sign, we said no word,   165.
We had no word to say;
For we did not meet in the holy night,
But in the shameful day.

A prison wall was round us both,
Two outcast men we were: 170.
The world had thrust us from its heart,
And God from out His care:
And the iron gin[123] that waits for Sin
Had caught us in its snare.

---

122 dock's] "Dock" refers to the platform in a courtroom upon which the accused party sits or stands. A dock may have a cage-like appearance, hence "dreadful pen."

123 gin] Snare.

❧

"An Irish Airman Foresees His Death"
WILLIAM BUTLER YEATS

W.B. Yeats was Ireland's national poet; he'd inherited the ballad tradition that's so conspicuous here, with its simplicity and its sometimes-metronomic regularity. But for the fact that airplanes were invented in the twentieth century, this poem could have been written at any point over the past 300 years, and perhaps even before that. This is what generates the poem's power: the use of an ancient mode to tell the tale of one man about to participate in a newfangled kind of catastrophe.

I know that I shall meet my fate
Somewhere among the clouds above.
Those that I fight I do not hate;
Those that I guard I do not love.
My country is Kiltartan Cross;   5.
My countrymen Kiltartan's poor.
No likely end could bring them loss
Or leave them happier than before.
Nor law nor duty bade me fight,
Nor public man, nor cheering crowds;   10.
A lonely impulse of delight
Drove to this tumult in the clouds.
I balanced all, brought all to mind,
The years to come seemed waste of breath;
A waste of breath the years behind   15.
In balance with this life, this death.

Once, in a less conspicuous passage, Aschenbach stated outright that nearly everything great owes its existence to "despites:" despite misery and affliction, poverty, desolation, physical debility, vice, passion, and a thousand other obstacles.
—Thomas Mann, *Death in Venice*[1]

---

1 Michael Henry Heim, trans., Ecco, 2004, p. 16.

ACKNOWLEDGMENTS

ANY THANKS to everyone associated with New English Review Press, including Rebecca Bynum, Theodore Dalrymple, and Kendra Mallock. Ms. Bynum deserves particular mention, not only for her editorial acuity, but also for her remarkable warmth and patience. Additional thanks are due Roy Bachar (for his friendship), Vincent Krivda (for his lifesaving sense of ironic detachment), Barry Spurr (for reading the manuscript and offering substantial editorial guidance), and all the lovely folks who constitute the home church hosted so hospitably by Josh and Emily Morris. I'm pleased also to acknowledge three up-and-comers who were my students when I was writing this book, and provided useful feedback: Emma Kuisick, Lincoln Stevenson, and Baden Wagner. My former student Joseph Colaizzi was a great help in reviewing the proofs.

So much of what I am (for better or worse) began to come into focus beneath the warm, thoughtful guidance of three great teachers, now all in heaven, where I suspect they're having a melancholy conference, attempting, in an abstracted daze, to discover how exactly I metamorphosed from an affable little postmodernist into the kind of creature who could write such a book as this. I revere their memory, nevertheless. These teachers are Robert Creeley, Victor Doyno, and Mark Shechner.

My old schoolmate, Ashvin Pulinthitta, was wont to refer to serious intellectual exertion as "the heavy lifting;" the title of this volume is an affectionate hat-tip to him. May he flourish always.

CPSIA information can be obtained
at www.ICGtesting.com
Printed in the USA
LVHW030551030323
740789LV00003B/30